KU-332-593

This book is dedicated to my parents, Ron and Kath,
who gave me a wonderful childhood

Marion Dowling

Young Children's Personal, Social and Emotional Development

4th Edition

Los Angeles | London | New Delhi
Singapore | Washington DC

Los Angeles | London | New Delhi
Singapore | Washington DC

SAGE Publications Ltd
1 Oliver's Yard
55 City Road
London EC1Y 1SP

SAGE Publications Inc.
2455 Teller Road
Thousand Oaks, California 91320

SAGE Publications India Pvt Ltd
B 1/I 1 Mohan Cooperative Industrial Area
Mathura Road
New Delhi 110 044

SAGE Publications Asia-Pacific Pte Ltd
3 Church Street
#10-04 Samsung Hub
Singapore 049483

Editor: Marianne Lagrange
Assistant Editor: Rachael Plant
Production editor: Rachel Burrows
Copyeditor: Audrey Scriven
Proofreader: Derek Markham
Indexer: Avril Ehrlich
Marketing manager: Lorna Patkai
Cover design: Wendy Scott
Typeset by: C&M Digitals (P) Ltd, Chennai, India
Printed and bound in Great Britain by Ashford
Colour Press Ltd

© Marion Dowling 2000, 2005, 2010, 2014

First edition published 2000. Reprinted 2003, 2004
Second edition published 2005. Reprinted 2007 (twice), 2
2009
Third edition published 2010. Reprinted 2011, 2013
This fourth edition published 2014

Apart from any fair dealing for the purposes of research or
private study, or criticism or review, as permitted under the
Copyright, Designs and Patents Act, 1988, this publication
may be reproduced, stored or transmitted in any form, or by
any means, only with the prior permission in writing of the
publishers, or in the case of reprographic reproduction,
in accordance with the terms of licences issued by the
Copyright Licensing Agency. Enquiries concerning
reproduction outside those terms should be sent to
the publishers.

Library of Congress Control Number: 2014930445

British Library Cataloguing in Publication data

A catalogue record for this book is available from
the British Library

ISBN 978-1-4462-8588-6
ISBN 978-1-4462-8589-3 (pbk)

MIX
Paper from
responsible sources
FSC
www.fsc.org   FSC® C011748

At SAGE we take sustainability seriously. Most of our products are printed in the UK using FSC papers and boards.
When we print overseas we ensure sustainable papers are used as measured by the Egmont grading system. We
undertake an annual audit to monitor our sustainability.

Contents

About the Author

Marion Dowling has been involved in the pre-school playgroup movement, has taught in London, and was also headteacher of a state nursery school. She was an educational adviser in two local authorities, a member of Her Majesty's Inspectorate, and has been involved in a number of government working parties on early years. She now works as a trainer and consultant in the UK and overseas.

Marion is an experienced author and is a vice president of Early Education, a national charity.

Acknowledgements

Many people have contributed to this new edition and thanks are due to Marianne Lagrange and Rachael Plant at Sage for their help and encouragement.

Thank you so much to the following people who gave permission to reproduce images in this book:

The directors of Siren Films and parents of the children photographed

Tachbrook Nursery School and the parents of Leonore for the photo of the 'Mud Girl'

Daniel Dowling and Tiffany Gordon for images of Ruby and Flora

All of the following photographs are taken from films produced by Siren Films – sirenfilms.co.uk

Loving attachment from *Communication Film – birth to three (forthcoming)*

Dexter enjoys a challenge and surprise from *The Power of Physical Play – the development of self regulation*

Dexter and Rae good friends share experiences from *The Power of Physical Play – the development of self regulation*

Girls in deep discussion from *Play and Learning at School – five years old*

Ava views her first full day at nursery with trepidation from *Life at Two – attachments, key people and shaping the brain*

Shared thinking about a dice game from *Play and Learning at School – five years old*

Peek a boo from *The Wonder Year – first year development and shaping the brain*

Once again, most of the case studies arise from my observations of young children over a number of years; some of these children are now young adults. In all cases their names have been changed, apart from when they have asked to keep them. Every effort has been made to obtain any copyright permissions and I apologise if, inadvertently, any sources are unacknowledged.

Finally, the book would not have been completed without Barry who has, as always, given me constructive criticism, time and constant support to write.

Foreword by Lilian Katz

For the fourth time in a row, Marion Dowling has provided us with an updated, comprehensive and practical approach to the most important aspects of the development of young children. In the 15 years since the first edition was published the accumulated research and professional experience has strengthened the case that Dowling clearly makes: that we have to get things right in the early years.

Each chapter summarizes the recent research related to the complexities of young children's personal, social and emotional development, and Dowling makes a convincing case for the importance of getting it right from the start. In addition, each chapter addresses the implications of recent changes in policies and national regulations and their implications for the organization and implementation of day-to-day practices in supporting young children's development.

As in the previous editions of this comprehensive coverage of the basics of human development, this book includes a rich set of case studies that address the large range of issues faced by all whose lives involve them in the care and development of young children. Those who work with young children in a variety of settings will easily find the cases clear, meaningful and useful. Each case is followed by practical suggestions about how to address the problems portrayed. In addition, Dowling encourages those who teach and care for young children to take time to engage periodically in self-examination to help them strengthen their own effectiveness.

Based on my own extensive experience of interacting with early childhood practitioners working in a wide range of facilities and conditions around the world, I am confident that Marion Dowling makes clear a wide range of effective practices that can be helpful to all of us.

Lilian G. Katz, PhD
Professor Emerita & Clearinghouse on Early Education and Parenting, University of Illinois

National References for Each Chapter

Chapter	EYFS Statutory Framework	EYFS Non-Statutory Guidance Development Matters	Teachers' Standards (Early Years)
1	Overarching principle p. 3, V1; p. 5, 1.6; p. 6, 1.9, 1.10; p. 7, 1.11; p. 8, 1.13; p. 10, 2.1; p. 18, 3.27–3.30	A unique child p. 2, Characteristics of effective learning p. 4, pp. 6/7, PSE self-confidence and self-awareness pp. 10/11	1.1, 1.3, 2.1, 2.2, 2.3, 2.5, 2.6, 2.7, 3.1, 3.3, 5.1, 5.2, 5.3, 6.1, 6.2, 6.3, 8.3, 8.5
2	Overarching principle p. 3, V1; p. 5, 1.6; p. 6, 1.9, 1.10; p. 7, 1.11; p. 8, 1.13; p. 10, 2.1, 2.2	Characteristics of effective learning p. 4, pp. 6/7, PSE self-confidence and self-awareness pp. 10/11	1.1, 1.2, 1.3, 2.1, 2.2, 2.3, 2.5, 2.6, 2.7, 3.1, 3.2, 3.3, 4.2, 5.2, 5.3, 5.4, 5.5, 6.1, 6.2, 6.3, 6.4, 8.3, 8.5
3	p. 7, 1.11; p. 8, 1.13; p. 10, 2.1, 2.2	Positive relationships p. 2, Characteristics of effective learning p. 4, pp. 6/7, PSE making relationships pp. 8/9	1.1, 1.2, 1.3, 2.1, 2.2, 2.3, 2.4, 2.5, 2.6, 2.7, 3.1, 3.2, 4.2, 4.3, 4.4, 5.3, 5.4, 5.5, 6.1, 6.2, 6.3, 6,4, 8.3, 8.5
4	p. 6, 1.8; p. 7, 1.11; p. 8, 1.13; p. 10, 2.1, 2.2	Positive relationships p. 2, Characteristics of effective learning p. 4, pp. 6/7, PSE making relationships pp. 8/9, Communication and language pp.15–21, Physical development pp. 22–27	1.1, 1.2, 1.3, 2.1, 2.2, 2.3, 2.4, 2.5, 2.6, 2.7, 3.1, 3.2, 4.1, 4.2, 4.3, 4.4, 5.1, 5.3, 5.4, 5.5, 6.1, 6.2, 6.3, 6.4, 8.3, 8.5
5	p. 6, 1.10; p. 8, 1.13; p. 9, 1.13; p. 10, 2.1, 2.2	Positive relationships p. 2, Characteristics of effective learning p. 4, pp. 6/7, PSE self-confidence and self-awareness pp. 10/11, Communication and language pp. 15–21, Physical development pp. 22–27, Literacy pp. 28–31, Mathematics pp. 32–36, Understanding the world pp. 37–42, Expressive arts and design pp. 43–46	1.1, 1.2, 1.3, 2.1, 2.2, 2.3, 2.4, 2.6, 2.7, 3.1, 3.2, 3.3, 3.4, 3.5, 5.1, 5.2. 5.3, 5.4, 5.5, 5.6, 6.1, 6.2, 6.3, 6.4, 7.2, 8.3, 8.5

(Continued)

(Continued)

Chapter	EYFS Statutory Framework	EYFS Non-Statutory Guidance Development Matters	Teachers' Standards (Early Years)
6	p. 6, 1.10; p. 8, 1.13; p. 9, 1.13; p. 10, 2.1, 2.2	Positive relationships p. 2, Characteristics of effective learning p. 4, pp. 6/7, PSE self-confidence and self-awareness pp. 10/11, Communication and language pp. 15–21, Physical development pp. 22–27, Literacy pp. 28–31, Mathematics pp. 32–36, Understanding the world pp. 37–42, Expressive arts and design pp. 43–46	1.1, 1.2, 1.3, 1.4, 2.1, 2.2, 2.4, 2.5, 2.6, 2.7, 3.1, 3.2, 3.3, 4.1, 4.2, 4.3, 4.4, 5.1, 5.2, 5.3, 5.4, 6.1, 6.2, 6.3, 6.4, 8.3, 8.5
7	p. 5, 1.6; p. 6, 1.8; p. 7, 1.11; p. 10, 2.1, 2.2; p. 18, 3.26	Positive relationships p. 2, Characteristics of effective learning p. 4, pp. 6/7, PSE managing feelings and behaviour pp. 12–14, Communication and language pp. 15–21, Understanding the world pp. 37–38, Expressive arts and design: being imaginative pp. 45–46	1.1, 1.2, 1.3, 2.1, 2.2, 2.3, 2.4, 2.5, 2.6, 2.7, 3.1, 3.2, 3.3, 4.1, 4.2, 4.3, 5.1, 5.2, 5.3, 5.4, 5.5, 5.6, 6.1, 6.2, 6.3, 6.4, 8.3, 8.5
8	p. 6, 1.8; p. 7, 1.11; pp. 7–8, 1.13	Positive relationships p. 2, Characteristics of effective learning p. 4, pp. 6/7, PSE making relationships, self-confidence and self-awareness, managing feelings and behaviour pp. 8–14, Communication and language: speaking pp. 19–21, Expressive arts and design: being imaginative pp. 45/46	1.1, 1.2, 1.3, 2.1, 2.2, 2.3, 2.4, 2.5, 2.6, 2.7, 3.1, 3.3, 4.1, 4.2, 5.1, 5.2, 5.3, 5.4, 5.5, 5.6, 6.1, 6.2, 6.3, 6.4, 7.3, 8.3, 8.5

Chapter	EYFS Statutory Framework	EYFS Non-Statutory Guidance Development Matters	Teachers' Standards (Early Years)
9	p. 6, 1.9; p. 7, 1.11, 3.26; p. 8–9, 1.13; p. 10, 2.1, 2.2	Characteristics of effective learning p. 4, pp. 6/7, PSE making relationships pp. 8/9, Self-confidence and self-awareness pp. 10/11, Managing feelings and behaviour pp. 12–14	1.1, 1.2, 1.3, 2.1, 2.2, 2.3, 2.5, 2.7, 3.1, 3.2, 3.3, 4.2, 5.1, 5.2, 5.3, 5.4, 8.3, 8.5
10	p. 3, V1; p. 5, 1.6, 1.9; p. 6, 1.10; p. 7, 1.11; p. 8–9, 1.13; p. 10, 2.1–2.5	Enabling environments p. 2, Characteristics of effective learning p. 4, pp. 6/7, Self-confidence and self-awareness pp. 10/11, Supporting each child's learning and development p.3	1.1, 1.2, 1.3, 2.1, 2.2, 2.3, 2.4, 2.5, 2.6, 2.7, 3.1, 3.2, 4.1, 4.2, 4.3, 4.4, 5.1, 5.2, 5.3, 5.4, 5.5, 6.1, 6.2, 6.3, 6.4, 8.3, 8.5
11	p. 6, 1.9, 1.10; p. 7, 1.11; p. 8, 1.13; p.10–11, 2.1–7	Positive relationships, Enabling environments p. 2, Characteristics of effective learning p. 4, pp. 6/7, PSE making relationships, pp. 8/9, Managing feelings and behaviour pp. 12–14	1.1, 1.2, 1.3, 2.1, 2.2, 2.3, 2.4, 2.5, 2.6, 2.7, 3.1, 3.2, 3.3, 3.5, 4.1, 4.2, 4.3, 4.4, 5.1, 5.2, 5.3, 5.4, 5.5, 5.6, 6.1, 6.2, 6.3, 6.4, 8.3, 8.5
12	p. 6, 1.7, 1.9, 1.10; p. 7, 1.11, 1.12; p. 8, 1.13; p. 10, 2.1, 2.5; p. 23, 3.50–1	Positive relationships p. 2, Characteristics of effective learning p. 4, pp. 6/7, PSE making relationships pp. 8/9, Managing feelings and behaviour pp. 12–14, Physical development pp. 22/23	1.1, 1.2, 1.3, 2.1, 2.2, 2.3, 2.5, 2.6, 2.7, 3.1, 3.3, 4.1, 4.2, 4.3, 4.4, 5.1, 5.2, 5.3, 5.4, 5.5, 5.6, 6.1, 6.2, 6.3, 6.4, 7.1, 8.3, 8.5
13	p. 6, 1.9, 1.10; p. 8; p. 9; p. 10, 2.1, 2.2	A unique child p. 2, Characteristics of effective learning p. 4, pp. 6/7, Making relationships pp. 8–9, Managing feelings and behaviour pp. 12–14, Expressive arts and design pp. 43–46	1.1, 1.3, 2.1, 2.2, 2.3, 2.4, 2.5, 2.6, 2.7, 3.1, 3.2, 4.1, 4.2, 4.3, 4.4, 5.1, 5.2, 5.3, 5.4, 5.5, 6.1, 6.2, 6.3, 6.4, 8.3, 8.5

(Continued)

(Continued)

Chapter	EYFS Statutory Framework	EYFS Non-Statutory Guidance Development Matters	Teachers' Standards (Early Years)
14	p. 6–7, 1.9, 1.10, 1.11; p. 8; p. 9; p. 10, 2.1, 2.2	Positive relationships p. 2, Characteristics of effective learning p. 4, pp. 6/7, Self-confidence and self-awareness pp. 10/11, Communication and language (speaking) pp. 19–21, Understanding the world pp. 37–42, Expressive arts and design pp. 4–46	1.1, 1.2, 1.3, 2.1, 2.2, 2.3, 2.5, 2.6, 2.7, 3.1, 3.2, 4.1, 4.2, 4.3, 4.4, 5.1, 5.2, 5.3, 5.4, 5.5, 6.1, 6.2, 6.3, 6.4, 8.3, 8.5
15	p. 2, I, III; p. 10, 2.1, 2.2, 2.3, 2.5; p. 24, 3.60; p. 26, 3.72, 3.73, 3.74	A unique child p. 2, Making relationships pp. 8–9, Communication and language (speaking) p. 19, Physical development (health and welfare) pp. 25–27, Understanding the world (The world) p. 40	2.7, 5.2, 6.2, 6.3, 8.2, 8.3, 8.5
16	p. 2, IIII; p. 10, 2.1, 2.2, 2.3, 2.5; p. 13–14, 3.4, 3.5, 3.6, 3.7; p. 24, 3.60		2.7, 5.3, 5.6, 6.3, 7.1, 7.2, 7.3, 8.2, 8.5, 8,6

Important Note

Development Matters

The status of 'Development Matters' as non-statutory guidance has not changed and has not been replaced by the DFE's new 'Outcomes' document. This is simply an extract from 'Development Matters' and unlike the full document does not inform on issues of child development.

Introduction

Since I wrote the last edition of this book the UK government has changed and there have been far-reaching innovations which affect provision for young children, their families and the workforce. In contrast to the substantial investment in early years experienced at the start of this century, the last five years have been a time of upheaval defined by breathless change and increasingly severe budget constraints.

A Climate of Austerity

The global financial crisis resulted in many developed countries experiencing a liquidity gap, with high unemployment, unsustainable debt and low growth (1). One outcome is the cut in funding to local authority children's services. By 2014–2015 the budget for local children's services will have fallen by more than a third since 2010, and further cuts are forecast for the following year (2). The coalition government has removed ring fencing for children's services and given responsibility to local authorities to decide where to make cuts. Councils are expected to provide more for families at a time when their financial resources have been drastically decreased.

Impact on Services

A review of eight local authorities with responsibilities for children's services showed that between 2011–2012 the cuts made in early years services included childcare services, early years consultancy, and advisory support for the voluntary, private and independent sector and Children's Centres (3).

These cuts have come when there is an increased need and demand for services. A census carried out recently by the charity 4Children revealed that for the first time over one million families are now using their local children's centre, including 320,000 disadvantaged parents. Despite this, the charity predicts that around 60 centres could close by the end of 2014 due to severe financial pressures. At the same time 31% of the 501 centres participating in the census expected to reduce their services due to diminished budgets (4).

As local authorities give priority for resources to the most disadvantaged families there are not the funds available to work with less vulnerable groups and prevent their needs increasing. Reducing preventative work can prove to be a false economy in the long term.

National Policy Initiatives

The framework

The format of the revised statutory framework for the Early Years Foundation Stage (EYFS) reflects today's economic climate. It is a brief document which simply spells out the legal requirements to support children's learning and development and safeguarding and welfare in all early years' provision; in order for practitioners to understand and meet these mandatory requirements however, they need to draw on other practice guidance, some of which I have referenced in this book.

Despite its brevity, the framework continues to be based on the themes and principles established in the previous framework and affirms the significance of children's personal, social and emotional development:

- as one of the prime areas of learning (recognising that it is central to all other areas of learning);
- in the characteristics of effective learning which emphasise how children learn rather than what they learn. References are made throughout this book to the three characteristics (playing and exploring; active learning; and creating and thinking critically) (5).

The section on Safeguarding and Welfare, which makes up half of the framework, rightly emphasises safeguarding and child protection with a view to protecting young children from harm. Following the serious case review relating to the Little Ted's Nursery and Vanessa George, the framework now requires safeguarding policies and procedures to cover the use of mobile phones and cameras in a setting. Staff are also required to be trained to identify and respond to signs of possible abuse and neglect which may be observed physically or from the adult's or child's behaviour (6). These necessarily stringent requirements highlight the serious responsibilities for practitioners having daily contact with young children.

Work with Families

The importance of close links with parents continues to be recognised. In 2011 the government set out its vision for services that should be available for families, stating that they are the most important influence on their young children (7). This ambitious and comprehensive document confronts us at a time when it is difficult to see how some of the services promised can be delivered. For example, the well-intentioned undertaking to recruit an additional 4,200 health visitors by 2015 has been greeted with some scepticism given the current shortage (8). However, the sensible insistence for various agencies to work closely together makes the best use of the resources still available.

Although it has long been recognised that young families benefit from professionals working together to offer a unified service, practice has been patchy. Some recent serious case reviews reveal that children have suffered when information has not been passed on to fellow professionals (9, 10). Acknowledging these weaknesses, a task group was commissioned by the government to disseminate good practice, identify the barriers to sharing information, and recommend how these barriers might be overcome. Authentic case studies demonstrate ways to achieve the sharing of information and useful fact sheets summarise key points (11). These recent documents have real potential to improve practice.

Ensuring a Quality Workforce

For some years the emphasis has been to recruit and maintain sufficient early years practitioners to work with very large numbers of babies and young children across the sector. The early emphasis on provision was more on 'never mind the quality, feel the width'. Poor pay and conditions of service still exist for the majority of practitioners. Too often private providers of childcare working on tight budgets and to required staffing ratios continue to employ the cheapest staff possible. Some (but by no means all) are young and inexperienced and sometimes lack interest in pursuing a career with young children. Many of these young adults do not have the appropriate skills, nor do they model appropriate attitudes, behaviour and language to impressionable young children. Moreover, fatigue and poor wages mean that hard-working and aspirational staff feel unsupported and undervalued; in these circumstances they have too little to offer children. It is not enough to rely on staff doing this work because of the intrinsic rewards of the job. High-level recruitment and retention of the best people are also dependent on those individuals being paid a realistic salary and working reasonable hours. Furthermore, a confusing mishmash of qualifications has meant that the routes to development and promotion have been unclear within the sector.

The Nutbrown Review

This review (*The Foundations for Quality*) was commissioned by the government to consider how best to strengthen qualifications and career pathways in the early years. Nutbrown's vision in her final report was that:

- 'every child is able to experience high-quality care and education whatever type of home or group setting they attend;
- early years staff have a strong professional identity, take pride in their work and are recognised and valued by parents, other professionals and society as a whole;
- high quality early years education and care is led by well qualified early years practitioners; and the importance of childhood is understood, respected and valued'. (12)

Her fair and measured messages were very well received by the workforce but the government's response (*More Great Childcare/MGC*) accepted only five out of her nineteen recommendations (13).

The introduction of both Early Years Teachers (EYTs) and Early Years Educators (EYEs) originated from Nutbrown's recommendations but delivered very different outcomes:

- Nutbrown's proposal to maintain and increase graduate leadership in settings has resulted in the government introducing EYTs who are not entitled to Qualified Teacher Status and therefore are also not eligible to teach children over five years old. Moreover, those practitioners who worked hard to achieve Early Years Professional (EYP) status are not able to transfer to become EYTs. We now have three routes to achieving graduate status but with different pay and conditions of service; this does nothing to clarify career routes for the workforce.
- More positively the former Level 3 qualification has been strengthened, with additional pedagogical elements, and the new status of EYEs is intended to be the equivalent of the highly respected Nursery Nurse diploma which was discontinued in the 1990s.
- Other recommendations to improve the quality of training for students by raising tutor qualifications, giving tutors access to professional development, and ensuring a good or excellent standard for students' practical placements received only a 'cagey' response from the government of 'Accepted in Principle' (14).

Nutbrown's take on this disappointing response was that the quality of early years provision is being undermined – a view that is shared by many.

Apprentices

Modest help is being given to those who are interested in starting out on a childcare career. An apprenticeship bursary scheme was introduced as a transitional system into the EYE qualification. It is also planned to support work with funded 2-year-olds and to be eligible apprentices must work in a setting which accommodates this age group. Basic GCSE qualifications are required and students have to carry out a combination of work and study (15).

The government has drip-fed funds in order to top up these bursaries, most recently making up to £3,000 available to 200 eligible students (16). This small investment has been welcomed as an incentive for selected students, but a greater subsidy is needed to make it an attractive proposition to all entrants.

Regulation

All early years provision continues to be regulated against a set of common standards. Ofsted inspections are slowly being recognised as a shared and active enterprise although there are misgivings about the recent more exacting inspection regime. A judgement of 'requires improvement' has replaced the earlier judgement of 'satisfactory'. Those settings requiring improvement are to be re-inspected within a year and have two years to become 'good'. If this is not achieved they will then be downgraded to 'inadequate' and face possible closure.

While rigorous standards of quality give parents peace of mind and rightly protect children who are entitled to benefit from 'good' practice, this tougher line comes at a worrying time when local authorities no longer have the capacity to support practice in weaker settings and help them to progress. At the same time in some areas there appears to be insufficient nursery places available. Freedom of Information data requested by Labour reveal that one in three councils believe that they do not have enough places to meet the government's free offer for less advantaged 2-year-olds (17).

Whereas nurseries face more stringent OfSTED judgements, there is a continuing and worrying move towards deregulation. The government has suggested that inflexible requirements for staffing ratios are restricting providers from being able to reduce the costs of childcare and education for parents. Given improved qualifications, it proposes allowing an increase in the number of children that each staff member can be responsible for. This is seen as a way of generating extra income which could be used to reduce fees for parents (18). It is simplistic to argue that a better qualification enables an adult to offer a high quality of care and support to more children. Nutbrown's succinct response to this proposal was that 'childcare may be cheaper but children will be footing the bill' (19).

There is also an attendant danger that the mandatory requirements for physical space allocated to young children will be removed, thereby giving scope for more 2-year-olds to be accommodated (20). There are sound reasons for the current regulation. Research findings suggest that floor space is critical for children's well-being (21, 22). For example, Legendre's study in France shows that five square metres of accessible floor space per child are required to minimise children's stress levels. His previous research had supported this, showing that access to sufficient space reduces altercations and encourages positive social relationships between children (23).

Research

One glimmer of light in this current gloomy scenario has been the introduction of a major new study to look at early education in England. The government is funding a large evaluation study, taking place over eight years, of 5,000 children from two years old until the end of Key Stage 1. The £4.7 million Study of Early Education and Development (SEED) is the first major piece of early years research since the Effective Provision of Pre-School Education (EPPE) study that began in 1997, the difference between the two projects being that SEED will follow children rather than beginning by identifying specific settings. Enquiries will focus on how much effect the early years can have on children's long-term education and look at:

- the difference for children between receiving an early education or not;
- whether different amounts of provision and the type of setting make a difference.

Home visits and interviews are currently being carried out as well as planned visits to 1,000 settings including child minders. Investigations will include a look at children's language development, the amount of TV they watch and the books they have. The intention is to use this information to produce a more detailed picture from the children and families involved in this project (24).

Findings from this substantial study should offer valuable information about young children's lives and what more can be done to improve them. Crucially, the success of the project will be dependent on the requisite action being taken at all levels, starting with the government.

Against this background early years practitioners are continuing their work. A nursery headteacher once told me that the aim in her school was 'to follow the child with love and help to grow the adequate person'. I agree with her wholeheartedly. Most of us would recognise an adequate person: we appreciate and admire those who have good interpersonal skills, live their lives by a clear moral code, and are able to show their feelings and empathise with the feelings of others. These people deal with the decisions they must take in life and bravely face up to difficult situations; they are enthusiastic and show sticking power in seeing things through, both at work and in their personal lives. Regardless of their intellectual abilities, these individuals seem equipped both to get the most out of life and to deal with problems. These are rough and ready definitions of 'adequacy' but it is surely these qualities that we want to respect, demonstrate, encourage and promote in young children. The type of person we become colours all else we do in life. The small baby lies ready to reciprocate and flourish in our loving care.

References

1. Hopwood, O. and Pharoah, R. (2012) *Families on the Front Line: Local Spending on Children's Services in Austerity.* London: Family and Parenting Institute.
2. Morton, K. (2013) 'Children's Centres closing despite high demand', *Nursery World*, 4–17 November.
3. Hopwood, O. and Pharoah, R. (2012) op.cit. (see note 1).
4. Morton, K. (2013) op.cit. (see note 2).
5. Department for Education (DfE) (2012) *Statutory Framework for the Early Years Foundation Stage.* London: HMSO. p. 6.1.10.
6. DfE (2012) op.cit. (see note 5), p. 14, 3.6.
7. DfE/DoH (2011) *Families in the Foundation Years.* London: HMSO.
8. Godson, R. (2011) 'Health visitor recruitment plans lack firm foundations', Nursing Times.net, March.
9. Boodhoo, B. (2012) *Safeguarding Children in Surrey: Lessons from Recent Serious Case Reviews.* London: NHS Surrey.
10. Mackie, P. (2013) 'Daniel Pelka: Missed but not forgotten', *BBC News*, Coventry and Warwickshire, 19 September.
11. DfE/DoH (2013) *Information Sharing in the Foundation Years: A Report from the Task and Finish Group chaired by Jean Gross.* London: HMSO.
12. Nutbrown, C. (2012) *Foundations for Quality: The Independent Review of Early Education and Childcare Qualifications Final Report.* Available at www.gov.uk publications. pp. 10–11.
13. Department for Education (DfE) (2013) *More Great Childcare.* London: HMSO.
14. Nutbrown, C. (2012) op.cit. (see note 12), recommendations 9, 10, 11.
15. Gaunt, C. (2013) 'Government funds early years apprenticeships', *Nursery World*, May.
16. Gaunt, C. (2013) 'Funding doubled for early years apprenticeship scheme', *Nursery World*, November.
17. Morton, K. (2013) 'A third of local authority councils do not have enough 2 year old places', *Nursery World*, 21 November.
18. DfE (2013) op.cit. (see note 13).
19. Nutbrown, C. (2013) *Shaking the Foundations of Quality? Why 'Childcare' Policy must not Lead to Poor Quality Education and Care.* Sheffield: School of Education, University of Sheffield.
20. DfE (2013) op.cit. (see note 13), p. 23.
21. Legendre, A. (2003) 'Environmental features influencing toddlers' bioemotional reactions in day care centres', *Environment and Behaviour,* 35 (July): 523–9.
22. Olds, A. (2001) *Child Care Design Guide.* New York: McGraw-Hill.
23. Legendre, A. (1995) cited in N. Eisenstadt, K. Sylva, S. Mathers (University of Oxford) and B. Taggart (Institute of Education, London), *More Great Childcare Research Evidence.* Available at www.ecers.uk.org, p. 4.
24. 4Children (2013) Presentation by Jane O'Brien, 'Study into Early Education and Development (SEED)', at Hallam Conference Centre ('Let's Talk Quality: Making Early Years Achievable For All'), NatCen, 10 October.

ONE The Seeds of Confidence and Competence

- Confidence is a catalyst supporting early personal growth. The young child develops confidence through becoming aware of herself as a separate and worthwhile person, as well as having a realistic view of what she can achieve.
- Children gain their self-esteem initially from the love and recognition that they receive from their family and other significant people in their lives, including whoever is their key person.
- On moving to an early years setting they gain confidence if their questions and comments are understood and their interests are recognised and strengthened as schemes of thought. They also become aware of themselves, what they are capable of doing, and what is approved behaviour.

Early childhood is a momentous time of life. Gazing at a newborn baby we can never be sure of how she will develop – what potential she has within her – but we know that there is everything to play for. And watching her grow up it is impossible to separate the different strands of development, as they are all interrelated. Increased physical movement leads to possibilities for growing independence, which in turn mean that the baby extends her horizons and strengthens her curiosity to discover more. But studies strongly suggest that the catalyst for these amazing achievements is the child's growing confidence (1, 2, 3). The Early Years Foundation Stage includes self-confidence and self-awareness as goals in the Prime Area of Personal, Social and Emotional Development. By the end of

Reception year in school it is expected that children 'are confident to speak in a familiar group, will talk about their ideas and will choose the resources they need for their chosen activities. They say when they do or don't need help' (4). Helen Moylett and Nancy Stewart usefully offer a broader interpretation: 'Self-confidence and self-awareness is about personal development – how we come to understand who we are and what we do. Within the early years children begin to understand themselves as people which supports developing confidence and motivation to engage pro-actively in the world' (5).

Confidence is a characteristic valued by all and one that parents most want for their children. Parents may deliberately send their young children to certain settings or schools, or arrange for them to join clubs, 'in order to give them confidence'. Many parents believe that the main role of care and education is to help children to acquire social skills and become confident before entering mainstream school. A confident person is well equipped to deal with life, whether in school or work or in social situations. Conversely, under-confident people often find coping with these aspects of life difficult and painful. Above all, truly confident people are comfortable with them-selves and have insights into their own strengths and weaknesses. This distinguishes them from the over-confident who, although they think well of themselves, may lack self-insight and have a false sense of optimism with regard to what they can achieve. In a world that demands so much of them, children do need to become confident from an early age. It is neces-sary for their early success in life and also for the future. In a 60-year study of more than a thousand men and women of high intelligence followed through from childhood to retirement, those most confident in their early years were most successful as their careers unfolded (6). What then is required to achieve this precious personal attribute, and how can we help young children to develop it?

Inherited or Genetic?

An interesting question here is whether confidence is an inherited trait and whether some children are blessed with it at birth. To some extent the lat-ter might be true: young babies show clear signs of personality traits, for example sociable and shy behaviours. However, being outgoing does not necessarily connect with a good level of confidence, while low key and seemingly unassuming persons can be quietly sure of themselves. So although babies may inherit certain traits we cannot leave it at that. The neuroscientist Colin Blakemore suggests that 'nurture shapes nature' (7), meaning that an inherited personality is shaped through experiences and relationships. Thus young children's levels of confidence are coloured by their successes and failures, the thoughts they have about themselves and other people's reactions to them. As Katz suggests, perhaps it is not what we are born with that counts so much but what we are allowed to do and who we are encouraged to be (8). Most people would admit that their confidence ebbs and flows according to the people they are with and the situations demanded of them. In this chapter I argue that a person's confidence is linked closely to three factors: becoming aware of oneself (self-concept); developing a view of oneself, either positive or negative (self-esteem); and getting to know one's strengths and weaknesses (self-knowledge). These all contribute to a child's growing sense of 'efficacy', which in simple terms means making a difference or having an impact. Children become aware of the first two at a very early stage; their experiences in a nursery will powerfully influence all three factors.

Becoming Aware of Oneself

We begin to recognise ourselves from early on. After about 18 months old a toddler will have a pretty good idea that the reflection shown in a mirror is a representation of herself. Shortly after that an infant will move from saying 'Dom do it' to 'I do it'. This heralds the early recognition of self. And even before that, babies will build a picture of themselves from the way in which they are regarded and treated, particularly by those people who are closest to them. Young babies will start to form this picture from their mothers, whose loving acceptance of them is the first signal that they are a person who matters. Rosemary Roberts describes this beautifully:

> The mother's face and body are like a mirror to the baby. This very early mirroring process which can reflect the mother's acceptance, forms the basis of the baby's self-concept; the mother's responses are the first 'brush strokes' for the developing picture. (9)

In order to establish a sense of identity it is crucial to have an image of oneself as a distinct person; this is most strongly established initially through ongoing contact with one person (see also Chapters 2 and 3). Selleck argues that only the presence of a parent or committed regular key person which is now required for every child in an early years setting can provide the continuity, attention and sensuous pleasure that a baby needs to make sense of her experiences and set in motion the process of mental development (10). For children under two years old, particularly those who are placed in daycare, their key person offers an essential warm attachment and the assurance that, despite being one of a number, that individual baby or toddler is special and unique. Young babies who have been institutionalised from birth and who lack regular contact with one carer may fail to recognise the 'brush strokes' described by Roberts. In certain circumstances a person's sense of 'self' can be eroded – for example, adults imprisoned in conditions of harsh confinement. Terry Waite wrote movingly of his long period in captivity and of the times when he wondered

Figure 1.1 Loving Acceptance
© Siren Films

who he was: 'How I yearn with a childish, selfish longing to be understood and cared for. I am frightened. Frightened that, in growing up, my identity may slip away' (11).

Attachment relationships are discussed in Chapter 7 where they are linked to children's emotional development. However, sound attachments are fundamental to a child's overall healthy development; a baby gains confidence in her identity when a few loving and significant people recognise and respond to her. Maria Robinson describes this process as attunement. She stresses the importance of learning to interpret the baby's signals and suggests that the parent is then able to attune their own responses to those of the baby. This responsive affirmation helps the child learn more about mum or dad and strengthens her belief in herself (12). As the infant develops into the pre-school years, other people contribute to a broader view of her identity. Through their various behaviours these people will help a child to know who she is. For example, Alison knows that she is dad's little daughter and she makes him laugh; her baby brother's loving older sister when she cuddles him and gives him his bottle; her older brother's noisy little sister when she dances and sings to his records; and Alison the artist at nursery when her teacher admires her paintings. By becoming aware of the way in which others view us we build up a composite picture of ourselves. We also learn to behave in character; we get a picture of how other people regard us and then adapt our behaviour to fit this picture. Because of their immaturity, a young child is both very open to and reliant on the opinions and views of other more experienced adults, particularly those adults who are familiar and loved, members of their immediate family, and later those others who care for and work with them. A child who recognises herself as distinctive feels that she belongs.

A stable family provides a child with a sense of personal continuity. Young children love to hear stories about when they were babies or to share recollections of past family events. They are also keen to share and listen to predictions of 'what will happen when you are a big girl'. These shared experiences and concerns help young children begin to have a sense of self within the larger family.

The family, then, has a powerful effect on each child's sense of identity, but when that child moves on to an early years setting the practitioners share this responsibility.

Self-esteem

When a child establishes her identity she is simply becoming aware of how others see her. Once we talk about self-esteem we start to place a value on that identity. Children do not gain a clear view of their self-worth until they are around six years of age, but their early experiences within the family and in early years settings provide the basis for them to make a judgement about themselves. Self-esteem is not fixed; it can change according to the people we are with and the situations we find ourselves in. Alison's self-esteem is mainly secure as she recognises that she is valued in different ways by her father, by her baby brother, and in the nursery. However, her esteem is lower when she is with her older brother, who makes it clear that she is often intrusive and a nuisance to him. So the views of others not only help a young child to recognise herself as a person who is seen in different ways, they also contribute to the regard she has for herself. Self-esteem is learned and again it is the people who are closest to the child and have an emotional link who will have the most profound effect. These are described as 'significant others' and they include the family and primary carers, the key person and other practitioners who have early contacts with the child.

One of the most important gifts we can offer young children is a positive view of themselves. Without this gift they will flounder throughout life and be constantly seeking reassurance from others as they cannot find it from within. However, as Siraj-Blatchford points out, positive self-esteem depends on whether children feel that others accept them and see them as competent and worthwhile (13).

Case Study 1.1

Four-year-old Eva had poor eyesight and after three weeks in her new reception class she was prescribed spectacles to wear. Eva was extremely self-conscious about her glasses and that same day was found weeping in the cloakroom after one child asked her why she was wearing 'masks over her eyes'. From that moment all efforts from her teacher Anna and later her mum could not persuade Eva to wear her spectacles in school, although she clearly had visual difficulties with mark making and when looking at picture books.

Four days later Anna arrived in school wearing a pair of ornate spectacles (with clear glass in the lens as she had perfect sight). As she had anticipated the children noticed the difference and this interest gave Anna the opportunity she wanted. At story time she asked the children what they thought about her new purchase – all of them thought the new glasses very pretty. Anna stressed how pleased she was with the spectacles and how well she could see with them. She involved other children in the class who also wore glasses and said how smart they looked. Eva said nothing but was clearly listening. The following day she hesitantly came into the class wearing her spectacles. Anna complimented Eva on her appearance and Eva was delighted to be able to identify and describe some fine detail in the picture storybook they shared as a group.

Comment

Having to wear spectacles severely affected Eva's self-esteem as she felt vulnerable and different. Anna's sensitive move to show wearing spectacles in a positive light and to model this herself was clearly effective. Eva resumed wearing the spectacles because she no longer felt different, but was finally persuaded of their benefit when she realised she could now see things more easily.

Reflection Point

Rachael has 4-year-old Sam in her reception class who, she believes, has hearing difficulties. He finds any group activity difficult to access including listening to stories, and is restless and disruptive. Other children are starting to avoid him. More and more often he hides under a bush in the garden with his head in his hands. Sam's parents refuse to accept that there is any problem, saying that their son is like any other boy. What actions can Rachael take to support Sam, his parents and the rest of the class?

Consequences of low self-esteem

When children constantly demand attention or boast about their achievements this is sometimes wrongly interpreted as over-developed self-esteem.

However, we should recognise that self-esteem is not conceit and this type of behaviour is more likely to reflect a lack of self-regard and a basic insecurity. In an article which stresses that self-esteem is basic to a healthy life, Murray White looks at the possible problems in later school life arising from its lack:

> If teachers examine what causes bullying and other chronic misbehaviours – the showing off, the fighting and the failure which some children have adopted – they will discover that low self-esteem is at the root of it. These children behave as they do because of strong feelings of inadequacy and internal blame, a belief that they do not possess the ability or intelligence to succeed. (14)

Interestingly, although low self-regard can lead to problems later in life, it appears that this is by no means conclusive. Evidence from a longitudinal study shows that relatively low self-esteem:

- is not a risk factor for delinquency, violence, alcohol and drug abuse and underachievement;
- is a risk factor (although one of a number) for suicide attempts, depression and teenage pregnancy (15).

Self-esteem in the Early Years Setting

The value that we place on ourselves is also affected by how secure we feel. Both adults and children are usually secure with people they know but also when they are in familiar situations. When we start a new job or a new course of learning, most of us feel very vulnerable being placed in the position of a novice. We do not even know where to get a cup of coffee, let alone really understand aspects of new work or how others will work with us.

Studies of young children at home show them to be comfortable and in control with mum or the main carer safely in sight. A 1-year-old is usually wary of anyone who comes between her and her mum and will use her parent as a secure base to explore wider territory (16). Tizard and Hughes' well-known study of 4-year-old girls conversing and questioning with their mothers gives a picture of children in a situation when they feel they are on sure territory (17). In nearly all families young children will recognise that there are loving adults who know them and care about them. This knowledge in itself helps children to feel secure.

Making a transition

When starting in an early years setting the young child faces new experiences including developing contact with people who are unknown to her and to whom she is unknown. She is placed in a similar position to an adult starting a new job but has much less experience of life to support her. Consequently the move to a group setting can be a momentous event children's lives and for some can result in considerable self-doubt; even the most confident child can find this move intimidating. When they start school, children's expectations of what it will be like often do not match the reality.

Those with older siblings or those who play with pupils from school may have acquired some understanding of school values and systems vicariously. Within role play they may have developed 'script knowledge' certain beliefs while they were exploring make-believe school ... However, for first-borns and many others, school will be a completely new experience. In presenting their picture of school, parents, siblings and friends shape children's thinking, but on arriving at school children may find the reality to be different (18).

The setting plays a key role in maintaining children's self-esteem when they are learning to work and play in a different environment from that of home. The size and type of setting can make a difference and there is specific evidence that moving into Reception at four years old is stressful. Barratt's classic study of children starting school in a reception class highlighted some of the feelings experienced by these new young entrants. By looking at photographs and in discussion children described feeling scared, fearful of getting things 'wrong', and not knowing what to do. Most of these feelings can be linked to not feeling in control (19). Although in many respects children are now better supported in their transition to school, a study from Bath University suggests that they still find the experience stressful and exhibit high levels of the stress hormone cortisol for three to six months beforehand. Most of the children in the study showed less anxiety and appeared to have adapted to school a few months later, but for some their cortisol level remained high (20). These studies show young children facing tremendous demands, both emotional and intellectual. Lately there have been genuine moves by schools to recognise the needs of their youngest children. Many settings and schools are now working closely together to ensure a gentle and phased transition into a reception class and from Reception into Year 1. Settings and schools are increasingly beginning to tailor-make a transition to meet each child's needs, rather than expecting every child to fit into one size of provision. It is now generally accepted that when young children make a transition they need easy access to a known adult (a key person) who can offer both reassurance and support that are tailored to each individual. This obviously requires a realistic number of staff to be available and is particularly important for infants under three years old. Findings from the 'Evaluation of the Graduate Leader Fund' show that these very young children need sufficient numbers of close adults to offer them bespoke care and support (21). Any attempt to increase the number of infants is highly likely to dilute the quality of adult attention. Dalli's international research and policy review supports this and concludes that 1:3 is the ideal adult-to-child ratio for infants under two years old (22). Fortunately, after a fierce debate with the government about increasing the number of children per adult, the ratio of 1:3 has remained mandatory (23).

The required ratios in Wales (24), Scotland (25) and Northern Ireland (26) are similar. However, all too often the staffing ratios in English reception classes remain inadequate. Try as they might teachers and assistants find it difficult to offer the bespoke care recommended in order to introduce each child to a multiplicity of new experiences gently and informally and interpret new requirements for them. The close involvement of parents in this process allows children to feel emotionally supported while they learn.

Practitioners also know that each child's self-esteem can be fragile. Self-esteem is not constant for any of us. As adults we can have a very positive view of ourselves in one circumstance only to have it knocked down in another. Given a new manager who makes unreasonable demands at work, an important project which proves to be unsuccessful or a failed relationship in our personal lives, our self-esteem can dip. A mature person with a sound self-concept should be able to cope with this over time and indeed seek out self-affirming situations in which she can succeed.

A young child does not have this ability. Her self-esteem is totally dependent on the people who matter to her and the situations that they provide. A young child will only really value herself fully if she knows that she has the unconditional love of a parent or carer. This knowledge is absolutely critical, and if for some reason it hasn't been acquired during the early years at home then the nursery practitioner has a heavy responsibility to demonstrate that love and care.

Knowing a child's thoughts and interests

Properly caring for a child means knowing about her, including how she thinks and what interests her. In order to feel comfortable and 'at home' in a nursery, a child needs to know that she is known and that her behaviour is understood. The first principle of the EYFS remains intact, emphasising that every child is unique, with their own particular personality and characteristics. Practitioners therefore need to have ways of tuning in to what lies behind children's thoughts, comments and actions. (Chapter 2 deals with the importance of closely listening to children.)

Practitioners can also start to understand children's interests by recognising 'schemes of thought'. Piaget claimed that children's patterns or schemes of thought are evident from babyhood in their early physical and sensory actions. These schemes are strengthened as children repeat their actions; through interactions with others they begin to make connections in their thoughts and so recognise cause and effect. Children's schemes or 'schema' are dealt with extensively in other literature (27, 28, 29).

Some children will have one schema while others will seem to have a number. Although around 36 schemes have been identified, Louis and colleagues have highlighted the most common ones. These are linked to straight lines (trajectory); circles (rotation); seeing things from different angles (orientation); joining things together (connecting); covering things (enveloping); creating and filling a space (enclosing) and moving things from one place to another (transporting) (30). Young children will demonstrate an abiding interest in these patterns of movement through what they do and how they behave. We will see this unfold particularly clearly when children play with open-ended materials. In a beautifully illustrated booklet published by Community Playthings, open-ended is defined as 'not having a fixed answer; unrestricted; allowing for future change' (31). When using these materials children create their own scenarios and are in charge of their learning. The booklet further suggests that these powers are at risk when children are fed a diet of ready-made entertainment, a heavy emphasis on use of commercial equipment and access to electronic activities. If we believe that young children learn initially through first-hand sensory experiences, 'a wealth of open-ended play – with simple materials – can set children on the road to being confident individuals with a lively interest in life' (32).

Case Study 1.2

Daisy at 15 months was introduced to heuristic play (providing her with an array of natural materials and containers which she has time to explore and investigate freely). Her key person observed her on three separate occasions engaged in the following:

- wrapping her teddy up, placing him in a bag, and carrying the bag around with her;
- collecting fir cones and placing them in boxes, taking great care to replace the lid on each box;
- attaching dolly pegs in a circle to the lid of a circular wooden container;
- covering small play characters with shawls and blankets which were placed nearby;
- repeatedly attempting to attach a necklace around her neck.

Comment

Sue, Daisy's key person, felt that she had some secure evidence to suggest that Daisy had an enveloping schema. She supported this by providing more drapes and bags and moving a large cardboard box into the area which Daisy then used as a 'hidey hole'.

Reflection Point

Rose observing Rudi, one of her key children, over a period of time, recognised that his actions revealed a pre-occupation with transporting. She had provided some bags and buggies for him to utilise as a means of transport which he did so happily, but after six weeks Rose needed advice as to what to do next.

(Continued)

(Continued)

Should she:

- give Rudi as much time as she needs to continue and deepen his current interest?
- talk with his parents to discover their son's actions and interests at home and build on these in the pre-school?
- attempt to interest Rudi in a different schema through providing additional resources and reading schematic related stories, e.g. *The Dirty Great Dinosaur* which covers an enclosure and different amounts inside it (33)?

Practitioners need to often take an imaginative leap into children's minds in order to keep in tune with them and make sense of their meanings. While this has always been good practice the statutory framework now requires that all provision made for babies and young children is based on practitioners' close observations of what they do on a day-to-day basis (34).

Supporting a child's behaviour

Although a child must be sure that she is loved at all times, part of the process of caring is also to help shape her behaviour (see also Chapter 11). A problem can arise where the expectations for behaviour differ from home to the setting. It may be that the basis for praise at home is 'to stand up for yourself and hit them back', or 'you make sure that you are the best in the class'. These are powerful messages for young children from people who are very important to them; all practitioners can do is attempt to modify these messages by presenting an alternative view and trying to provide the conditions in the nursery to demonstrate them. Hopefully, then, over a period of time a child learns to use language instead of fists to maintain her rights and to understand that every single person in the nursery community can be 'the best' at something. Again, a confident, bright and creative 4-year-old whose parents have encouraged her non-contingent thinking and activity may find it difficult to conform in any group setting; she will certainly find life extremely hard in a nursery which puts a very heavy emphasis on a narrow definition of correct behaviour. She risks being herself and receiving constant reprimands for her responses, or complying with the requirements and feeling herself to be in an alien and unreasonable environment in which she has no opportunity to show her strengths. In this situation self-belief will ebb away unless a watchful practitioner understands the behaviour that has been encouraged at home and is prepared to be flexible with the requirements in the setting.

Having a positive esteem for oneself is dependent on having a clear view of who one is; this is often difficult for children from minority groups. Tina Bruce points out that too often people from minorities are stereotyped into an identity with which they are not comfortable (35).

Case Study 1.3

Kofi was black and an adopted child. His younger two brothers were white as were his parents. Kofi was only aware of being the much loved oldest child in the family – his colour was incidental although he was proud of it. He was the only black child when he started at the nursery. When one or two children there started to call him 'black boy', Kofi was taken aback. He started to wash obsessively at home. After a week he asked his dad if he could have medicine to change colour. When the parents informed the nursery of their concerns the teachers realised that all the children needed help to see different aspects of their identities. Kofi, with others, was recognised as an important member of his family and the nursery community. Children were encouraged to describe each other in terms of their physical appearance and made a display of their differences and common features.

Comment

Kofi's teachers were initially not prepared for the children's reactions to a child of a different colour. They felt strongly that the comment 'black boy' was simply descriptive and therefore not discriminatory. However, the incident made them more aware of the need to avoid stereotyping, and they were careful to avoid any possibility of discrimination when, shortly afterwards, the nursery admitted a child with cerebral palsy.

Reflection Point

Some young children will react negatively to difference; as they grow up these attitudes may harden into prejudice.

In order to combat intolerance and discrimination consider how well you promote a culture of being similar and belonging?

Moving a child who does not appear to be thriving during the early years at school is not to be considered lightly, although this was eventually seen as the right decision for James. Andrew Pollard, in his social study of five children starting school, describes James who stayed at the local state primary school for the first two years of his school career, after which his parents transferred him to an independent school. James found the move to infant school difficult and his self-esteem suffered. He was not accepted by other children although he badly wanted friends; overall he could not adapt to the robust climate of school life. His teachers supported him, but perceived him as cautious and 'nervy'. There was a clash of culture between the school and the parents who were strongly supportive of James, had high academic aspirations for him, and provided him with home tuition. It was apparent that he could not meet the requirements of both school and home. When he started to be influenced by the other children at the end of the reception year, the parents became alarmed and described his new behaviour as 'rude' and 'cheeky'. Pollard suggests that this little boy's unhappiness sprang from the poor home/school communications. The parents had always aspired for James to move to an independent school where more formal teaching methods were seen to be in keeping with what they wanted for their son. Most importantly, James subsequently flourished in his new school, both in his learning and social life (36).

So, optimal conditions to promote children's self-esteem include care and respect for their ways of thinking and an appreciation of difference, which enables children coming from different backgrounds and cultures to experience feeling good about themselves. Self-esteem is only likely to be fostered in situations where all aspects of all children are esteemed, including their gender, race, ability, culture and language.

Practical Suggestions

Observe

- Observe how babies signal their needs through crying, wriggling with discomfort, and responding to attention.
- Observe a child's emerging schema, demonstrated through her patterns of play, e.g. lining up small animals in a row, covering objects, wrapping herself in a blanket.

Get to know your children

- Consider your group/class and note how much you know about each individual child: their personal characteristics (likes, dislikes, interests, talents and learning dispositions). Ask yourself 'What is this child like and how do I know'?
- Fix a clipboard and pencil in all the areas of provision. Encourage all staff to note significant comments, questions and actions from different children as they work in these areas. At the end of the day, the key person can collect these observations in regard to his/her children, reflect on any noted behaviour that is significant, and decide on any implications for next steps.
- Plan a regular time at the end of each day/week when you meet as staff and share any other information about children that you have gathered.

Create a climate to promote self-esteem

- Consider how your spoken and body language can affect small children, e.g. pursed lips, a tensed body, toe tapping and an abrupt tone of voice communicate irritability; a genuine smile, relaxed body posture, eye contact, gentle touch and warm voice communicate approachability and friendliness; a tight smile and rigid body posture communicate a mixed message and can confuse.

- Demonstrate that you are interested in, and have time for, each child, e.g. bend down to their level when speaking and listening to them; give them time to talk; and try not to interrupt to cut across their thinking.
- Make each new baby and child feel special, e.g. ensure that babies are held in ways that they prefer and are soothed by tapes of rhymes and music that are familiar to them; ask each new child to bring in a photograph of herself and her family; display this on a large board and use it as a topic of conversation.
- Arrange for each new child to have their photograph taken and enlarged. Attach the photograph to a card and cut to form a jigsaw. Older children will enjoy working in small groups and sorting out their own photograph and those of their friends.
- Pronounce children's names correctly – if this is difficult, be honest with parents and ask for their help.
- Remember and refer to important details in the child's life, e.g. 'How is your new kitten, Isaac?', 'Did you enjoy the fair, Angelo?', 'I like your new haircut'.
- Provide mirrors in different parts of your environment to enable children to view themselves when working at different activities.
- Have artefacts and scenarios that reflect children's circumstances, e.g. books where the main characters look like them; dolls which resemble their colour and characteristics; domestic play scenarios which depict familiar contexts; posters and jigsaws which make people like them and their families appear important.

Help children to talk about themselves

- Ask children to do a painting/drawing of themselves and take time to listen to them talking about their picture.
- Ask children about their likes and dislikes about the food they eat, the clothes they wear and their favourite activities at home and in the nursery; these views can be scribed and displayed together with each child's self-portrait or made into individual books.

Provide for those children who are less secure

- Position coat pegs with each child's personal clothing so that they can see them during the day.
- Encourage children to bring a familiar toy to the nursery, in order to maintain a link with home.
- Support a child to separate from his parent/carer; suggest that he carries with him a personal memento that he can refer to during the session, e.g. a photograph of the parent or a personal item such as a scarf which carries a familiar perfume.
- Ensure that an adult is available to less secure children, particularly at vulnerable times of the day, e.g. the start and the end of the session; at transition times; when children are outside.
- Make it possible for these children to be physically near to an adult during group activities.

Professional Practice Questions

1. How do my daily routines make it possible for me to get to know and treat my key children as individuals?
2. How does my environment demonstrate to children that they are welcome in the setting?

Work with Parents

- Encourage parents to understand that the way in which they view their child will influence that child's self-image.
- Suggest how they can boost their child's self-esteem by praising him for achieving small responsibilities, e.g. posting letters, sweeping up leaves.

References

1. Siren Films (2008) *Attachment and Holistic Development: The first year.* DVD and User Notes, Siren Films Ltd.
2. Siren Films (2002) *Exploratory Play.* DVD and User Notes, Siren Films Ltd.
3. Meggitt, C. (2006) *Child Development: An Illustrated Guide.* London: Heinemann.
4. Department for Education (DfE) (2012) *Statutory Framework for the Early Years Foundation Stage,* 1.13. Available at www.education.gov.uk/education.gov.uk/publications/standard//All Publications/Page/1/DFE-00023–2012
5. Moylett, H. and Stewart, N. (2012) 'Understanding the revised Early Years Foundation Stage', *Early Education,* p. 3.
6. Holahan, C.K. and Sears, R.R. (1999) 'The gifted group in later maturity', in D. Goleman (ed.), *Working with Emotional Intelligence.* London: Bloomsbury, p. 71.
7. Blakemore, C. (2001) 'What makes a developmentally appropriate early childhood curriculum?', lecture given at the Royal Society of Arts, 14 February.
8. Katz, L.G. (1995) *Talks with Teachers of Young Children.* Norwood, NJ: Ablex.
9. Roberts, R. (1995) *Self-esteem and Successful Early Learning.* London: Hodder & Stoughton, p. 8.
10. Selleck, D. (2006) 'Key person in the Early Years Foundation Stage', *Early Education,* Autumn.
11. Waite, T. (1993) *Taken on Trust.* London: Hodder & Stoughton, p. 297.
12. Robinson, M. (2003) *From Birth to One: The Year of Opportunity.* Buckingham: Open University Press, p. 128.
13. Siraj-Blatchford, I. (2006) 'Diversity, inclusion and learning in the early years', in G. Pugh and B. Duffy (eds), *Contemporary Issues in the Early Years* (fourth edition). London: Sage, p. 115.
14. White, M. (1996) 'What's so silly about self-esteem?', *TES,* 26 April, p. 3.
15. Emler, N. (2001) 'The costs and causes of low self-esteem', Joseph Rowntree Foundation, www.jrf.org.uk/publications-costs-and-causes-low-self-esteem

16. Thomas, S. (2008) *Nurturing Babies and Children under Four*. London: Heinemann.
17. Tizard, B. and Hughes, M. (2002) *Young Children Learning* (second edition). Oxford: Blackwell.
18. Fabian, H. (2002) 'Empowering children for transitions', in H. Fabian and A.-W. Dunlop (eds), *Transitions in the Early Years*. London: Routledge and Falmer, p. 123.
19. Barratt, G. (1986) *Starting School: An Evaluation of the Experience*. Norwich: AMMA, University of East Anglia.
20. Turner-Cobb, J., Rixon, L. and Jessop, D.S. (2008) 'A prospective study of diurnal cortisol responses to the social experiences of school transition in four-year-old children: anticipation, exposure and adaptation', *Developmental Psychobiology*, 50 (4): 377–89.
21. Mather, S., Ranns, H., Karemaker, A., Moody A., Sylva, K., Graham, J. and Siraj-Blatchford, I. (2011) *Evaluation of the Graduate Leader Fund Final Report*. Bath: Bath University ERSC.
22. Dalli, C., White, E.J., Rockel, J., Duhn, I., with Buchan, E., Davidson, S., Ganly, S., Kus, L. and Want, B. (2011) *Quality Early Childhood Education for Under-Two-Year-Olds: What Should It Look Like?* New Zealand: Ministry of Education.
23. Department for Education (DfE) (2012) op.cit. (see note 4), 3.28.
24. Welsh Government (2012) *National Minimal Standards for Regulated Child Care*. Available at www.wales.gov.uk, 5.12.
25. The Scottish Government (2005) *National Care Standards: Early Education and Care up to the Age of 16* (by R.R. Donnely). Scottish Government, B5394 11/07. Available at www.scotland.gov.uk
26. Department of Education in Northern Ireland (2004) *Review of Pre-school Education in Northern Ireland* (Department of Education pre-school review @ deni.gov.uk, para 118).
27. Athey, G. (2007) *Understanding Schemas in Young Children: A Parent Teacher Partnership*. London: Sage.
28. Nutbrown, C. (2011) *Threads of Thinking* (fourth edition). London: Sage.
29. Atherton, F. and Nutbrown, C. (2013) *Understanding Schemas and Young Children from Birth to Three*. London: Sage.
30. Louis, S., Beswick, C. and Featherstone, S. (2013) *Understanding Schemas in Young Children: Again! Again!* Edinburgh: A. and C. Black.
31. Community Playthings (2008) *I Made a Unicorn*. Robertsbridge, East Sussex: Community Playthings. Available at www.community playthings.co.uk, p. 3.32.
32. Community Playthings (2008) op.cit. (see note 31), p. 20.
33. Waddell, M. and Lord, L. (2009) *The Dirty Great Dinosaur*. London: Orchard Books.
34. Department for Education (DfE) (2012) op.cit. (see note 4), 2.1.
35. Bruce, T. (2005) *Early Childhood Education* (third edition). London: Hodder Arnold.
36. Pollard, A. and Filer, A. (1996) *The Social World of Children's Learning*. London: Cassell, pp. 225–44.

TWO   Confidence and Competence for Learning

- Children's self-esteem and self-knowledge link closely to the ways in which they see themselves as learners and develop a sense of efficacy. This leads them to show either 'growth' or 'fixed' mindsets.
- Their success as learners is dependent on them feeling secure and also having opportunities to experiment in play contexts and try things out for themselves.

Self-knowledge

When people are acknowledged and respected, this contributes to their self-regard. However, this must also go hand in hand with them getting to know themselves. As young children develop they start to learn about themselves and what they can do; they begin to recognise those things that they find easy and where they need help and support.

Initially, however, children have limited self-insight and they look to others to provide information; a young child is dependent on the adults around her to gain a view of her strengths and weaknesses. Nevertheless, although guidance should be given and boundaries for behaviour established, ultimately, as Pat Gura suggests, the main aim must be to help children develop a sense of control over their lives and build their own aspirations (1).

In a setting where adults control, children can only respond and their self-knowledge is stunted.

As always, an educator's actions are a powerful influence on the way in which a child develops. Questions which allow children to give open-ended answers and which spring from a genuine interest in all that they do will encourage individuals to think about their achievements.

The ways in which adults respond to children will also have a powerful effect on their developing knowledge about themselves. For example, a skilled practitioner sensitively balances giving positive affirmation to her children, while establishing clear messages about acceptable behaviours. Drawing on studies of work with different age groups (2, 3) the following types of responses are suggested which can either hinder or help children.

Responses which hinder children's self-knowledge

1 Evaluating through praise

Nursery settings are usually defined by the constant use of praise and encouragement; comments such as 'That's wonderful' and 'I'm really pleased with you' are commonly heard. Praise is important, but as Lawrence warns 'whilst there is a place for genuine praise in self-esteem enhancement, this has to be realistic praise, otherwise the child will be in danger of developing a faulty self-image' (4). Where adults always take the responsibility for judging what a child has done, believing that this is their job, this restricts the child from forming her own view. Lafferty, the director of High/Scope UK, usefully distinguishes between 'praise' and 'encouragement'. Lafferty suggests that praise comes from 'outside' the child and is an external judgement of approval, while 'encouragement' is about motivating the child within and creating the ongoing desire to learn (5). Praise can also encourage conformity when it leads to children becoming dependent on others rather than on themselves. Gura suggests that the constant use of praise can be high on warmth but low with regard to information (6) and that this is particularly the case when praise is general. Moreover, overdoses of lavish praise do become devalued even by young children. Robert, age five, told me confidentially, 'It doesn't matter really what you paint because she [his teacher] always says it's really very lovely'. Young children deserve more than a comforting and benign environment.

Nevertheless the use of praise is very effective when used with discretion. It is particularly helpful to encourage those children who are not well motivated, to help set the limits of behaviour, and for young children who are learning to socialise and become one of a group. The Unit for Parenting Studies at Leicester University encourages parents and carers to give their children 'five praises a day' to improve their behaviour and self-image and to redress the attention that so often is given to misbehaviour (7).

Use of praise is particularly helpful when children are being introduced to an early years setting, but it should be seen as a means to an end. Specific praise that is focused can help children become aware of the processes of their achievements, for example 'Using those elastic bands to fix the two boxes together is really clever, Dean'.

2 Evaluating with criticism

Negative comments are inevitably going to leave children feeling inadequate and that they have failed. Importantly, if a child is criticised this usually shuts down her learning. Early years practitioners are very aware of this and negative responses are rarely used in early years settings.

Responses which help children's self-knowledge

1 Using silence

Often in a busy nursery, and particularly when adults feel under the pressure of time, young children are not given sufficient time to reflect on and collect their thoughts. However, if when asking a question an adult pauses to allow a young child time to respond, the chances are that, as with older children, the time allowed for thinking means that the response given is of greater quality. It also demonstrates the adult's faith that the child will be able to respond, which in turn fosters that child's confidence. Young children will learn to recognise that they are not expected to come up with quick answers and that it is more important to have the time to explore what they really feel.

2 Clarifying

Young children often find it difficult to put their thoughts into words. Sometimes, in their eagerness, they will rush to communicate and then tail away as they struggle to recall the sense of their message. Adults can actively accept children's contributions by paraphrasing or summarising what they have said. Although a practitioner may use different words she will make sure that she maintains the child's intention and meaning: 'I know what you are saying, David. Your idea is ...' In this way a practitioner can show that she has both received and understood what a child has said.

3 Asking for information

If practitioners show a genuine interest in children's views about what they have done, this helps children to become confident in making judgements.

4 Providing information

If young children are helped to see how their paintings and constructions have developed over a period of time they will start to understand that achievements and progress are linked to growing up. A child will take pleasure in recalling her limitations as a baby and contrasting them with what she is doing now.

Self-esteem, Self-knowledge and Self-efficacy

A child who has sound self-esteem is well placed to learn. The Early Years Foundation Stage (EYFS) stresses that educational programmes must involve activities and experiences which encourage children to have confidence in their own abilities (8). Feeling good about yourself though is not sufficient in itself; self-knowledge is important in order for people to develop not only an optimistic view of themselves but also one which is realistic. However, in order to learn young children must believe that they are able to do so. If this belief is not secured during the early years of life it is unlikely to blossom later. In a study to accelerate learning in science with pupils of secondary age, about half made impressive progress while the others did not. One of the main reasons for this difference was that the latter group of children were afraid of failing in thinking tasks and so gave up the mental challenges required (9).

Some children on admission to an early years setting will not regard themselves as learners. Their thoughts and views may have been disregarded by adults; caring and protective parents may not have trusted children to try out things for themselves and so learn from their mistakes. These children will have learned to accept that they are not important or competent enough to do things for themselves. By comparison, other children on admission shine as eager and capable learners who brim with self-belief. Their early experiences have included opportunities to try things out and discuss the outcomes with adults. They have been gently helped to frame their ideas in words and their increasing command of language has helped them to feel 'in control' of events. Bandura's research ascribes this self-belief as supporting self-efficacy (effectiveness) where a person:

- approaches new encounters as something to relish and tackle;
- becomes committed to a task;
- persists even in the face of difficulty (10).

Siegler et al. suggest that 'how children think and feel about themselves plays a role in how they respond to their successes and failures' (11). Dweck supports this view and illustrates it with her reference to mastery and helpless behaviour (12).

Growth and fixed mindsets

Children who follow a mastery approach are confident and have a positive view of themselves. They seek new and challenging experiences and believe that if they persevere they can succeed even in the face of difficulties.

Other children are unsure of themselves; because their self-esteem is not secure they constantly look for approval from others. These children show helpless behaviour in that they 'give up' easily, and when things go wrong they believe that it is their own fault because 'they are no good'. They attribute their failures to factors that are outside their control. Dweck links mastery and helpless behaviours to 'mindsets'. She suggests that master learners adopt a growth mindset; they wrestle with problems and delight in the effort of thinking and learning. Duckworth and colleagues summarise how master learners persist in their enquiries and show 'grit' in their determination to succeed (13). While the 'master learners' forge ahead in learning, often on their own initiative, the 'helpless children' adopt a fixed mindset: they avoid the challenge of uncertainty and stick to the familiar where they feel safe and know what to do. They need constant reassurance and support from parents and key persons (see also Chapter 5). Although Dweck's work was with older children, similar patterns of behaviour are evident with 3- and 4-year-olds as they begin to recognise who they are and what they can do. Young children's beliefs about themselves as master learners who can be effective are closely linked to their emerging self-regulation, described as 'a deep internal mechanism that enables children as well as adults to engage in mindful, intentional and thoughtful behaviours' (14). Moreover, the consequences can be profound as children move into school. Those showing helpless behaviour with fixed mindsets are unable to adopt strategies to help themselves. The descriptors for mastery behaviour chime closely with the Characteristics of Teaching and Learning in the EYFS which require practitioners to be aware of how children learn as well as the content of learning. When children develop positive mindsets and persist to overcome difficulties they begin to see that, by their efforts they can make a difference. They relish being in control, experiencing the 'skill, will and thrill of being learners' (15).

Bandura's work made it clear though that this self-efficacy is not necessarily constant or permanent, rather it is strengthened by experiences of

Figure 2.1   Dexter enjoys a Challenge and a Surprise
© Siren Films

successful outcomes where persistence and self-belief are seen to pay off. It can also be weakened when there is no support or encouragement for commitment and perseverance and endeavour is undermined (16). In the same way strong learning characteristics are dependent on what young children experience:

> When they are encouraged and supported to follow their curiosity, to feel the satisfaction of meeting their own challenges, to think for themselves, and to plan and monitor how they will go about their activities, they become self-regulated learners who later outstrip children who may have developed more early subject based knowledge but are more passive in their learning. (17)

Play and learning

Although all of the characteristics of learning are critical as a means of learning, 'Playing and Exploring' offers the greatest scope for confidence building. When young children get to the point of being willing to 'have a go' they then access more and more experiences and grow as learners. Practitioners now have firm support from the EYFS to provide for play which is described as being 'essential for children's development, building their confidence as they learn to explore, to think about problems and relate to others' (18).

This description sums up a masterly approach to play where children make their own judgements, take initiatives, and seek resources and information when they require these. However, there has long been an ongoing tension between masterly play which is under the control of the player and the role of the adult. The EYFS raises the issue but offers no guidance, merely referring to 'planned, purposeful play' and the need for 'an ongoing judgement to be made by practitioners about the balance between activities led by children or guided by adults' (19). There remains an understandable degree of uncertainty in schools and nurseries about how play methodology aids learning and the practicalities of planning and provision (see Chapter 10).

Case Study 2.1

Pascale and Jeremy were the same age, three years 11 months, and they had started nursery at the same time during the previous term. Pascale sat at a table drawing. She was clutching the pencil in a pincer grip and her movements were repetitive. Try as I might I could not gain eye contact with her or get her to respond in any way. On mentioning this to the teacher she said that she was not surprised. When Pascale was admitted to the nursery, her name was Cheri. A month later, her mother requested that the name be changed to Amanda. On returning to the nursery that term the staff were further informed that Amanda was no longer to have that name but was to

(Continued)

(Continued)

be called Pascale. The little girl was not sure who she was. Her teacher reported that every day Pascale refused to move from the drawing table and join in any other activities in the nursery.

On passing through to the next room I met Jeremy who was with a fairly large group of children listening to a story about a little boy who was walking along a very long road. Jeremy, having grasped the conventions of being a pupil in a group, raised his hand to make a comment. When invited to do so he politely asked if the road in the story went on and on into infinity! The teacher, somewhat taken aback, said that it might do but suggested that Jeremy explain what the word meant. 'Well', said Jeremy, confidently raising his voice so that all in the group might hear, 'if it goes on into infinity, it might never, ever end!'

Comment

Despite being of a similar age and having had a similar amount of time in the nursery, these two children were poles apart. Pascale, alias Cheri alias Amanda, was not even able to recognise herself in her name, and showed helpless behaviour and a fixed mindset in her refusal to accept new challenges. Jeremy's high regard for himself as a learner was evident in his active participation in the story. Having a growth mindset he was keen to question and make links in his learning using a fascinating new word he had acquired. Jeremy showed all the elements of a master player, using the teacher as a resource for further learning.

Before they arrived at the nursery, home experiences had already had a potent effect on Pascale's and Jeremy's views of themselves as learners. The staff were faced with different challenges for these two children. Pascale needed the security and consistency provided by a predictable programme and the attention and care of one adult in whom she could learn to trust. Close and sensitive links with Pascale's mother would hopefully enable her to recognise her daughter's needs and try to meet them at home. Jeremy's inner resources for learning were already firmly in place. The nursery's task here was to ensure that staff respected Jeremy's contributions, provided additional stimulus to motivate him, and extended his skills and knowledge based on what he understood already.

Reflection Point

- Consider your children and those among them who show helpless behaviour and have fixed mindsets.
- What three actions could you take to help them adopt growth mindsets and a 'can-do' attitude to learning?

The psychologist Carl Rogers says that children need two conditions in order to be creative learners: psychological safety and psychological freedom (20).

Pascale's future progress depended initially on the first condition being met. Rogers suggests that psychological safety is dependent on having total trust in a child and accepting all that that child does; encouraging the child to become self-aware; and trying to see the world from the child's perspective and so getting to understand how she feels. It will only be when Pascale feels safe that she will make any progress towards mastery learning. Jeremy shows that he has already benefited from positive support at home: this now needs to be sustained in the nursery, at the same time Jeremy requires the psychological freedom to try out new things and ideas.

Practical Suggestions

Help children to recognise what they have learned

- Publicise children's achievements, e.g. 'Liam is really good at doing up his buttons – would you like to show everyone, Liam?'
- Encourage children to teach others, e.g. showing a friend how to use the mouse on the computer, or how to hang their painting to let it dry.
- Build into your session relaxed and informal recall sessions when older children demonstrate and discuss with others what they have experienced, e.g. six children with a key person when each child talks about and shows any outcomes of her most recent activity. It is important that each child feels free to opt out or to make a minimal response. As children grow accustomed to the session they can be encouraged to comment on other children's contributions.

Professional Practice Questions

1. How are my children helped to consider critically what they achieve?
2. How well do I help children to appreciate the processes of their learning, e.g. progress stages in learning how to mix paints/ tie their shoelaces?
3. How often do I praise my key children and for what purpose?

Work with Parents

- Discuss with parents how they might help their children feel good about themselves but also start to develop a realistic view of their capabilities.
- Give parents one or two examples of responses to use which aid self-knowledge (from the list given earlier in this chapter) and suggest that they let you know how these were received.

References

1. Gura, P. (1996) 'What I want for Cinderella: self-esteem and self-assessment', *Early Education*, 19 (Summer).
2. Sylva, K. (1998) 'The early years curriculum: evidence based proposals'. Paper prepared for NAEIAC Conference on Early Years Education.
3. Costa, A.L. (1991) *The School as Home for the Mind*. Australia: Hawker Brownlow Education, pp. 53–66.4.
4. Lawrence, D. (2006) *Enhancing Self-esteem in the Classroom*. London: Sage, p. 21.
5. Lafferty, P. (2007) 'A desire to learn or a desire to please', *Eye*, 9 (4): 8.
6. Gura, P. op.cit. (see note 1), p. 7.
7. Gaunt, C. (2008) 'Give them "five a day" in praise, parents advised', *Nursery World*, 20 November, p. 6.
8. Department for Education (DfE) (2012) *Statutory Framework for the Early Years Foundation Stage*. London: HMSO, p. 1.6.
9. Gold, K. (1999) 'Making order out of chaos', *Guardian Education*, 11 May, p. 2.
10. Bandura, A. (1997) *Self-efficacy: The Exercise of Control*. New York: W.H. Freeman.
11. Siegler, R., Deloache, J. and Eisenberg, N. (2003) *How Children Develop*. New York: Worth, p. 428.
12. Dweck, C. (2006) *Mindset: The New Psychology of Success*. New York: Random House.
13. Duckworth, A., Matthews, M. and Kelly, D. (2007) 'Grit, perseverance and passion: long-term goals', *Journal of Personality and Social Psychology*, 92 (6): 1087–1101.
14. Bodrova, E. and Leong, D.J. (2008) 'Developing self-regulation in kindergarten: can we keep all the crickets in one basket?', *Beyond the Journal: Young Children on the Web,* March. Washington, DC: National Association for the Education of Young Children, p.1.
15. Moylett, H. (2013) 'How young children learn', in *Characteristics of Effective Early Learning*. Maidenhead: Open University Press, p. 1.
16. Bandura, A. (1997) op.cit. (see note 10).
17. Moylett, H. and Stewart, N. (2012) 'Understanding the revised Early Years Foundation Stage', *Early Education*, p. 10.
18. Department for Education (DfE) (2012) op.cit. (see note 8), p. 1.9.
19. Department for Education (DfE) (2012) op.cit. (see note 8), p. 1.9.
20. Rogers, C. (1961) *On Becoming a Person*. Boston, MA: Houghton Mifflin.

THREE Living with Others

- Babies are attracted to others from birth and grow up initially in a social world made up of immediate family.
- Young children learn to relate to a key person and a wider group of adults when they move from the security of home into a nursery setting.
- Their developing friendships are dependent on them acquiring and practising complex social skills.

'Being good with people' has always been recognised as a strength in people's work and personal lives. This is even more important today when the pace of life does not allow time for personal contacts. In the late 1990s Philip Zimbardo of Stanford University told the British Psychological Society that we were entering a new ice age of non-communication, and there was what he called an emerging worldwide 'epidemic of shyness'. Zimbardo's theory was that there was less of the personal contact and small talk that held communities together (1).

Fourteen years later Sigman supports this view referring to young children's home lives. Quoting research on families, he asserts that time spent on the internet reduces time spent in face-to-face relationships and that social engagement is rapidly disappearing (2). Sherry Turkle summed this up succinctly in the *New York Times* with a stark message that we are designing technologies that give an illusion of companionship without friendship (3). However, although mobile phones and screen technology are now more readily available to young children a lack of personal contact is certainly not evident in early years settings. Children are open and friendly. They chatter as they work and play.

Disputes that flare up are usually settled amicably. Any newcomer visiting a nursery notices immediately the sociable aspect. However, this social environment is not achieved easily. We know that young children are brimming with potential but lacking in life experience; interpersonal skills only develop over time. Around the age of two years old young children start to respond with caring gestures towards a person who is upset or hurt and begin to take some part in role play with others. Considerable social learning is required in negotiating to become part of a group. This aspect is highlighted in the Early Years Foundation Stage (EYFS) as one aspect in the prime area of Personal, Social and Emotional Development (4).

Why do Social Relationships Matter?

When we consider the basic attributes young children need to acquire, social skills must be a priority. Our children live in a democratic society and in order to survive they must learn to rub along with others. We may know of adults who are able and attractive but for some reason they are not able to relate easily: they are uneasy with people and consequently people find them difficult. This can be a serious disability in life. Practitioners know that they have an important task to ensure that children are equipped to live with and relate easily to others. A good experience of transition can enhance a young child's well-being and learning while a poor experience can be damaging. For a child to have a friend is a strong factor in supporting a positive transition to a new setting. Children who move into a reception class or Year 1 alone can feel unsure, isolated, nervous, anxious and afraid. A friend (even a temporary one) can offer companionship, physical closeness, shared past experiences and reassurance. Howes showed that children who made transitions in day-care with friends found it easier than those who came alone (5). This emerged as a major theme in Dunn's research. She asked children who had been in a reception class for six weeks what advice they would offer to a child who was just starting school. One boy gave a clear message: 'get a friend' (6). Dunn had also found that when children had moved with friends into new settings, they remembered that those friends had helped them feel happy (7). There are wider claims that positive relationships with those around us and sustaining friendships are important factors in our gaining the desirable state of being happy (8).

Psychological Perspectives

When working with children we face the question of how the world that surrounds those children supports or hinders their social development. In this chapter we highlight the work of four important theorists: Vygotsky, Bruner, Bronfenbrenner and Bandura.

Vygotsky lived during the Russian revolution and only worked in Russia for ten years before his death from tuberculosis. His work was largely unknown in the West until it was published in 1962. Despite this short career his ideas were critical in emphasising that children construct their learning in a social context (9):

- Vygotsky focused on the connections between people and the ways in which they interacted in shared experiences (10). He believed that social learning preceded development, i.e. the child learns first with people and then functions by herself.
- He developed the notion of the more knowledgeable other (MKO). This describes anyone who has a better understanding or skill than the learner in respect to a particular concept or task. For a young child this may be a close adult, an older child or a peer.
- He introduced the Zone of Proximinal Development (ZPD) which is the distance between a person (young child) operating independently and the potential for learning given guidance from another.

These three theories have important implications for children learning with adults and other children (see later in the chapter):

- Bruner, born in New York in 1915, built on and developed some of Vygotsky's work. Like Vygotsky, Bruner emphasised the social nature of learning and the role of the adult in supporting children's learning.
- Bruner's concept of scaffolding is very similar to Vygotsky's ZPD. Scaffolding was first introduced by Bruner in 1976 (11). It refers to an adult observing what a child can do by herself and then offering specific and bespoke support to help that child achieve a more challenging task. This support is gradually withdrawn as the child becomes competent His concept of a spiral curriculum outlines how children learn through discovery with the aid of adults and then deepen their thoughts and ideas by re-visiting their experiences and ideas.
- Bruner believed strongly that close adults, and particularly parents, support children's cognitive development through scaffolding everyday play.

Bronfenbrennner, also working in the 1970s, followed these theorists, reminding us that young children do not develop by themselves. He is well known for promoting an ecological approach where he identifies four different environmental systems that can influence child development and impact on social growth:

- The microsystem covers the innermost circle of the child's life, namely relationships with close family and friends and daily experiences in nursery settings and school. All of these contacts help to socialise children.
- The mesosystem refers to two microsystems linking together, e.g. home experiences which offer rich opportunities for social learning echoed in the nursery.

- The exosystem is concerned with the conditions that can affect family life and which impinge on the child, e.g. a parent is stressed and irritable with her children having lost her job and been forced to rely on benefits.
- The macrosystem involves the wider context such as government policies and cultural beliefs, e.g. racist attitudes in a society may impact on the lives of children from immigrant families.

Although each system can be viewed separately, in reality they interconnect. They can be seen as a nest of Russian dolls with each doll fitting inside another. The child is seen as the smallest doll supported or restricted by a series of larger dolls, each of which represents one of the systems.

Bronfenbrenner's key message is that each child's development and their social experiences are influenced by the values and expectations of their family and the immediate and wider community (12).

Bandura's work on self-efficacy was referred to in Chapter 2. However, he is probably best known for his earlier work on Social Learning theory published in the 1970s. This follows the views of the other three theorists in stressing the importance of social interactions and learning from others (13).

Bandura demonstrated the significance of role models in child development. He highlighted how young children learn to behave by observing others. He also showed worryingly that this applied equally to children imitating observed aggressive, anti-social behaviour. His acclaimed Bobo doll experiment involved three groups of nursery age children observing a film where a plastic doll was hit with a mallet. Each group viewed a different ending. One group saw the behaviour rewarded, one saw it punished, and the third group saw that no action was taken. The children were then observed playing with the doll: the two groups who had witnessed the rewarded behaviour or where nothing was done about it showed higher levels of aggression towards the doll. The researchers concluded that the children were motivated to imitate what they believed were valued ways of behaving (14). These findings are a powerful reminder of the need to show children consistent examples of positive and loving relationships.

Simply offering models of pro-social behaviour is not enough though. Young children need to be alert and responsive to the models around them, to remember what they have seen and heard, and over time, to try out this behaviour for themselves.

Social Skills in Early Personal Development

To ensure their healthy growth and development, babies and very young children need to feel securely attached and become socially competent.

Attachment

The EYFS recognises the fundamental importance of attachment, which is dealt with later in the book (see Chapter 7). For the purposes of this chapter, we recognise that a secure initial attachment underpins any further relationships. Significant people who are special, and who forge a primary link with a young child, gently introduce her to the wider world: the special person or key person encourages the child to branch out, meet new people and learn to trust others. This is beautifully illustrated in the DVD *Life at Two*, where at 26 months Ava's very secure relationship with her mum helps her to adjust to her key person in the nursery (15). Maria Robinson suggests that children who are loved, encouraged, respected and comforted are able to learn about the world within a context of emotional safety and about themselves as fundamentally loveable (16).

Social competence

Babies are primed to be social and to communicate. Within a very short time babies are 'reading' eye contacts, facial and body gestures, and the tone of voice of those significant people who care for them. Some babies and toddlers are particularly keen to interact. My experience suggests that these are the small individuals who have already had their early attempts at conversations valued: they quickly learn that the sounds they make are of interest to adults and they want more of this affirming experience. The adult's task is to tune in to the baby's intentions and efforts and maintain this social dialogue. This applies even if the baby does not share a common spoken language with the practitioner, as babies are able to tune in rapidly to other languages and will be reassured by warm gestures, expressions and tone of voice (17).

In order to communicate, babies, young children, and indeed all of us need to have someone to communicate with. Piaget (an educational giant in his time) encouraged us to believe that the very young child was a little scientist; the role of the practitioner was predominantly to provide interesting and stimulating resources and then observe the child as she freely interacts with them. (Whilst affirming active learning, this belief led to the adult's role being marginalised.) As we have seen, other theorists have emphasised that all of us, children and adults, grow up and learn more with others. As a result, practitioners have an important responsibility to pave the way for young children to reach out and communicate with a widening circle.

Social relationships with peers develop very early out of the family. Babies will respond to other babies. Goldschmeid and Selleck have shown in their studies that children from a few weeks old are able to use sound, gazes and touches (later they exchange objects) to develop loyalties and attachments to other children in their group (18). From this very early start, other children continue to be important.

Infants already show considerable interest in what people do. They tune in to how adults react to different situations and use these reactions as a point of reference for their own behaviour. All parents and other close adults will have experienced a toddler's delight when she is praised for an activity or her knowing look when an adult says 'no'. By three years old, friendships start to become of interest although at this stage they are transitory. *Development Matters* suggests that children as young as two to three years old are keen to share experiences with others and may form a special friendship with another child (19). However, we should bear in mind the very wide gap in development between a child of 24 and 36 months. This makes it much less likely that a 2-year-old will yet have the social competence to sustain a friendship with another. The development of relationships has always been a fundamental part of early childhood education. Young children are recognised not just as individuals but also as part of their family. Practitioners recognise that the development of close links between the home and the setting is essential in the interests of the child (see Chapter 15). Depending on their family experiences, children will also have learned a great deal already about getting on with people. They may be used to warm loving relationships within the family and have had many and varied chances to meet a wide circle of different adults and children. Other children may have been sheltered from social contacts, been reared in a culture of privacy, or live in geographically isolated areas with no other young families nearby. Parents are usually keen for their children to spread their social wings: for most parents, an important reason for sending their child to a nursery is to help them learn to mix with other people which they recognise as a key factor in living a happy and successful life.

Regardless of the social experiences young children will have had before coming to an early years setting, it is likely that many relationships will have been established since babyhood and will have developed with the support of parents. Moving into a new environment and facing often a completely unknown group of children and adults is a challenge for any child. For those who have experienced only a small social circle of contacts at home this experience can be daunting. Most children now have some early experience in a nursery setting, but for those few who make a direct transition from home to a reception class in a mainstream school, this will probably prove to be the *most* challenging move for a child during her school career. In Pollard's study of five children who started school very shortly after their fourth birthday, the children's parents provided constant emotional, practical and intellectual support in the early days of school. Pollard emphasises the vital role that parents and carers play as the reference point and interpreter for their children as they move into a wider social context (20).

Reflection Point

When welcoming a new child, how far do I take account of information from parents and former practitioners about that child's friendships?

Relating to adults

Babies and infants are very concerned with themselves and they must have their particular needs met. Most will receive this and continue to benefit from it at home as part of a loving upbringing. Parents and other close family members and friends will have listened, responded, and demonstrated their interest in all that the child does. Within this secure and interested environment children thrive. On moving to a group setting the child's first need is to develop a link with new adults whose task it is to provide a similar framework of security. When they first separate from their parents, children must be able to feel confident in the care of the people who are temporarily taking the place of their parents.

Children need to make this close relationship with at least one adult in the setting who they know is there for them. This is no longer left to chance as it is now required for every baby and child in a setting to have a key person. Roberts clearly describes the importance of a key person for babies and young children. She suggests that a key person in a setting and significant people at home often do the same things. They help the very young child manage during the day: they think about her; they get to know her well; they sometimes worry about her; they get to know each other; they talk about the child (21).

Confident and sociable children who are already socially experienced may rapidly 'branch out' to relate to other children. Other children, however, will continue to have a greater need for adult attention throughout their early years.

It may be that for various reasons, some children have been denied the time of an adult at home. Other children who initially may require a great deal of the practitioner's attention and time may be those who are used to having a great deal of attention, possibly an only or first child. Some children will need the practitioner more at specific times when they are vulnerable: for example, this can happen when a new baby arrives or if there is illness or turbulence in the family. In all these cases it is important for the practitioner to be aware of and to respond to individual needs and give the message that she is consistently there for the child.

Good communication is at the heart of any successful relationship. Petrie suggests that 'Whether it involves children, babies or adults, interpersonal communication is a two-way process. Listening to children shows our respect for them and builds their self-esteem' (22). Adults tune in to all that young children are trying to convey. This involves using professional skills and developing attitudes which are at the heart of good practice. The Reggio approach has made a significant contribution by using the Pedagogy of Listening. The approach developed by Carla Rinaldi is described as a relationship where adult and child construct knowledge and make meaning together. Rinaldi stresses that in order to listen to children, adults need to focus deeply on the context of the dialogue, i.e. what is happening at that moment in time (23).

The Listening to Young Children Project and Training Framework developed in England (24) began because of concerns that young children were not being given a voice. The project concluded that this was largely to do with a belief that children under eight years old were too inexperienced to have a view or make a useful contribution about matters that concerned them. The Training Framework suggests ways in which children can be encouraged to communicate both verbally and through the visual and expressive arts. Six years on, the project acknowledges that there is a revised focus on listening to children, embedded in the Children Act 2006, which requires local authorities in England and Wales to take account of young children's views and actively listen to them (25). In Scotland 'The Child at the Centre' echoes a similar message, recognising that young children can provide thoughtful views about their learning experiences and what is important for them (26).

Developing Understanding and Friendship Skills

Making friends is very important to young children: they approach other children openly, often asking 'Will you be my friend?' They also show great distress if they are refused friendship. Common and heart-rending cries from some young children are 'Peter won't play with me' or 'Zareen says that she is not my friend'. One small-scale study demonstrated that when a number of children in a kindergarten left for their new school, both the group transferring and the group left behind showed signs of negative behaviour and mild distress. Although the researcher admitted that the agitation demonstrated by the leaving group may have been due to the anticipated transfer, the group of children remaining appeared to have missed their 'friends' after they had gone (27).

Studies suggest that the first six or seven years of development are critical for the development of social skills. By four years old a child should easily be able to deal with several peer relationships. If that child fails to learn to relate to other children during this time, this can lead to great unhappiness. Nurseries and schools are social communities. If a child is condemned to attend school daily without the support of friends she is unlikely to learn well: studies show that a lack of friends can ultimately result in children refusing to attend school (28).

Dunn reminds us however that some children are content being without a friend, that they are quite happy with their own company. Nevertheless, she admits that this is rare (29). More usually children will want a friend but have difficulties with friendships, particularly if they are shy or not inclined to co-operate. Other reasons may be less obvious, and the fact that most young children in the settings do make friends easily and quickly sometimes makes us overlook the complexities involved in establishing relationships. These complexities include developing certain understandings which are explored below.

Becoming aware of others' viewpoints

Piaget tested young children in a formal situation and consequently found that most individuals under four years old were not able to appreciate any view other than their own. However, as Donaldson has shown, when they respond in everyday situations that make sense to them, children show a higher level of understanding (30). The most familiar context for children is the home. Dunn's earlier work with young families in their homes shows that even babies in their first year are sensitive to those who are close to them. Infants less than two years old show some understanding of how older siblings will react when teased or annoyed (31.) They observe and are able to 'tune in' to quarrels between members of their family. Their own behaviour is sympathetic and supportive to the member of the family who is upset, but they are also able to recognise and join in with a shared joke. By three years of age the children in one of her studies were able to recognise, anticipate and respond to the feelings of their baby brothers or sisters (32). (See also Chapter 7.)

These studies offer powerful evidence for how, even before they can talk, very young children take a real interest in and begin to understand how other people behave. Although they are not able to appreciate another's perspective in an intellectual task, they already work from a sharp social intelligence. However, during these first three years of life, this understanding of people's behaviour is largely influenced by children recognising feelings that they themselves have. In the best circumstances young children are able to observe family interactions and have been encouraged to take an active part in them. They are then able to take their social learning into a group setting.

Case Study 3.1

Jodie brought into the nursery her new teddy, which she had received for her fourth birthday. She proudly showed it to the other children but became very upset when Gary, a new 3-year-old, grabbed it from her and sat on it. The other children pushed Gary away and returned the bear to Jodie. Later she was observed going up to Gary and offering for him to borrow the bear. Jodie

(Continued)

(Continued)

explained to her teacher that Gary was only little and she knew that he really wanted a bear like hers.

Comment

Jodie's generous response showed her mature ability to recognise, empathise and respond positively to Gary's envy and longing for a similar toy.

Reflection Point

How might you use Jodie's response to encourage generous behaviour in other children?

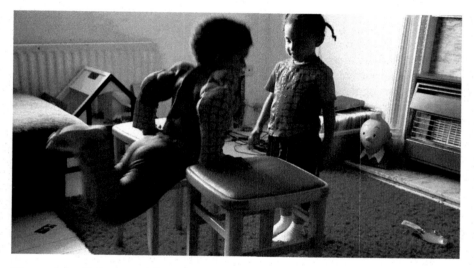

Figure 3.1   Dexter and Rae, good friends
© Siren Films

Understandings about friendships

Young nursery-age children regard their current playmates as their friends. When a 3-year-old says 'I'm your friend now', this is likely to mean that 'I am playing with you now'. By age four a friendship is becoming more stable, based on shared experiences over a period of time. At this age children look for each other in the nursery and may spend considerable amounts of time together. It is at this stage that 'friendship' has a much more sociable meaning, although a long-lasting relationship is rare until a child is around seven or eight years old.

These social understandings are linked to a child's level of maturation. Generally speaking, the more practice that young children have in making and playing with friends the more experiences they will have of both rejection and acceptance. In this way they come to understand what is involved in being a friend and maintaining that friendship. However, it is not always simply a matter of providing the experience as there are powerful factors which affect relationships. Young children are differently equipped to make friends and have friendship preferences.

Ramsey suggests that young children's social behaviour can be grouped into four categories (33):

- **Popular** children are usually very capable and more intellectually, socially and emotionally mature than their peers. It is also a sad truth that popular children are often more physically attractive and this is particularly noticeable with little girls (34).
- **Rejected** children may show aggressive or withdrawn behaviour. They may angrily retaliate or avoid other children.
- **Neglected** children appear to take little part in the social life of the group and are often quite content with their own company.
- **Controversial** children are described as having a major impact on the social group, i.e. socially and intellectually talented but often in trouble for aggressive behaviour and rule breaking. Although these children are often group leaders, they are regarded with caution by some of their peers.

It can be helpful to recognise these behaviours, although Ramsey points out that these are crude descriptors and many children may be well adjusted socially but unable to fit into any of these categories. When looking at friendship preferences research indicates that, for whatever reason, girls find it a little easier to make friends than boys. Children also tend to select friends who are like them. Thus the popularity of an individual child may be affected by that child being in a group with others from the same ethnic origin, or with those of a similar level of maturity or ability. Moreover, while little girls will play with either boys or girls, boys prefer to be with other boys.

Rubin's study of nursery-age children suggests that there are intricate social skills involved in making friends. These include the ability to gain entry to group activities, to be approving and supportive of one's peers, to manage conflicts appropriately and to exercise sensitivity and tact. The most popular children were seen to be particularly accomplished in using these skills (35).

The more experiences young children have of relationships and contacts with others in their play, the more they gain from it. Rubin's work and his reference to other studies show that the children who make friends easily display generous behaviour, i.e. they involve others in their play, praise them, and show affection and care. These socially experienced children also learn that, in order to maintain a friendship, they need to recognise when others are upset and do something about it. They start to learn the skills of reconciling arguments and negotiating roles.

It is very noticeable when young children find it difficult to relate and establish friendships, and it is important to distinguish between 'aloneness' as a matter of choice rather than necessity. 'Neglected' 4-year-olds might have all the social skills to communicate and play with others, but may prefer to spend time alone. Practitioners will quickly learn the difference between that autonomous and self-sufficient behaviour and behaviour demonstrated by a child who is longing but unable to relate to others. 'Rejected' children are the ones who become socially isolated, although this is not their choice.

Scarlett's study of nursery children suggests that socially isolated children spend a considerable amount of time 'on the side-lines', observing others at play but without the strategies for joining in. When they do become involved, they are necessarily inexperienced players and they need direction from other children. This can mean that they are devalued in the group and they are very often the individuals who end up in a role-play being the dog or the baby (36). When these children do try to make friends, their overtures to others are often either too timid or over-effusive and other children will 'back off'. Paley vividly describes her concern about the social exclusion that operated in her class when some children announced to others 'you can't play' (37).

Practical Suggestions

Observe developing social relationships

- Observe how babies make contact with others, through gazing, imitating and responding to interactions, particularly from their key person.
- Observe how toddlers reach out to other children, initially by playing alongside them, and handing out and receiving objects.
- Observe how children aged three to five years approach others to make friends.

Learn more about children's relationships

- Note the patterns of young children's friendships to find out who are the most popular and who are the children who have difficulties in making relationships.
- Note children in a role play and identify the leaders, followers and those on the sidelines. Note friendship patterns in various activities: which children are constantly together; which children share similar interests (schema); and how they share this in their construction/drawing/painting/movement/stories.

Strengthen your relationships with children

- Consider the kind of messages you send to babies and children through non-verbal communication. Think about the signals you convey at the start and end of the day, when you hold a baby to feed her, and when you prepare a toddler for a rest time.

Support children's friendships

- Place babies lying and seated alongside one another and offer treasure baskets for them to 'share'.
- Model caring and sharing skills in role play, e.g. comforting a sad doll, sharing a cake with teddy.
- Give new children a 'friend' on their arrival in the nursery. Emphasise the importance of this role and encourage the 'friend' to take real responsibility for showing the new child the nursery routines.
- Provide a large stuffed animal and place it in a quiet corner of the nursery. The animal is introduced as a friend to anyone who is feeling lonely.
- Give children 'access strategies' to enable them to join a group: encourage hesitant children to join in with an activity by imitating what other children are doing. By doing this the child is often accepted as part of the group.

Help children to appreciate the effect of external events on friendships

- Support those children whose friends move away with their families. Encourage two friends to each make a gift by which they can remember one another, e.g. a special shell or stone which they found in the nursery garden or a photograph in a frame.
- Help children to accept that although they will feel lonely if they are parted from their friend (on account of holidays or illness), this is an opportunity to try out new friendships.
- Encourage a child to keep a scrapbook of nursery activities while a friend is in hospital. This can then be given as a present.
- Encourage children to think of their friends whilst they are on holiday and to send them a postcard.

Provide specific support for those children who lack friendship skills

- Work with small groups of children and use puppets and miniature dolls to enact scenarios and provoke discussion. Help children to develop their understandings about relationships. Use events and comments that occur in the nursery as a starting point, e.g. taking turns, being kind and offering to play with a new child, ensuring that no one is lonely.

Professional Practice Questions

1. How well do we communicate with babies and very young children during daily routines?
2. How does my room arrangement encourage babies to be with others, children to talk together, to share and co-operate?

Work with Parents

Suggest that parents:

- allow their very young child time to observe others at play without being pressurised to 'join in'.
- share their memories of friendships that they had when they were little and the activities they enjoyed together.

References

1. Zimbardo, R. (1997) quoted in the *Guardian,* 22 July, p. 8.
2. Sigman, A. (2011) 'Screen technologies in early years education', in *Too Much Too Soon.* Gloucestershire: Hawthorn Press, p. 282.
3. Turkle, S. (2012) 'We have sacrificed conversation for mere connection', *New York Times Sunday Review,* p. 21.4.
4. Department for Education (DfE) (2012) *Statutory Framework for the EYFS.* London: HMSO, para 1.13.
5. Howes, C. (1987) 'Peer interaction of young children', in T. David, K. Gooch and L. Abbott (eds), *Birth to Three Matters: A Review of the Literature.* London: Department for Education and Skills (DfES), p. 66.
6. Dunn, J. (2004) *Children's Friendships: The Beginnings of Intimacy.* Oxford: Blackwell, p. 77.
7. Dunn, J. (1993) *Young Children's Close Relationships: Beyond Attachment.* Newbury Park, CA: Sage.
8. BBC 2 (2006) 'The Science of Happiness', in the BBC series *The Happiness Formula,* 30 April.
9. Vygotsky, L. (1978) *Mind in Society: The Development of Higher Psychological Processes.* Cambridge, MA: Harvard University Press.
10. Crawford, K. (1996) 'Vygotskian approaches to human development in the information area', *Educational Studies in Mathematics,* 31 (1–2): 43–62.
11. Wood, D., Bruner, J. and Ross, G. (1976) 'The role of tutoring in problem solving', *Journal of Child Psychology and Psychiatry,* 17 (2): 89–100.
12. Bronfenbrenner, U. (1979) *The Ecology of Human Development.* Cambridge, MA: Harvard University Press.
13. Bandura, A. (1969) 'Social learning theory of identifactory processes', in D.A. Goslin (ed.), *Handbook of Socialisation: Theory and Research.* Chicago, IL: Rand McNally.

14. Bandura, A., Ross, D. and Ross, S.A. (1961) 'Transmission of aggression through imitation of aggressive models', *Journal of Abnormal and Social Psychology*, 63: 575–82.
15. Siren Films (2006) *Life at Two: Attachments, Key People and Development*. Siren Films Ltd, available at www.sirenfilms.co.uk
16. Robinson, M. (2003) *From Birth to One: The Year of Opportunity*. Buckingham: Open University Press.
17. Department for Children, Schools and Families (DCSF) (2007) *Supporting Children Learning English as an Additional Language*. London: DCSF. Available at www.dcfs.gov.uk
18. Goldschmeid, E. and Selleck, D. (1996) *A Framework to Support Children in their Earliest Years*. London: DfES.
19. Early Education (2012) *Development Matters in the Early Years Framework*. Available at www.early-education.org.uk, p. 9.
20. Pollard, A. and Filer, A. (1996) *The Social World of Children's Learning*. London: Cassell.
21. Roberts, R. (2002) *Self-Esteem and Early Learning* (second edition). London: Paul Chapman.
22. Petrie, P. (1997) *Communicating with Children and Adults: Interpersonal Skills for Early Years and Play Work* (second edition). London: Arnold, p. 25.
23. Rinadi, C. (2006) *In Dialogue with Reggio Emilia: Listening, Researching and Learning*. Abingdon: RoutledgeFalmer.
24. Coram Family Sure Start (2004) *Listening to Young Children: A Training Framework*. Buckingham: Open University Press.
25. Lancaster, P. and Kirby, P. (2010) *Coram Family: Listening to Young Children* (second edition). Maidenhead: Open University Press.
26. The Scottish Executive, Education Scotland (2007) *The Child at the Centre: Evaluation in the Early Years* (second edition). Available at www.educationscotland.gov.uk/early yearsmatters/t/genericcontenttcm 44533334
27. Field, T. (1984) quoted in R.K. Smith and H. Cowie (1991) *Understanding Children's Development*. Oxford: Blackwell, p. 102.
28. Parker, J. and Asher, S. (1987) 'Peer relations and later personal adjustment: are low accepted children at risk?', *Psychological Bulletin*, 102: 358–89.
29. Dunn, J. (2004) *Children's Friendships*. Oxford: Blackwell.
30. Donaldson, M. (1978) *Children's Minds*. London: Fontana.
31. Dunn, J. and Kendrick, C. (1982) *Siblings: Love, Envy and Understanding*. Cambridge, MA: Harvard University Press.
32. Dunn, J. and Munn, P. (1985) 'Becoming a family member: family conflict and the development of social understanding in the second year', *Child Development*, 56: 480–92.
33. Ramsey, P.C. (1991) *Making Friends in School*. New York and London: Teachers College Press.
34. Vaughan, B.E. and Langois, J.H. (1983) 'Physical attractiveness as a correlate of peer status and social competence in pre-school children', *Developmental Psychology*, 191: 561–7.
35. Rubin, Z. (1983) 'The skills of friendship', in M. Donaldson (ed.), *Early Childhood Development and Education*. Oxford: Blackwell.
36. Scarlett, W.G. (1983) 'Social isolation from age-mates among nursery school children', in Donaldson op.cit. (see note 35).
37. Paley, V.G. (1992) *You Can't Say You Can't Play*. Cambridge, MA: Harvard University Press.

FOUR   Learning with Others

- Young children learn from within the family, with adults and children in the nursery setting.
- Practitioners will develop and monitor children's growing social competence and abilities to regulate their play in the company of others.

The Family as a Social Context for Learning

Piaget's view of the child making sense of the world through her own investigation emphasised the importance of the environment rather than other people. His views have since been modified to take account of the importance of social contacts. We all need other people to help us learn and young children need adults and other children. Thus, a child's ability to form good relationships not only enhances her personal development but also helps her to progress intellectually. Despite the quantity of day-care and the length of time babies and young children spend in day-care, many still spend the bulk of their time at home, particularly those who are under two years old. During this time they learn a great deal from daily social interactions. One of the great strengths of family relationships is that they are founded on mutual interests and shared past experiences. Tizard and Hughes' classic study vividly describes the rich and easy conversations that can take place between parents and young children as a result of daily routines and social contacts (1). Any practitioner who has visited young children in their homes will be aware of most children being comfortable and confident on known territory and with people who know them. One of the most challenging tasks for the practitioner visiting a home for the first time is to develop a relationship with the child, given that she knows little about her. She will take care to be a gentle presence, only following a lead from the child, observing her interests and willingness to be approached. She will carefully note a parent's ways of holding, soothing and interacting with the child. This information is invaluable to pass on to the child's prospective key person, although ideally the key person should home visit as part of her role.

Learning with Adults in the Early Years Setting

This task of really getting inside children's minds and understanding them can only be properly achieved through observing their actions and conversing with them. Increasingly, practitioners recognise that observation is the basis for planning young children's future development. Where this work is taken seriously, time is set aside to observe children at play and note their social behaviour. Young children's social development will be most noticeable in situations where they make decisions in self-chosen play experiences. The EYFS Framework requires practitioners to review children's progress and share a summary with parents at two points: in the prime areas between the ages of 24 and 36 months (the Progress check at age two) and at the end of the EYFS (the EYFS Profile). These summative assessments provide an overview of the child's progress over a period of time. However, ongoing or formative assessments allow a view of moment-by-moment learning and provide information to plan for the young child to move forward. The non-statutory guidance offers ways to support these processes. For example, it suggests that a young child between two and three years old is likely to demonstrate his interest in others' play and seek out other children to share experiences. Adults may support these developments by ensuring that children have scope to join in group activities and become aware of the rules for being together, such as joining in and taking turns (2). However, we must be aware of the huge amount of progress that occurs in a child's social development between 24 and 36 months old: by age three many children will be experienced group players.

Access to communication is every young child's entitlement and of course involves much more than talk. We know that long before young babies can communicate verbally, they listen to and respond to intonations in adults' voices. Bruce and Spratt suggest that babies and children note and use:

> the sounds and subtle messages of non-verbal communications, to do with pauses, the music of anger, lovingly, affectionately muttered sounds, surprise, fear, protective shouts, a sudden look, meeting someone's gaze, or avoiding eye contact, pulling someone to look and share a focus, pointing. (3)

Daily routines of meal times and nappy changing offer wonderful opportunities for informal social conversations with babies and infants. For those very young children who are new to English it is particularly reassuring if they can hear practitioners use a few words of their home language, but above all practitioners will take their cues from the baby and respond to their sounds, expressions and gestures. The overall experience should be relaxed and enjoyable for both parties.

By two years old children start to use language to make sense of social boundaries such as telling others not to do things. Most 3- and 4-year-olds who are settled and secure in their setting are keen to talk and by listening to them we can gain insights into their interests and ideas. But adults also need to contribute in order to develop and sustain a conversation. Too often dialogues with young children have been dominated by practitioners using management talk, linked with routines such as clearing up, the organisation of snack time and washing hands, with children not being encouraged to have a voice (4, 5). Increasingly, practitioners recognise that a successful conversation with a child or small group of children needs to be reciprocal and based on that child's interest. And this is dependent on using similar interactions to those we would have when chatting with an adult. Early Education training materials designed to support young children's thinking suggest some useful common conversational ploys which include:

- tuning in – listening carefully to what the child is saying or conveying through gesture and expression;
- showing genuine interest – giving eye contact, affirming, smiling, nodding;
- respecting a child's own decisions and viewpoint;
- inviting a child to elaborate on an idea – 'I really want to know more about this ...';
- gently recapping or clarifying what has been said – 'so what you are saying is ...';
- speculating on what might happen – 'I wonder ...';
- offering an alternative viewpoint – 'maybe he wasn't the baddie ...';
- sharing your own experience – 'I was scared of that bit as well ...';
- asking open questions (but sparingly to avoid the impression of interrogation).

The training materials emphasise that adults who engage young children in worthwhile talk have established warm trusting relationships with them: 'They can enter the child's world, recognise his/her interests, dilemmas and concerns and have a conversation which encourages further thinking' (6).

Case Study 4.1

Leila, in her first term in a reception class, decided to make a box for her teddy to use as a hidey-hole. Margaret, a teaching assistant, observed her cutting out squares of thin cardboard to make the different faces of the box.

Simon approached and commented that Leila would not be able to make a box like that because the pieces wouldn't stick together. Leila ignored him but became upset when she was clearly not succeeding with her construction. Margaret suggested that the three of them think of an alternative approach. Simon said that he had seen boxes stacked flat in the supermarket and the sides had been folded. He suggested that folding was a good idea. Margaret collected a box and together they looked at its construction. Leila was delighted to find that she could produce a box through a combination of folding and cutting. 'We're friends aren't we', she said. 'That's what friends do – they help each other'.

Comment

Margaret observed carefully and only intervened when Leila was upset. When she helped, it was to work alongside Leila and Simon as an equal partner. Her main role was to support both children on the basis of what she had observed. Leila's comment at the end shows how her experience of being helped confirmed in a practical way her view of what constituted friendship.

Reflection Point

When are the best times in the day to have easy conversations with your children?

The adult's potent role is further exemplified in the Italian pre-schools in Reggio Emilia. Warm, supportive relationships underpin all of the work with children coupled with scaffolding of learning. This scaffolding is likened to a game of ping-pong where the educator helps the child to clarify and articulate her ideas; she also picks up one child's idea and offers it for consideration within the group; other children then throw back their responses. The educator also encourages conversations that help children to reflect, exchange and co-ordinate points of view: she acts as the 'memory' of the group by making tape recordings and taking photographs of the children's discussions and activities. The continuing relationship between the practitioner and child is recognised as so significant that in these schools children stay with the same teacher for three years (7).

This way of working is not limited to Italian schools. The best nursery settings in the UK support practitioners to develop easy social relationships with children and skilfully use these as a means of helping children learn more.

Learning with Other Children

For years we have accepted the need for children to be with other children, to play together and learn how to live with others. In addition we now recognise how important children's relationships with one another are in assisting their thinking. These developments probably happened more easily in the past where children mixed with others of different ages. Rubin reminds us that today young children remain in age-separated groups longer than they have done at any point in history (8). Vygotsksy strongly supported social learning and claimed that mental activity begins with social contacts and exchanges between people. Eventually these exchanges will be taken on board: a child will use conversations as a basis for her own thinking. Vygotsky suggested that what the child does in co-operation with others she eventually learns to do alone (9).

Learning with and from their peers starts early. Babies often observe with interest the play of other children and from around 15 months may play alongside others. From around 30 months they start to play in a group, suggesting ideas and joining in what others are doing (10).

Azmitia's work also highlighted the value of shared thinking. She observed 5-year-olds working in pairs and produced the following conclusions.

- Having a partner can increase the amount of time children work on a task.
- The presence of a partner can prevent children from giving up in a difficult situation and it can also provide added enjoyment to the activity.
- Moreover, when children work together this can increase their total work strategies as different children bring different skills to a task.
- Finally, when less mature or less experienced children are paired with an older or more able partner, the 'novice' learns a great deal from observing her partner and benefiting from 'expert' guidance (11).

Children in Reggio schools also recognise the benefits of group learning. They suggest that:

- Working in groups is faster because you can decide things together and it's more fun for everyone.

- Once you all agree on something you can do it together.

- Group work means that your brain works better. When you say your ideas out loud they come together; and when all the ideas come together you end up with a huge idea (12).

A child who is new to a setting with English as an additional language (EAL) can be helped greatly by another child (13). The EYFS requires practitioners to enable these children to use their home language in play and learning (14). By sharing and strengthening their first language they can use this understanding to develop English.

Figure 4.1 Girls in Deep Discussion
© Siren Films

Case Study 4.2

Antoni, aged three, had recently arrived in England and started at a nursery class attached to a primary school. He appeared very confused and his key person, Marie, despite trying different approaches, found it difficult to communicate with him. Although there were no adults in the school who spoke Polish there was one Polish boy in Year 1 who had adapted very well to school life. Marie introduced Brunon to Antoni and asked him if he would be a buddy to the younger boy. Brunon was delighted to be asked and to have the chance of conversing with another in his mother tongue. Brunon initially visited Antoni in the nursery daily for half an hour. He read stories with him and played with construction which was proving to be Antoni's favourite activity. Brunon also stayed near Antoni at lunch times, often eating with him and encouraging him to play outside. During these times Antoni proved to be a different child, one who was vivacious, chatty and interested. By the end of half term the little boy was mixing with others, understood most of the routine of the day, and used a few words of English. At that stage Brunon reduced his visits to once a week.

Comment

Brunon played a crucial role in helping Antoni settle into nursery life. Although he did not usurp Marie's role as a key person, initially Antoni trusted Brunon

(Continued)

(Continued)

to interpret the nursery conventions for him and to represent his thoughts and views. Antoni's parents spoke very little English and it was Brunon who told Marie about Antoni's interest in animals and how he longed for a dog of his own. Marie built on this by showing Brunon photographs of her dog and later bringing the dog to the nursery. Brunon also taught Marie several Polish words which were a great help in establishing early spoken conversations with Antoni.

Reflection Point

How often do you encourage a new child with EAL to receive support from a more experienced child who shares the same language? What are the benefits and possible pitfalls of this approach?

Learning to collaborate

However, not all young children will socialise naturally and for some, as we have seen, acquiring social skills will prove difficult. In order for children to work collaboratively they have to learn the skills of turn taking and sharing. Sally Thomas suggests that young children are gently introduced to these skills through a progression: first helping the child to 'wait a minute' with adult support and then with a resource such as an egg timer, then taking turns in a structured game and finally in a freely chosen activity. The aim should be for the child by five years old to share confidently but always with the proviso that maturation levels and circumstances may differ (15). The environment will also be influential. Elizabeth Jarman's materials, 'Communication Friendly Spaces', encourage practitioners to look critically at how well their environments are designed to support children to communicate with one another (16).

The Reggio Emilia schools deliberately foster social knowledge via their project work and the way in which the building is planned: dressing-up areas are situated in a central area; classrooms are connected by phones, passageways and windows; dining areas and cloakrooms are designed to encourage children to get together; and the daily menu for lunch is a vivid display of close-up colour photos of the food to be served that day, encouraging children to comment on the shape of the pasta or the colour of the vegetable.

Furthermore, these Italian pre-schools believe passionately in the effectiveness of learning in small groups: the staff consider that this is the most favourable type of organisation for an education which is based on relationships.

These small groups are not set up as a convenient way of managing learning but as the best way. Staff assert that contact between children can provide opportunities for negotiation and communication that can be at least equivalent to that achieved when an adult is working with a child, and sometimes greater. When children are with children the contacts are equal: although children can learn a great deal with an adult there can be the relationship of authority and dependence, which can detract from a child's confidence. This approach to group work empowers children and strengthens their developing self-regulation (17).

When children form their own groups they often choose to work with others who share their interests or schemes of thinking. Arnold found that children played in this way in her family group at the Pen Green Centre: she also noted that when disputes arose, this was often because these interests or schemas conflicted (18). My own observations of 4-year-olds revealed some particularly concentrated work from pairs of boys who shared the same schema.

Case Study 4.3

Mark and Ben, at three years and six months old, used large brushes and buckets of water to paint patterns on stone paving slabs. They painted long, straight lines and matched them for length. Mark noticed nearby pine trees and commented that their lines were like 'lying down trees'. Ben said that they could make their trees stand up and he rushed off for some drawing paper and pencils. The boys drew their trees, and compared them as horizontal lines and as vertical lines when they held the paper up. Mark drew two short vertical lines on a separate piece of paper which he described as 'baby trees which are just standing up'.

Comment

The boys shared a strong interest in up and down (vertical schema). They rubbed ideas off against one another, and through his intellectual search Ben discovered how to transfer one means of representation to another.

Reflection Point

How can I encourage children who share similar schema to play together?

Monitoring the Development of Social Skills

Children's social development is dramatic during the first six years of life. The experience of being alongside other adults and peers means that all children 'pick up' some of the conventions of living and learning in a group. Depending on their starting point, for some individuals this will be a hard and slow lesson, while others will sprint ahead with their interpersonal skills and show an ability to lead and influence others. Most practitioners are broadly aware on a day-to-day basis of their children's various levels of sociability. Others dig more deeply; they closely observe and reflect on a child's play and activity in order to acquire a properly informed and more detailed picture. The Social Play Continuum developed by Broadhead (19) provides a useful tool for observing and assessing children's social play. It highlights four domains of play, i.e. associative, social, highly social and co-operative. The emphasis in the observations is on the children's activity and use of language, with a stress on continuity and progress as play moves across the four domains. Some helpful signals of progression are identified, one being when children's actions and language become reciprocal. Another sign is the impact of altercations on play: for example, in the earlier domains the adult is often called on to resolve a dispute which inevitably halts the momentum of the play; when children play more co-operatively, they tend to resolve their disputes and start to regulate their actions rather than call on an adult to intervene.

The Social Play Continuum both provides a good structure for observations, and encourages practitioners to assess the level of play in a particular area of provision and to reflect on which action might help children to move into a higher social domain.

Practical Suggestions

Provide activities and opportunities which encourage children to share and take turns

- Purchase wheeled toys which are for two children to ride. Help children to agree that each should have a set number of turns jumping down from the climbing frame. Have a large, illustrated rota for cookery to allow each child to see when it is her turn.
- Provide 'treasure boxes' which contain props and dressing-up clothes to suggest different types of role play.
- Provide for small-scale play, e.g. identify a designated and preferably secluded area.
- Provide a selection of attractively decorated boxes which contain small-scale people, animals and vehicles. Include ready-made floor layouts or a sheet and felt tip pens for children to create their own floor map.

Encourage younger children to learn from older ones

- Provide for infants to sit with older children at meal times to observe their behaviour.
- Give older children specific responsibilities to support younger ones, e.g. helping them dress to go outside.

Professional Practice Questions

1. Have I sufficient apparatus to enable children to have reasonable opportunities to share and take turns?
2. How well does the layout of my outside area and the resources promote children's social skills?
3. How well do I tune in to children's thoughts and concerns by listening to what they say, noticing their actions, and reflecting on their meanings?
4. How do I extend my relationships with children to share thinking with them?
5. What model of social behaviour do I provide for my children when I interact with them, their parents and other adults?
6. How successfully do I establish a community of friends in my setting?
7. How closely do I monitor children's social development and use the information gained to improve it?

Work with Parents

Ask parents what they do to encourage their child's friendships.
   Suggest that parents:

- invite their child's friend to come to play over the weekend (the child's parent should be invited as well to ease the initial visit);
- encourage their child to bake a small cake/draw a card for their friend who is unwell.

References

1. Tizard, B. and Hughes, M. (2002) *Young Children Learning* (second edition). Oxford: Blackwell.
2. Early Education (2012) *Development Matters in the Early Years Framework*, www.early-education.org.uk, p. 9.
3. Bruce, T. and Spratt, J. (2008) *Essentials of Literacy from 0–7*. London: Sage, p. 16.
4. Woods, D., McMahan, L. and Cranstoun, L. (1980) *Working with Under-Fives*. London: Grant McIntyre.
5. Sylva, K., Roy, C. and Painter, M. (1980) *Child Watching at Playgroup and Nursery School*. London: Grant McIntyre.
6. Dowling, M. (2005) *Supporting Young Children's Sustained, Shared Thinking: An Exploration*. Early Education, available at www.early-education.org.uk
7. Gandini, L. (1993) 'Fundamentals of the Reggio Emilia approach to early childhood education', *Young Children*, November: 4–8.

8. Rubin, Z. and Thomson, A. (2002) *The Friendship Factor*. London: Penguin Books.
9. Vygotsky, L.S. (1978) *Mind in Society*. Cambridge, MA: Harvard University Press.
10. Early Education (2012) *Development Matters in the Early Years Framework*, op.cit. (note 2), pp. 8–9.
11. Azmitia, M. (1988) 'Peer interaction and problem solving: when are two heads better than one?', *Child Development*, 59: 87–96.
12. Guidici, C., Rinaldi, C. and Krechevsky, M. (2001) *Making Learning Visible: Children as Individual and Group Learners*. Reggio Emilia: Reggio Children and Harvard College.
13. Department for Children, Schools and Families (DCSF) (2007) *Supporting Children Learning English as an Additional Language*. London: DCSF, p. 10.
14. Department for Education (DfE) (2012) *Statutory Framework for the Early Years Foundation Stage*. London: HMSO, para 1.8.
15. Thomas, S. (2008) *Nurturing Babies and Children Under Four*. London: Heinemann, p. 34.
16. Jarman, E. (2013) *Communication Friendly Spaces Approach*. Available at www.elizabethjarmantraining.co.uk
17. Reeve, J., Ryan, R., Deci, E.L. and Jang, H. (2008) 'Understanding and promoting autonomous self-regulation: a self-determination theory perspective', in D.H. Schunk and B.J. Zimmerman (eds), *Motivation and Self-Regulated Learning*. Mahwah, NJ: Lawrence Erlbaum.
18. Arnold, C. (2010) *Understanding Schemas and Emotion in Early Education*. London: Sage.
19. Broadhead, P. (2004) *Early Years Play and Learning: Developing Social Skills and Cooperation*. London: RoutledgeFalmer.

FIVE   Becoming Independent

- Babies are born with the powerful urge to be independent but early experiences strongly influence their later ability to take responsibility for themselves.
- A young child's independence is reflected in his readiness to separate from home and move into a group environment. He also learns physical and practical self-help skills.
- Young children develop as self-regulated learners by making choices and decisions and asking questions.

Practitioners recognise that independence is an essential life skill that needs to be nurtured from the earliest age; however, the term is often taken to mean different things. For example, some consider that the main aim should be to support a child to separate from his family for periods of time or become self-sufficient in personal care such as toileting, washing and dressing; others believe that the priority is for a child to think for himself. In fact all aspects of independence are important in order for a child to become a self-regulating individual.

Psychological Perspectives

One meaning of independent learning for young children is defined as 'children's development of self-reliant ways of dealing with problems and difficulties' (1).

Vygotsky believed that children are naturally self-reliant in that they construct or build their own knowledge and don't simply follow and replicate what is offered to them. Piaget had similar views, the difference being that for Piaget the child's building of knowledge occurred when he interacted with the environment: for Vygotsky the construction was in the company of others (social constructivism).

Vygotsky's beliefs are best recognised in the Zone of Proximinal Development (see Chapter 3). Although this clearly describes how children can move from an independent level of learning to higher achievements the theory does not specify how this might happen.

Bruner's theory, using the metaphor of scaffolding, provides a method whereby close adults support children to achieve the Zone of Proximinal Development. Both theories:

- totally respect what children are able to do independently and allow them to do as much as possible alone;
- emphasise that the adult can build on children's independent actions and support them to achieve higher challenge.

Susan Isaacs, a psychologist and pioneer supporter of nursery education, also believed passionately that exercising independent judgement was beneficial for children's development. Like Vygotsky she understood that this was best achieved through play with the adult offering support and guidance (2). Isaacs enabled this as headteacher of the Malting School in Cambridge in the 1920s where she observed children closely and gave them great scope to develop responsible autonomy: 'Children learn to take responsibility by having it' (3).

Independence Starts Early in Life

Although very young children are necessarily dependent on their caregivers for their physical needs, as Winnicott stresses babies are 'going concerns' whose growth and development are 'inevitable and unstoppable' (4). It quickly becomes noticeable that babies do exercise choices in what they play with, what they like to eat, and when they sleep. These decisions about their physical needs and their subsequent levels of independence are significantly affected by the style of care-giving. Winnicott suggests that when adults feel responsible for shaping and forming a child without knowing the importance of developing autonomy, they make life difficult both for themselves and for the small person with whom they are living. Winnicott's views are borne out when we see adults either restricting children's development or pressurising them into achieving developmental milestones too early.

Case Study 5.1

Two-year-old Elise was an only child and was fiercely protected at home. She was never allowed to try to climb stairs or steps and only allowed to walk outside on a rein with an adult. These restrictions continued until Elise was three years six months old when she started at the nursery. By this time her movements were poorly co-ordinated and tentative. For the first term in the nursery Elise was hesitant about joining in any activities and refused to go outside.

Comment

Elise's parents had failed to trust her to learn through trial and error. The key person explained to them that their small daughter needed support in order to develop her physical skills, make her more independent, and build her confidence. Working together the nursery staff and parents helped Elise to achieve small progress steps towards physical independence.

Reflection Point

As a senior member of staff how do you practically encourage a new colleague who overprotects children to give them scope to become independent?

Elise's parents were over-protective. At the other extreme some parents are very keen to accelerate their child's independence. Sitting up, walking and becoming dry at night become milestones that are immensely important to achieve early. Both of these shaping approaches stem from loving parents who genuinely want the best for their children. Parents who pressurise their child do not understand that independence only grows from a time of dependence and so they push their child towards maturity before he is ready, and risk him experiencing failure and losing confidence. Both approaches can lead young children to become over-dependent. Jenny Lindon states that 'We need to resist over-loading young children with stimulation and to avoid the "build better baby" type products that have emerged, especially in the United States'. Lindon suggests that babies and toddlers need time to use their physical abilities and apply their ideas: 'The clear preference of very young children for "do it again" is ideal for their learning' (5).

Given scope, babies and toddlers are capable of making decisions for themselves. For example, a baby will decide which items to select in a treasure basket. Mobile babies may choose a new area of the room to explore or, according to their sleep patterns, may move in and out of sleep nests or use sleep mats as needed. Opportunities for these choices reflect the respect that staff give to such young children, and also their belief that even at this age babies are capable of deciding what is best for them.

Social and Emotional Independence

As children develop from birth they move from home to a different learning environment. Each transition is a major event for a baby or child and during the early years it is likely that children experience more 'handovers' than they ever will in later stages of their lives. Moreover, every baby and child will encounter a transition differently.

In Chapter 1 we considered the potential stresses for some young children who move to a new setting. In this chapter we follow them as they move through common stages in transition, which Manchester Education Partnership usefully identify as Trying to Let Go, Being Uncertain, and Taking Hold (6).

Trying to Let Go

Trying to Let Go is when young children can feel confused and overwhelmed as they leave a secure and familiar context for new horizons. For a baby or infant making a first move away from home this is a huge step as they are pitched into a welter of new sensory experiences, i.e. different sights, sounds and smells. The greatest change of course for the very young child is the move away from her parent to a stranger (albeit her key person). The role of the key person is explored further in Chapter 7, but her primary responsibility here is to support the young child through forming a similar (but not identical) attachment to the one which the child has already with a parent or primary carer. We know now that a successful initial attachment helps the child to move from being dependent on a close family member to a widening social contact; a child who has made a sound initial attachment within the family is more likely to bond happily with another significant person. Nevertheless a very young child under two years old can experience high levels of stress when he moves into a group setting. A Cambridge study of babies (11–20 months) during the first nine days of full-time daycare, after being cared for at home, showed doubled levels of the stress hormone cortisol. Even five months later, these levels were still significantly high (7). Although the authors of the report emphasised that there was no evidence of long-term effects of high cortisol levels this alerts us to how very young children can be psychologically challenged. If we are surrounded by strange people and unknown events, we are really in survival mode, namely unsure, suspicious, disempowered and so unable to start to 'feel our feet'. This disempowerment can apply equally to babies and older children during the early days of separation although responses can vary. When a child starts in an early years setting, ideally any family should feel that the staff are doing everything possible to accommodate their needs. Practitioner time spent with the family may well avoid anxieties and problems arising at a later stage. In order for a new child to feel comfortable about leaving mum or dad he must be at ease in the new setting. Such rituals as finding coat pegs, learning how to hang up a coat, moving into a room with other children and saying goodbye, take time. Some small individuals will respond to these new procedures easily and rapidly. Others will be unsure and each new step will prove a burden: in this circumstance any moves to try to jolly the child into separating from the parent or carer is misguided, as the child is not yet ready to make this tremendous move on his own and patience, sensitivity and more time are needed.

Being uncertain

Even when a young child is able to separate from his parent he may still feel apprehensive about the new experiences on offer, particularly when he has to contend with something new. Babies and children can face transitions daily when they are moved from one provision to another. Within a Children's Centre where all the provisions are often under one roof an infant may arrive early for a breakfast club, move onto core provision in a different room, into the hall for lunch and onto day-care in the afternoon. At the end of the day the infant may join a wider age group in a different room for teatime and a story. Each one of these transitions can require the child to mix with different adults and children, recognise and adjust to different expectations and routines, and adapt to a new environment. To avoid these considerable and confusing challenges staff need to work closely together to provide common and constant approaches which will allow a child to feel on familiar ground wherever he is during the day.

Figure 5.1   Ava's First Full Day at Nursery
© Siren Films

Travelling through the Early Years Foundation Stage (EYFS) involves babies and young children moving into different groups or classes. Each move is a rite of passage and potentially a celebration of children's progress and achievement. Any rite of passage involves change and disequilibrium. It can cause us to be excited and full of anticipation but can equally stir up feelings of anxiety, trepidation, uncertainty and fear. These negative feelings can very effectively diminish self-esteem (see Chapter 1) and can mean that a child doesn't feel in control. While any transition will provide new challenges, these can easily prove to be overwhelming. Initially a child needs to recognise and feel reassured by elements of the familiar.

Practitioners should expect to spend more time with the child who is still insecure in a new setting and is emotionally dependent on one adult. Although we know that a young child needs to be helped to make a gentle and comfortable initial transition, there will still be instances when he does not have enough adult support once his parent has left. An early study of transition from home to pre-school found that the total adult time given to all new children was less than 10 per cent (8). Thirty-nine years later, my own study of pre-school settings showed that, although never neglectful, in some cases practitioners were not being sufficiently proactive: a new child was more likely to be left to his own devices unless there were noticeable signs of distress. At this point a child was always comforted and often encouraged to stay with an adult for the rest of the session. However, that was often too late: experienced and good quality early years practitioners are very aware that young children can appear to be coping with situations but are in fact finding them very stressful. During the early days in a setting a child should be observed closely by the key person who understands that some children and parents find transition times stressful while others will enjoy the experience (9). It is helpful if each child knows that at all times there is one adult in particular who is there for them and this is now assured through the requirement for a key person. In this way children are reassured that they are never on their own, and this reassurance prevents the bottling up of anxiety which can then give rise to problems at a later stage. Over time, and given initial help, children will delight in learning that they can cope for themselves in many new situations.

Older children being uncertain

Older children can face similar challenges. It is now over twenty years since we adapted a common policy of admitting children at just four years old into reception classes and yet there is no clear evidence to show that the pressure for children to attend school early is worthwhile. Indeed, Caroline Sharp's paper relating to school starting ages for children across the world indicates that a late start to school appears to have no adverse effect on children's progress (10). This early start of course has a knock-on effect and children can move into Year 1 when they are barely five.

These young children in particular can receive a huge jolt when they move from Reception at the end of the EYFS into a different culture in Year 1. Uncertainties occur when children encounter difference. Increasingly, staff recognise that they should minimise change during this experience. Reception and Year 1 teachers try to look at the transition from the child's perspective and consider useful questions such as 'What do our children see, experience and encounter that is the same and that is different when they move from Reception into Year 1 (11)? We should also remember that children may respond differently to a transition. In an early study of 4-year-old children moving into reception classes (12), parents recounted their children's diverse responses. For example, one child was hesitant about lining up with others in the playground, while another self-reliant child complained to his mum about her accompanying him into school. Although it is usually desirable for parents initially to spend some time in the setting with their children, this last comment highlights the need for rules to accommodate individual needs. Consideration of the child's previous experience in being separated from home and observations of her levels of confidence and independence in the new reception class should always play a part when deciding when it is appropriate for parents to leave their child. The teachers in the reception class study made great efforts to help children into school. This was easy when admitting small groups initially on a staggered basis. One or two upsets were reported as later groups of children were admitted into a larger class group.

Taking hold

Helping children to feel secure and comfortable with others is a basic requirement for any sound transition. But only when a child shows that they want to branch out and investigate on their own or with others can we be sure that the transition has been successful. This might include:

a baby who crawls away from her key person, but turns back just to check that the adult is still there;

a 2-year-old who plays happily alongside other children, observing and mirroring their actions;

a 4-year-old who enters a classroom and wanders over to join a group of other children in the construction area.

These observations indicate that young children are starting to feel that they belong. The baby trusts his key person to remain in sight and support his adventures. Infants and children are beginning to feel part of a group.

A child becomes more sure of his new identity as a member of the setting when he gets to know the pattern of the day. This helps him to feel in control of what he experiences; he is able to predict what will happen next rather than being simply a passive recipient. A young child shows that he is familiar with the setting by placing events into a sequenced framework. When a child recounts his 'script', this tells us about his understanding of what he is experiencing during the day.

Case Study 5.2

I visited a reception class three days after the children had started school. I wanted to find out how much of an understanding children had about school life in this short space of time. I approached Gavin and asked him, 'What do you do in this school?' He paused for a moment and then told me 'Well, we paint and draw and go outside to play. Sometimes we have a story and we must try to sit and cross our legs'. After another pause, Gavin continued, 'That's not all. We have lunch and then we go to the hall. I like that. We have to take off our clothes and put them together, 'cos they will get lost. Then our mummies come to take us home'. Over the other side of the class I approached Joe with the same question. Joe avoided looking at me. He simply hung his head and muttered, 'I dunno, I dunno'.

Comment

After only three days in school Gavin already possessed a wonderfully clear grasp of some main school events. His detailed script and understanding of what was required and why showed that he was rapidly feeling himself to be a member of the class community. Joe, on the other hand, was lost. He was unable to talk to me about his life at school because at this stage he had no clear understanding. Things happened during the course of the day over which he felt he had no control. For Joe, school life is still a buzzing confusion; he needs considerable support from a caring adult who will help interpret events for him.

Reflection Point

What support would you offer to help children like Joe develop a clear mental map of the pattern of daily activity in a new class?

Physical and Functional Independence

Healthy babies and infants strive to develop skills that enable them to become less physically dependent upon adults: a 1-year-old may start to use a feeding cup and want to feed himself; infants will insist on trying to dress and feed themselves, they start to control their toileting habits and they want to move to explore new territories; 3- and 4-year-olds will then progress and refine these skills. They will learn the sequence for dressing themselves and develop their fine motor skills to enable them to deal with zips and buttons on clothes. They will also learn to go to the lavatory unaided. Their co-ordination improves and they are able to pour a drink and carry a plate of fruit to the table. As they gain confidence they practise their physical skills using apparatus both inside and outside. A child who is physically able to climb by himself to the top of the climbing frame has achieved a considerable milestone in independence.

Loving parents recognise that each developmental step towards physical independence is a significant achievement for their child. They proudly recount to friends and family each new example of what their child has managed to do for himself. Despite this, however, some parents are not always aware of their role in encouraging self-sufficiency. Although their child often surprises them they are understandably not sure of what to expect. They know that at two and three years old children do not write or draw representational pictures, and so it may not occur to them to give their child a pencil or crayon in order to practise making marks. Moreover, time is often the enemy. Naturally, young children's lack of manual dexterity does not allow them to do things swiftly. Small, fumbling fingers will struggle with buttons when dressing and turning on the tap. In the bustle of daily life it is much easier to do things for children rather than wait for what seems endless time to allow them to try for themselves. Parents and carers are also rightfully protective of their children. This sometimes leads them to be over-anxious about their physical safety. Elise, as we saw earlier, was protected from potential hazards both inside and outside the home. Her parents could not bear to think of her tumbling down a step, or even falling in the garden. Many parents worry about safety issues of being outside. Traffic has increased immensely in residential areas and despite efforts to clamp down on speeding many cars pose a hazard to children playing in the streets. Although there is no direct evidence that children today are in more jeopardy from encounters with strangers, the grim stories sensationalised in the media cause parents to think that their children may be in danger and they are understandably not prepared to allow them to play out of sight. Young children thus have less chance to enjoy 'risky freedom' – that heady feeling of tasting adventure which encourages personal growth (13).

Other families will promote and celebrate their child's physical independence in different ways. Infants are encouraged to feed themselves early on, even though the initial results are messy. Parents will show their child how to put on his vest and not worry if socks are put on inside out. They will provide equipment for drawing, painting and sticking and simply let their child experiment. They will allow their child to take some small physical risks in learning to climb and balance on equipment in a playground, while standing by alert to prevent any real danger. Moreover, some parents will help their young children to become practical and useful members of the family, e.g. they will be shown how to take responsibility for small tasks such as watering the plants, laying the table, and helping to wipe up pans in the kitchen. They may also help to fetch and carry things for a new baby.

As a consequence of their different home experiences, when children start at a nursery setting their physical independence will differ vastly. Some 3-year-olds will have had little opportunity to practise physical skills for themselves. They have learned to be dependent and their initial drive and confidence to try for themselves have lessened and they expect others to try for them. Other children of the same age are agile and physically confident. They can cope with their personal needs and are very keen to apply their physical skills in the new experiences offered in the nursery. They are also keen to extend their functional skills and take messages or a piece of apparatus to another room or help to mix the paints. Some children are particularly adept at doing these things and will become known for their reliability.

Practitioners realise that a physically independent child is likely to adapt more easily to life in the setting. A more dependent child needs time and encouragement. Children also need to know that although they will be helped, it is expected that they will become physically self-reliant. Usually, once they recognise this, the vast majority of children grow in confidence and will fulfil expectations by the end of the reception year to 'manage their own basic hygiene and personal needs successfully, including dressing and going to the toilet unaided' (14). *Development Matters* links children's developing physical skills to their ability to act independently, not only in self-care but also in taking risks and knowing how to keep safe when playing in challenging but safe environments (15).

Case Study 5.3

Andrew had adapted reasonably well to the nursery except for periods of outdoor play. Whenever these times were voluntary for children, Andrew opted to stay indoors, even in very warm weather. On the one daily occasion when all children were expected to have time outside, Andrew did all he could to hide, or pretended that he had lost his shoes. His key worker Sue noticed this at an early stage and made a particular effort to stay and chat with him during outside sessions. It eventually became clear that Andrew was afraid that if he played outside he would not be able to locate the lavatories (which were situated inside the building). Sue reassured him that if in need, he should simply let her know and she would return inside with him. This worked successfully, and after one week when Sue accompanied Andrew to the lavatory he told her that he 'knew the way now to have a wee' and didn't need her.

Comment

Sue's early observations of Andrew's behaviour resulted in her spending time with him to forge a relationship and gently find out the cause of his concern. Her practical support allowed Andrew to cope with outdoor play and also to practise finding his way round the new nursery building. Once he had become familiar with the location of the lavatories he was keen to demonstrate his independence.

Reflection Point

Consider the reasons why some children are reluctant to branch out into different territory or explore new experiences.

For future reference, keep an archive of reasons, the support you have offered and the child's response.

A degree of physical and functional independence assists young children to feel more in control of their own lives and gives them self-respect. It is also extremely helpful to busy parents and practitioners if children are able to cope with their own physical needs. However, these skills are not acquired out of thin air; they need to be taught gently and systematically with plenty of encouragement. Thomas refers to a helpful technique known as backward chaining (16). This is a form of scaffolding where the adult initially offers close support and gradually withdraws it as a child becomes competent enough to cope for himself. Adam, at nearly three years old, was keen to learn to dress himself. His key person demonstrated and talked through each step, including folding each item of clothing in turn when undressing in order to retrieve each item easily and the sequence in which to dress. Gradually this scaffolded support was lessened as Adam became more competent and his achievements were celebrated. Schools have traditionally always stressed the desirability of new children having physical self-help skills and most emphasise this in school brochures for new parents. However, it does not just rest there. If we consider independence in a broader sense it should include children's development as independent learners.

Intellectual Independence

Most practitioners would agree that it is helpful for both children and adults if children learn to tidy away resources after playing with them, or to take messages. There remains less certainty about the extent of intellectual independence that should be encouraged, and yet this wider issue of intellectual independence is possibly more crucial to children's futures.

This view was officially supported by the government, probably most famously in the Plowden Report in 1967, when Lady Plowden recommended that 'children should be agents in their own learning' (17). The belief that young children should be supported to act for themselves is now strongly represented in the EYFS through the characteristics of effective learning (18). We still have to recognise this. A report from the Joseph

Rowntree Foundation stressed how important it is to involve young children in making decisions about all aspects of their lives. It made a key point that often our youngest citizens are ignored. They have very different needs and interests from those of older children and yet many consultations effectively exclude anyone under eight years of age (19). Since that report however it has been heartening that practitioners increasingly regard listening to children as essential (see Chapter 3).

Anyone who has been employed in or visited a setting where young children are working autonomously, making decisions about what they are doing with whom and where, cannot fail to be impressed with the control that these children have over their lives. When a child is encouraged and expected to use his mind he shows himself to be very capable. It is also accepted that babies and young children are already powerful and persistent thinkers. Although they lack experience of the world, they compensate for this to a large extent by their inner drive to make sense of all that they experience. Given the opportunity they will self-direct themselves.

Case Study 5.4

Carl, at three years and four months old, had taken great care to build a construction of blocks which he proudly described as his house. He told his teacher that he wanted to show it to his mum. Rosemary, his teacher, explained gently that this would not be possible, as today his neighbour would be collecting him from the nursery at the end of the session. Carl persisted that he wanted his mum to see his work. Rosemary suggested that he thought carefully about how this might be possible. After a pause, Carl declared that he would draw his construction. He spent 20 minutes on his drawing ensuring that the representation was completely accurate. Rosemary provided him with ribbon and helped Carl present his drawing as a scroll.

Comment

Instead of providing Carl with a solution to his problem, his teacher made it possible for him to make his own decision. The amount of time spent on the drawing and the quality of the work reflected Carl's investment in his self-directed learning.

Reflection Point

How often do you encourage children to solve their problems rather than taking responsibility for this yourself?

As with any new learning, though, children have to be introduced to the skills of independence and given the opportunity to practise and apply them. Some of the most important skills include children being able to use the environment for themselves, and to make choices and decisions.

Using the Environment Independently

Space is essential to enable children to be physically independent. A setting which is organised as a workshop can increase opportunities for children to use their initiative. A practitioner who takes the view from Reggio Emilia that the environment is the third teacher, plans the setting to promote independence and will take great care with the management and layout of physical space. This applies to all age groups. Babies who are learning to crawl should have enough comfortable floor space to move around freely but they also need boundaries to feel safe and help them to concentrate. Very young children can easily be overwhelmed by a bombardment of sensory stimulation and an overly busy space is more likely to bewilder rather than excite a toddler.

The quality of children's self-chosen play is hugely influenced by the quality and range of continuous provision, i.e. the resources that are made available on a daily basis. Practitioners understand that the resources are there for children to use in their own way to represent their thoughts and ideas. Commonly, room spaces are organised in areas of learning. If so, we should understand that children will not play neatly in each of the seven areas. They must be aware of what is available for them and feel free to mix and combine materials and resources. Various philosophies of early childhood are reflected through the environments they provide to enhance independence. The Montessori philosophy emphasises self-reliance and decision-making; consequently most Montessori nurseries will encourage children to select apparatus for themselves rather than have it readily available on tables. The High Scope programme particularly stresses the importance of the physical arrangement of a room and the need for resources to be accessible to children. The programme requires that resources in each area are logically organised and clearly labelled. Steiner settings put great store on children developing their ideas through using open-ended and natural materials.

Having prepared the environment, children need to be supported and trusted to use it. A toddler may be encouraged to use a handrail to support him in being mobile. Older children arriving new to a class or group need to be carefully introduced to what is available for them and where it is located. Sometimes it is helpful to model ways of using equipment in the spirit of suggestion. In order to use space and resources for themselves new children need to understand the sorts of experiences and activities they can have, what they are allowed to use, and how they return materials after use. Tidying up is part of children learning to be responsible and even infants will enjoy putting away blocks after playing with them. This can be a contentious issue though and should not dominate a session, as tidying up works best if adults have reasonable expectations of what should be achieved, work with the children, make it fun, allow sufficient time, and offer lots of encouragement for effort. Importantly, any induction should concentrate on helping children recognise that the environment is there for them to use. However, while young children should be able to get on with their activities without interruption, Fisher stresses that this does not mean that independent learners should be abandoned. Although young children need time to themselves the adult needs be watchful and available when required to support their endeavours (20).

Making Choices and Decisions

Active learners are not dependent on just doing what others tell them but bring their own ideas and initiative to situations. Mathieson suggests that by saying out loud the thinking that we go through before making a choice, this can support very young children in making their own decisions (21). The statutory framework for the EYFS recognises the importance of play, notably in the characteristic of effective learning: Playing and Exploring (22). This strand emphasises for example that young children learn through making decisions about taking a role in play, how to represent their experiences in play, and deciding on (initiating) new activities. Not all children find it easy initially to make decisions, particularly when making the transition from home to an early years setting. Bronfenbrenner states that this move is probably the first major ecological transition in children's lives (23). Indeed some new entrants may be overwhelmed by the amount of choice in the activities available to them. At this stage it is helpful to make suggestions as to what they might start to do and watch out for signs of children being at a loss as to what to do next. As they become comfortable and at ease in the nursery they will respond to gentle encouragement to try different options.

Self-initiated play

This offers young children many opportunities for choice. Children act within the self-imposed rules or decisions that they make for themselves. They engage in 'private speech' (i.e. talking to themselves about what they have chosen to do and how they are going to do it) as an early step toward self-regulation (24, 25).

Choices are available to babies when they are introduced to treasure baskets and select objects of interest. Heuristic play, providing a rich array of natural and open-ended materials, invites infants to move around and decide on something particular to explore and investigate. Older children need to be able to select what materials or tools to use. Before children are able to describe materials, make considered choices or consider similarities and differences, they need to have had many and varied opportunities to observe and handle materials and listen to descriptive language (26).

Practitioners observe individual children at play and provide these opportunities in a way that meets specific needs. Initially, young children will act on impulse taking the first thing available or opting to use everything. This is a necessary stage, as over time children can be encouraged to reflect on their choice and so become more intentional and selective.

Organisation in the setting should make it possible for children to make decisions about with whom they wish to play (see Chapter 3) and also to determine what they do with their time. Some young children have their lives at home heavily programmed by adults and they are subjected to a relentless timetable of outings, shopping and planned activities such as swimming, dancing and music lessons: in these cases the gift of time is particularly precious. Others, of course, are provided with large chunks of time for themselves, but the only choice available to them is which DVD or television channel to view. Again, a carefully planned programme in a setting should give scope for the child's enterprise but also provide a place for adult guidance and, when appropriate, adult involvement and intervention. Tina Bruce's wise suggestion is still valid: 'At times the adult leads and at times the child. Each takes note of and responds to the other's actions and words' (27). Children who are given choices and real opportunities to take responsibility for their actions are more likely to understand that adults are there as a resource to support their enterprise. Their confidence as decision makers is strengthened as they begin to understand how they can have a stake in their own lives.

Practical Suggestions

Listen and observe

- Observe signs to show that a baby/infant has made a strong second attachment and a secure transition to a setting, e.g. content with a handover to the key person; shows interest in surroundings and new experiences; happy to greet mum or dad at the end of the session and not overly distressed.
- Observe when babies/infants convey a preference, e.g. when exploring treasure baskets, in heuristic play or when selecting books, and use these resources when you play with them.
- Observe the experiences offered to children that encourage them most to be independent.

Support social and emotional independence

- Make it clear to each child new to a setting that he is known by referring to some aspect of his life that you shared with him during a home visit, e.g. discussing his dog, his favourite toys, sharing some photographs of his family and home.

(Continued)

(Continued)

- Ensure that a key person pays particular attention to each new child until it is evident that he has made a sound transition to the setting, e.g. be alert to times when a child does not understand instructions, cannot remember where to find things, cannot remember routines, and is confused and tense when making a transition from one activity to another, when clearing away or going outside.
- If children are to stay full-time or for extended day-care, encourage parents or carers to join them for breakfast/lunch/tea sessions during the early stages of transition.

Support children in separating from their parents (see also Chapter 7)

- Be alert to when a parent needs to leave the nursery and be nearby when this happens.
- Agree with the parent a procedure for saying goodbye such as waving from the window or taking the child's teddy shopping with her.
- Talk through with the child the daily routines that will take place until 'mummy' returns.

Promote physical and functional independence

- Provide easy-grip feeding cutlery to encourage older babies to feed themselves and an environment that allows babies to move easily and comfortably to different areas.
- Play games that need buttons, zips and buckles to be fastened.
- Encourage children to take responsibility for their own possessions, e.g. clipping wellington boots together with a named wooden peg.
- Provide older children with areas of responsibility, e.g. keeping the book area tidy, checking that all the jigsaws are intact, checking the painting aprons for repairs.
- Encourage less confident children to take messages; as a safeguard provide a written version for the child's pocket which he can produce if he wishes.
- Help children to be tidy, e.g. sew large curtain rings onto painting aprons to make it easy to hang aprons onto pegs, provide a dustpan and brush for clearing up dry sand, and provide a floor cloth or short-handled mop for coping with spillages.
- Provide pictorial notices which will help children to remember self-help skills, e.g. a picture of two large hands displayed with the caption 'Please wash your hands'.
- Check how well the storage of your resources makes it possible for children to access them easily. Provide easily fitting lids on containers and low shelves with sufficient space for each piece of apparatus. Space for individual jigsaws can be marked out and symbols/colours used to match each puzzle to the space allocated.
- Check that children know where things are. Play a game in the group called 'Can you find where it lives?' Prepare a drawstring bag containing

various objects, e.g. pencils, blocks, counters, scissors. Ask children in turn to withdraw an item from the bag and return it to its home.

- Build in choice and decision-making in experiences.

Promote intellectual independence

- *Painting*: provide a range of paper of different shapes, sizes and colours. Make the paper easily accessible by having it available on a low table in the painting area.
- *Collage*: provide a range of materials and adhesives to allow infants simply to explore and older children to compare the different properties.
- *Storytime*: provide two alternatives for a story and ask children to state their preference.
- *Snacks*: provide alternative options of fruit or crackers; allow children to pour the amount of milk, water or squash they wish to drink rather than be expected to consume a standard measure.
- *Displays*: consult children about whose work is going to be displayed on walls (ensure, through gentle encouragement, that all children's work is eventually presented).
- *Outings*: provide alternative suggestions for a walk and ask children to select.
- *Planting bulbs*: ask children to browse through bulb catalogues in order to select their favourite colour bulbs.
- *Celebrations*: consult children about what food to have for a summer picnic or Christmas party.
- Support children to choose how they use their time:

  o make clear what resources are available by having the room/outside area clearly organised and displayed;
  o introduce children gradually to each part of the room in turn, and the resources that are available to be used;
  o encourage older children to record their decision of where they decide to play by sharing this with an adult who acts as a scribe for them or by asking them to attach their name card to a picture/photograph of their chosen activity.

Professional practice questions

1. What scope do babies have to handle and control items when lying on their backs or their tummies?
2. How well do the storage space and labelling make clear to children where to access and return resources?
3. How many of the following things have I done today that children could have tackled just as well:

(Continued)

(Continued)

- o dressing and undressing themselves;
- o sending and delivering messages;
- o preparing materials, e.g. making playdough, mixing paints, combining ingredients for cookery;
- o tidying away equipment?

4. What decisions and choices are my children encouraged to make about:

- o the experiences they have;
- o the materials/apparatus they use;
- o how they use their time;
- o who they work with;
- o when they go to the lavatory;
- o when they have a mid-morning snack;
- o playing inside or outside?

Work with Parents

Suggest that parents support their children's independence by encouraging them to:

- tidy away their toys at bedtime;
- carry out simple household tasks such as helping to clear away and wash dishes, sweeping the floor, polishing the table.

References

1. Hendy, L. and Whitebread, D. (2000) 'Interpretations of independent learning in the early years', *International Journal of Early Years Education,* 8 (3): 245–52.
2. Isaacs, S. (1930) *Intellectual Growth in Young Children.* London: Routledge.
3. Isaacs, S. (1971) *The Nursery Years: The Mind of the Child from Birth to Six Years.* London: Routledge, p. 102.
4. Winnicott, D.W. (1964) *The Child, the Family and the Outside World.* Harmondsworth: Penguin.
5. Lindon, J. (2003) 'Good practice in working with babies, toddlers and very young children', in *Birth to Three Matters: A Framework to Support Children in their Earliest Years.* London: DfES.
6. Manchester Education Partnership/Sure Start (2004) *Effective Transitions in the Early Years,* Manchester City Council, Manchester Education Partnership, 3rd Floor, Fujitsu Tower, Wenlock Way, West Gorton, Manchester M12 5DR.
7. Ward, L. (2005) 'Hidden stress of the nursery age: childcare study', *Guardian News,* 19 September, p. 3.

8. Blatchford, P., Battle, S. and Mays, J. (1974) *The First Transition: Home to Pre-School*. Slough: NFER/Nelson.

9. Department for Education and Skills (DfES) (2007) *The Early Years Foundation Stage: Principles into Practice Cards, 3.4: Supporting Every Child*. London: DfES.

10. Sharp, C. (2002) 'School Starting Age: European Policy and Recent Research'. Paper presented at the LGA Seminar, *When Should Our Children Start School?* NFER/Local Government Association.

11. Qualifications and Curriculum Authority (QCA) (2005) *Continuing the Learning Journey*, QCA online order ref: QCA/05/1590. Available at www.naa.org.uk/naa17856

12. Ghaye, A. and Pascal, C. (1988) 'Four-year-old children in reception classrooms: participant perceptions and practice', *Educational Studies*, 14 (2): 187–208.

13. Ouvry, M. (2000) *Exercising Muscles and Minds*. National Early Years Network.

14. Department for Education (DfE) (2012) *Statutory Framework for the Early Years Foundation Stage*. London: HMSO, para 1.13.

15. Early Education (2012) *Development Matters in the Early Years Foundation Stage*. Available at www.early-education.org.uk, pp. 27–8.

16. Thomas, S. (2008) *Nurturing Babies and Children Under Four*. London: Heinemann, p. 12.

17. Department of Education and Science (DES) (1967) *Children and Their Primary School*. Report of the Central Advisory Council for Education. London: HMSO, para 529, p. 2.

18. Department for Education (2012) op.cit. (see note 14), para 1.10.

19. Willow, C., Marchant, R., Kirby, P., and Neale, B. (2004) *Young Children's Citizenship: Ideas into Practice*. York: Joseph Rowntree Foundation.

20. Fisher, J. (2013) *Starting from the Child* (fourth edition). Maidenhead: Open University Press, p. 96.

21. Mathieson, K. (2013) *I am Two! Working Effectively with Two Year Olds and Their Families*, Early Education, p. 45.

22. Early Education (2012) *Development Matters in the Early Years Foundation Stage*. Available at www.early-education.org.uk, p. 6.

23. Bronfenbrenner, U. (1979) *The Ecology of Human Development*. Cambridge, MA: Harvard University Press.

24. Berk, L. (2008) quoted in an article by Alex Spiegel, 'Old Fashioned Play Builds Serious Skills', on National Public Radio, 21 April.

25. Kuvalja, M. (2009) 'Private Speech, Play and Self-Regulation', quoted in David Whitebread (2009) *Play and Self-Regulation in Young Children*, in European Association for Research on Learning and Instruction (EARLI) Conference, Amsterdam, August.

26. Dowling, M. (1995) *Starting School at Four: A Shared Endeavour*. London: Paul Chapman.

27. Bruce, T. (1987) *Early Childhood Education*. London: Hodder & Stoughton, p. 23.

SIX   Independent Thinkers

- Given scope, young children are powerful thinkers.
- Using spoken language they begin to make complex thoughts more precise and explicit.
- As children mature they learn to self-regulate their behaviour and use and apply their thoughts more deliberately, particularly in self-chosen play.

In an encouraging climate young children constantly lay bare and invite adults to share their thoughts and ideas, original, quirky and so very often insightful. The most ambitious aim in fostering young children's independence is to recognise, support and extend their thinking.

The growing interest in young children's thinking derives from:

strong support from research evidence;

imperatives in National Frameworks;

increased insights from practitioners in their day-to-day work;

listening to the voice of children.

Support from Research Evidence

During the last twenty-five years research has recognised that thinking starts very early; very young babies are primed to think in their unceasing efforts to make sense of the world. We do not have to teach babies to think because they are born with mental abilities that fully function, which allow them to make sense of experiences and anticipate future events (1). Studies also show that babies and young children strengthen their thinking through warm social contacts with people who are close to them. Sue Gerhardt, in her wonderful book *Why Love Matters*, suggests that being lovingly held is the greatest spur to development. Her work points up the importance of babies forming close attachments both with immediate family members and then with a key person in day-care, nursery, and in a reception class. These significant people are able to 'read' a young child's behaviour and provide a 'tailor-made' response to individual needs (2).

Support for children's thinking is showing some long-term benefits. Previous findings from two major research projects, EPPE (Effective Provision of Pre-School Education) and REPEY (Researching Effective Pedagogy in the Early Years), stated that one of the ways in which we could identify high quality early years practice was where children were helped to improve their thinking skills. In the most effective early years settings staff provided opportunities to sustain and challenge children's thinking and to model this for children to share their thoughts with other children (3, 4). Since then the EPPE project has followed the same children from pre-school into Year 5. The study found that these older children had continued to benefit from attending good quality and effective early years provision and this was reflected in their achievements in mathematics and reading. This was particularly noticeable for the most vulnerable groups of young children who have had a poor start to life. EPPE also recognises the strong influence of home and stresses that the greatest impact on a child's progress is likely to be improving the quality of learning (which includes encouraging thinking) in both the home and the early years setting (5).

The issue of improving thinking is important. Resnick suggests that young minds are better thought of as developing muscles rather than fixed capacity engines (6). This statement has clear implications for the role of adults in providing scope to strengthen the muscles.

Many studies now acknowledge that two determinants of children's success as independent learners are their abilities to develop metacognitive skills (that is, be aware of, reflect on and control their thinking) and have growth mindsets about themselves as thinkers. These two factors combined result in self-regulation (7, 8, 9). David Whitebread, who has made a study of self-regulation, suggests some key criteria to support this in the early years. They include:

- providing a warm, secure and encouraging climate for children's initiatives;
- allowing scope for autonomy;
- encouraging children to talk about their learning (10).

These link closely to statutory requirements to support independent thinking.

National Frameworks

The statutory framework for the Early Years Foundation Stage (EYFS) in England gives clear statements about the need to have a regard for and offer support to young children's thinking. In Wales the Foundation Phase Framework, which covers children from 3- to 7-years-old, includes developing their thinking as part of a non-statutory Skills Framework (11). In Scotland, the guidance highlights active learning as a key curriculum component; as part of this practitioners are encouraged to support young children's sustained, shared thinking (12). In Northern Ireland, thinking skills and personal capabilities are considered to be at the heart of the curriculum and include thinking, problem solving and decision making (13).

Taken together these documents issued in the four countries of the United Kingdom offer consistent messages about the importance of young children developing as thinkers. More recently, the current and revised Early Years Framework in England contains some brief but clear messages which relate to young children's thinking, highlighted in one of the three Characteristics of Teaching.

Creating and Thinking Critically states that practitioners must (i.e. are required to) show that children are given scope to:

- have and develop their own ideas;
- make links between these ideas;
- develop strategies for doing things (14).

These messages are vital but are mere bullet points, and therefore do not do justice to the essential role that young children's thinking plays in their total learning and wellbeing, and nor do they offer guidance for practice. Other authors have offered support linking theory to practice (15, 16, 17).

Increased insights from practitioners in their day-to-day work

These research findings and requirements in national frameworks which point up the significance of young children thinking really reinforce what so many practitioners have intuitively long known to be true. In recent years those who work directly with young children have been required to give priority to planning and 'delivering' the curriculum. Early years workers recognise that in these endeavours to *provide* for children they may be in danger of missing what children are interested in and where they are investing their energies.

Practitioners also realise that, unless we understand the ways in which children express their ideas and thoughts, we may be in danger of underestimating their potential for learning. Commonly we look at children's mark making as an indicator of their achievement. However, a child may have poorly developed fine motor skills, he may have little pencil control, and his drawings, paintings and models may be immature. In this case the representations may not reflect that child's complex and original ideas which perhaps are revealed in self-chosen role play or when he is engaged in constructing outside.

Practitioners also know first-hand, from experience, that where young children are good thinkers this is a pre-cursor to their later achievement. In order to write clearly and imaginatively, and solve problems by using and applying mathematics at Key Stage 1, children must first become clear and inventive thinkers. If young children learn to reflect on their actions and recognise the link between cause and effect, they start to regulate their behaviour and are less likely to act impulsively: this is surely a lesson for life. Above all, children who are encouraged and become able to think for themselves are likely to become eager and autonomous learners.

Listening to the voice of children

Finally, if given the opportunity, young children will share with us their intimate thoughts, for example about growing up in today's society. The interim findings of the Cambridge Primary Review revealed through interviews with children that some as young as four years old think deeply about issues in the world that confront us all (18). They try to make sense about the worrying turmoil in their family lives, the effects of climate change, crime, violence and the tragedy of wars that they witness daily on the media. They are concerned about the distress caused to their parents who separate and anxious about their own safety and their futures. High quality practitioners recognise how critical it is to encourage children to share and discuss their thoughts and concerns with us in the interests of their well-being and their learning. Emotional issues take up a great deal of space in our working memories (see Chapter 7). If young children spend time dwelling on worries, they are not in a frame of mind to make a good transition in a group setting or to learn effectively.

What is going on?

Mental disequilibrium: Thinking causes a mental imbalance or disequilibrium. We can be going about our daily affairs cheerfully when we come up against something new that causes us to pause. It doesn't quite fit in with what we know already. This challenges our current understanding and we have to mentally adjust, absorb and assimilate the new idea. As we adjust and accommodate to new thinking we can once more achieve a state of equilibrium. Piaget developed this concept of the three processes of assimilation, accommodation and equilibrium to describe how a child's thinking moves forward (19).

Making connections: A baby is playing with a rattle when suddenly he drops it and it falls to the ground. Someone returns it to the baby; he repeats his action and the rattle is returned again. The baby relishes this new game and tests it out again and again before he starts to make a tentative connection between cause and effect, what he does and what happens as a result. Babies and infants show their thinking when they remember such familiar routines, games and rhymes. Each time these enjoyable experiences are repeated they support and strengthen early connections.

We cannot force new thinking. It can take considerable time for young children to give up their current understanding and move on to adjust to a new idea. Sometimes they are just not developmentally ready to make the leap in their thinking, for example a child who insists that shopkeepers give money, not change, cannot understand the concept of exchange.

Children's thinking develops as they are exposed to the ways of the world, and note how things work and what people say and do. They are alert to the conduct of adults and other children and reflect this social intelligence in their behaviour.

These descriptors make us realise that we cannot directly teach children to think independently. There is no package of structured materials that will achieve this. We can only provide supportive conditions to encourage thinking. Kahil Gibran, in his book *The Prophet*, describes this so well: he gives a profound and perceptive definition of a wise teacher who 'does not bid you enter the house of his wisdom, but rather leads you [the child] to the threshold of your [the child's] own mind' (20). Practitioners might consider how far their provision provokes young children to engage in the above types of mental activity.

How do we recognise young children's thinking?

It is relatively easy to gain insights into the thinking of an older child; he will lay his interests and views before us in writing and in discussion. We can ask him questions about his concerns and difficulties and expect to receive some responses. A younger child's thoughts are less visible, and we need considerable skills to spot and understand them. The following are important signals.

Levels of involvement: We now recognise that when children are deeply absorbed in what they are doing this assumes that there is mental activity going on. We can usefully spot a child's body language and facial expression as well as the time he spends persisting at that activity. If we note his behaviour carefully we may move closer to gain insights into what he is interested in (see the section on levels of involvement in Chapter 10).

Preoccupations or schemes of thinking: Young children develop deep interests from a very early age. Babies and toddlers can become absorbed by patterns of movement. Cathy Nutbrown describes these as 'Threads of Thought' which capture so well the fragile nature of a baby's mental activity (21). These early 'threads' are linked to young children's fascination with aspects of space and movement, such as inside, outside, near and far, up and down, over and under. They are strengthened when young children have opportunities for similar experiences where they can repeat their actions again and again as they work through their interest.

Case Study 6.1

Carol worked with a group of children ranging from two to four years old who were accommodated in one room in a Children's Centre. She set up richly resourced role-play environments, particularly to challenge the older children's ideas, including a shoe shop, a pirate ship and a builder's yard outside. However, Carol became frustrated and demoralised when too frequently three of the youngest children invaded the role play and created 'chaos'. They collected up many of the resources and carted them off to other areas; in turn, dough and small-scale vehicles were brought into the role play. The older children were sometimes resentfully forced to abandon their play in the ensuing disorder. Carol sought advice and soon learned that the 2-year-olds were simply playing appropriately. They all shared a preoccupation with transporting things from one place to another. The difficulty was overcome when Carol ensured that these children had other transporting experiences. For example, she introduced them to sturdy wheelbarrows outside and with the children she gathered piles of fir cones and leaves which could be moved around.

Comment

When Carol learnt that the 2-year-olds were demonstrating their schema in transporting she recognised that she needed to respect the needs of both groups of children, and so allow them scope for their thinking. This was difficult as the setting only had one room but she made full use of the outside area.

Reflection Point

How do you provide for children's different schema when they are accommodated in mixed age groups?

Representations: Children will relish rich curriculum experiences and then represent their understandings and ideas in many different ways, for example, through dance, role play, constructing, painting and drawing. All children will have a preferred way to characterise or record what they have gained from the experience; a broad range of media and resources will allow children good scope to demonstrate their thinking.

Talk: Given a receptive audience, young children are keen to share their ideas and thoughts in conversations. The High Scope programme encourages children to review their activities and learn over time to become reflective and self-critical.

In the process of recalling what they've done, children attach language to their actions. This makes them more conscious of their actions and more able to refer to these and draw upon them for later use. Talking about, recalling and representing their actions will help children evaluate and learn from their experiences. When planning and doing are followed by recall, children can build on what they've done and learned and remember this for the next time they plan an activity (22).

Many young children (like adults) are inhibited to share talk in large groups. Being with many other children in a semi-formal situation can be stressful: even when given gentle encouragement to participate, these children's responses are often limited and compliant as they try to tune in to what they are expected to say and marshal their thoughts into language. Children are most likely to reveal their ideas when they believe that they are working away from adults. Given an illusion of privacy, particularly when playing in dens, they relax and chat easily as they set up their own scenarios. In these circumstances they argue, negotiate, sort out roles, and freely share their beliefs and views. The National Strategies programme *Every Child a Talker* is still available online and offers lead practitioners useful guidance to support young children to converse with others (23).

Young children spend a great deal of time trying to figure things out in a fascinating and puzzling world. In an encouraging and familiar climate they are persistently curious and questioning as they search for explanations. Sometimes their questions can appear bizarre and irrelevant to the matter in hand, but there is always a link back to their own logic. When playing outside, 5-year-old Ana suddenly asked her key person, Sue, if there were restaurants under the ground. Later, Sue discovered that Ana's granddad had recently died and Ana was understandably trying, with difficulty, to make sense of his burial.

In 1992, Dr Karin Murris developed a way of helping young children to think their way through big issues by using picture books and asking questions. She described this activity as philosophical enquiry and this way of working is now widespread in reception and Year 1 classes. Murris believed that young children could play around and engage with ideas in a way that was more difficult for older children (24). In providing the conditions for philosophical enquiry it is important that: children set the agenda for discussion through their questions and responses to the story; each child's contribution is fully respected; the adult remains strictly neutral and avoids steering the discussion. This approach has developed as 'Philosophy for Children' which, although founded on similar principles, is managed more clearly by the adult who negotiates the ground rules for speaking and listening and engages the entire group of children in the discussion (25, 26). This adult-led method makes it more relevant for older and more mature children.

In order to access the treasures in young children's thoughts, we must be prepared to observe their behaviour, note their actions, listen to them closely, and then take an inspired leap into their minds.

Which conditions best support young children's thoughts and ideas?

Here I have adapted some circumstances described by Tina Bruce which help children's thoughts to take root and flourish (27):

When they are in a familiar setting with adults they trust. If children do not make a really secure transition to a setting they will not have the confidence or emotional vigour to develop their own ideas.

When they are exposed to a wide range of thought-provoking experiences. If children are intrigued by what they encounter they are likely to invest their mental energies into investigating further.

When they are supported to make their own decisions and select resources and materials for themselves. In situations where they take responsibility for their learning children learn to plan, negotiate, consider and reflect on their actions.

When they have time to pause, re-visit and re-consider, make connections and practise and apply what they know.

When they are free to make mistakes and are encouraged to see these as a valuable way of learning.

When they are encouraged to share their ideas with others.

Two educational thinkers, Sternberg and Vygotsky, offer further guidance which supports many of the points above. Sternberg argues that children (and indeed all of us) need to learn to plan, monitor, reflect on and transfer in developing powers of thinking. They also need opportunities to use these skills and strategies through problem solving and making choices and decisions. Vygotsky stresses the role of language in thinking and making meaning from experience. Both Sternberg and Vygotsky emphasise that

Figure 6.1   Shared Thinking About a Dice Game
© Siren Films

children will only be able to think well in familiar situations when they make use of their previous experience and knowledge (28, 29).

The above conditions for independent thinking are most likely to be found when children have opportunities to freely choose their experiences. Where this happens children will: concentrate on their interests rather than what is decided for them; make choices and decisions about what they are going to do, how and where they are going to do it and who they will work with; be free to make mistakes and come to see these as a valuable way of learning; practise and apply what they know and start to explore new possibilities (30).

Case Study 6.2

Richard had made a fire engine using junk materials. He proudly showed his nursery nurse and the seven other children during small group review time: 'I nearly didn't make it so good though' Richard admitted, 'I stuck the wheels with glue but they fell off'. In response to a question from Lynda, his nursery nurse, Richard thought that he had made a good mistake: 'My good mistake helped me to fix the wheels right – and look they can turn'. (The wheels were attached with split pins.)

Comment

Richard recognised that his first solution to provide wheels for his construction was not going to work. During his activity he had seen another child use split pins to attach two pieces of card. This gave him an idea for attaching his wheels. Richard persevered with a different approach which proved to be successful. He understood that his first mistake had been useful. He had learned that one approach to attach wheels was less successful than another. Richard would use this lesson in a future activity.

Reflection Point

How do you balance respect for young children to work spontaneously while encouraging them to reflect on what they have learned?

Practical Suggestions

Recognise independent thinkers

- Be alert to when babies and children appear to be making a connection in their learning, e.g. through their repeated behaviour/schema/ or a question/comment.

- Note the experiences and environments which encourage young children to grow and develop thoughts and ideas, e.g. small-scale play, exploring nature outside, simple science investigations.
- Ensure a daily programme which protects uninterrupted time for children to try out and share new ideas and mull things over.
- Provide spaces in your setting or class which are specifically designed for quiet reflection, e.g. placing a baby in a pram underneath a tree.

Offer older children

- The spaces and varied open-ended resources which encourage den making, displays of models, drawings and paintings that are particularly completed, and engage children in a discussion about what might be added next.
- Prompts to develop a structure for independent thinking, e.g. provide an attractive pictorial chart with the following headings: What do I want to do? Who do I want to do it with? What do I need in order to do it? How well did we do it?
- Encourage opportunities for an open and reflective discussion, e.g. the children to ask the questions, and make suggestions about the features in a picture or aspects of a story that are unresolved or puzzle them.

Professional Practice Questions

1. What opportunities do my children have to:
   - o make and share judgements about their representations;
   - o respond to what others think or do and have others respond to their ideas;
   - o have their views respected?

2. How well does my continuous provision allow children to use resources in ways which enrich and deepen their ideas?

Work with Parents

Share examples with parents of how their child makes connections in his thinking and conveys these at home and in the nursery.

Suggest that parents support their child's thinking by encouraging him to:

- help remember what foods need to be purchased at the supermarket;
- plan what things they need to take to nursery tomorrow.

References

1. Gopnik, A., Melzoff, A. and Kuhl, P. (1999) *How Babies Think: The Science of Childhood*. London: Weidenfeld and Nicolson. p. 178.
2. Gerhardt, S. (2004) *Why Love Matters*. London: Brunner-Routledge.
3. Sylva, K., Melhuish, E.C., Sammons, P., Siraj-Blatchford, I. and Taggart, B. (2004) The Effective Provision of Pre-School Education (EPPE) Project: *Technical Paper 12 – The Final Report: Effective Pre-School Education*. London: DfES/Institute of Education, University of London.
4. Siraj-Blatchford, I., Sylva, K., Muttock, S., Giden, R. and Bell, D. (2002) *Researching Effective Pedagogy in the Early Years (REPEY)*, DfES Research Report 356.
5. Sammons, P., Sylva, K. et al. (2007) EPPE (3–11) *Influences on Children's Attainment and Progress in Key Stage 2: Cognitive Outcomes in Year 5*, Research Brief No: RB8, 28 February.
6. Resnick, L. (1999) 'Making America smarter', *Education Week Century Series*, www.edweekorg/ew/vol18/40/resnick18, pp. 18–40.
7. Berk, L.E., Mann, T.D. and Ogan, A.T. (2006) 'Make-believe play: wellspring for development of self-regulation', in D.G. Singer, R.M. Golinkoff and K. Hirsh-Pasek (eds), *Play = Learning: How Play Motivates and Enhances Children's Cognitive and Social-Emotional Growth*. Oxford: Oxford University Press.
8. Bronson, M. (2000) *Self-Regulation in Early Childhood*. New York: Guilford Press.
9. Perry, N. (1998) Young children's self-regulated learning and contexts that support it, *Journal of Educational Psychology*, 90(4): 715–29.
10. Whitebread, D. (2013) 'The importance of self-regulated learning from birth', in H. Moylett (ed.), *Characteristics of Effective Early Learning from Birth*. Maidenhead: Open University Press, p. 28.
11. Department for Lifelong Learning and Skills (2008) *Foundation Phase; Framework for Children's Learning*. Cardiff: Welsh Assembly Government.
12. Learning and Teaching Scotland (2007) *Building the Curriculum 2: Active Learning in the Early Years*. Available at www.educationscotland.gov.uk/Images/150553%20Building%202%20Final_tcm4-628333.pdf
13. Northern Ireland Curriculum Key Stages 1 and 2 (2007) *Thinking Skills and Personal Capabilities: CPD Materials*. Available at www.nicurriculum.org/key_stages_1_and_2
14. Department for Education (2012) *Statutory Framework for the EYFS*. London: HMSO, para 1.10.
15. Dowling, M. (2012) *Young Children's Thinking*. London: Sage.
16. Chilvers, D. (2013) 'Creating and thinking critically', in H. Moylett (ed.), op.cit. (see note 36), pp. 72–90.
17. Robson, S. (2012) *Developing Thinking and Understanding in Young Children: An Introduction for Students*. London: Routledge.
18. Esmée Fairbairn Foundation/Faculty of Education, University of Cambridge (2007) *The Primary Review: Community Findings*. Available at www.primary-review.org.uk
19. Piaget, J. (1953) *The Origins of Intelligence in Children*. London: Routledge and Kegan Paul.
20. Gibran, K. (1926) *The Prophet*. London: Heinemann, p. 67.
21. Nutbrown, C. (2011) *Threads of Thinking* (third edition). London: Sage.
22. Hohmann, M., Banet, B. and Weikart, D.P. (1979) *Young Children in Action*. Ypsilanti, MI: High/Scope Press, p. 88.

23. The National Strategies Early Years (2008) *Every Child a Talker: Guidance for English Language Lead Practitioners*. London: DCSF.
24. Murris, K. (1992) *Teaching Philosophy with Picture Books*. London: infonet.
25. Bowles, M. (2008) *Philosophy for Children*. London: A. and C. Black.
26. Stanley, S. and Bowkett, S. (2008) *But Why? Developing Philosophy in the Classroom*. London: Continuum.
27. Bruce, T. (2004) *Cultivating Creativity in Babies, Toddlers and Young Children*. London: Hodder & Stoughton, p. 71.
28. Sternberg, R.J. (1985) *Beyond IQ: A Triarchic Theory of Human Intelligence*. Cambridge: Cambridge University Press.
29. Vygotsky, L.S. (1978) *Mind in Society: The Development of Higher Psychological Processes*. Cambridge, MA: Harvard University Press.
30. Dowling, M. (2008) *Young Children Thinking through their Self-chosen Activity*, Training Materials (DVD and Training Guidance), Early Education, www.earlyeducation.org.uk

SEVEN Emotional Well-being

- People's emotional lives are increasingly seen as critical to their success in life.
- Young children's emotional development is emphasised in national frameworks and is closely tied to other areas of development.
- Children's feelings are affected by the environment, the quality of relationships, and their communication and language.
- Having experienced and expressed different emotions children grow to understand these.

We may be puzzled as to why a friend or family member who is academically very able fails to make a success of his career or family life. After all, it appears that he has so much going for him. Or maybe another person who has modest intellectual qualities seems to accomplish so much in her personal and professional life. One clue may be to do with the emotional abilities these people have rather than their rational or academic competencies.

There is increasing recognition that emotional abilities have been underrated in the role that they play in helping to ensure a successful and fulfilling life. Regardless of intellectual capacities, some people are blessed with emotional stamina which helps them to withstand the stresses and difficulties in life and have insights into and empathy with others. Others who lack this stamina and are emotionally fragile are likely to experience problems in dealing with both their own and others' feelings. Both rational and emotional abilities are now seen as being equally influential in determining how people enjoy and what they achieve in life. Denham quotes evidence which emphasises that emotional competence is important both in its own right and its contribution to social competence and mental health (1).

Feelings affect everything we do and impact on children's well-being. Well-being refers to the quality of people's lives and this chapter focuses on emotional well-being. Allen's independent report to the government on 'Early Intervention' stated that 'enabling children to become rounded, capable people results in great and lasting social benefits through a lifetime that includes happiness and security in childhood, achievement in education, readiness for productive work and successful parenthood' (2). However, Allen warns, if we fail to provide this for children they will never develop the social and emotional strengths they need – leading to a cycle of wasted potential, low achievement, drink and drug abuse, and low work aspirations. A report from the Children's Society echoes this message, stating that 1 in 11 children (from a sample of 500,000 children aged eight to fifteen years old) has low subjective well-being. The report's focus on subjective data measures how children feel about their lives. It concludes that low levels of subjective well-being are associated with problems of poor mental health, social isolation and participation in risky behaviour. This focus is in response to growing recognition from prominent political and intellectual leaders that people's views on the quality of their lives are as important as measuring their standards of living or economic well-being (3). The report reflects the views of older children but surely strengthens the importance of working in the early years to make certain that children grow emotionally strong and have an optimistic view of their lives.

In other fields of corporate life and medicine there is clear acknowledgement of the significance of emotions for people's well-being and learning. The many forms of alternative medicine take account of people's feelings and how they are linked to physical health. Holistic remedies such as yoga and aromatherapy are used increasingly as part of treatment for cancer patients. On modern management courses we hear that 'feminine' stereotype qualities which include sensitivity and intuition are requirements for effective leaders regardless of the gender of a leader.

Daniel Goleman summarises the view from the business world:

> The rules for work are changing. We're being judged by a new yardstick: not just by how smart we are, or by our training and expertise, but also by how well we handle ourselves and each other. This yardstick is increasingly applied in choosing who will be hired and who will not, who will be let go and who retained, who is passed over and who is promoted. (4)

Goleman lists a number of studies that highlight both the worrying consequences when people are not emotionally competent and the great benefits when they are. He also refers to brain studies which suggest that a person's emotional state of mind is closely linked to his ability to think more effectively (5, 6).

Young Children's Emotional Development

This informed awareness tunes in well with practitioners' belief that, when working with young children, they are educating more than their intellect. The link between children's emotions and other aspects of their learning is increasingly recognised. Laevers' project, 'Experiential Education' (EXE), identifies the degree of a child's emotional well-being as one of two key factors to be considered when judging the means of a child learning effectively and the quality of an educational setting. His definition of emotional well-being is broad:

> the degree to which children do feel at ease, can be spontaneous and are satisfied in their physical needs, feel the need for tenderness and affection, the need for safety and clarity, the need for social recognition, the need to feel competent and the need for meaning in life and moral value. (7)

Some of these factors are explored elsewhere in this book (see Chapters 1, 2, 5, 6 and 13); here we concentrate on the importance in regard to feelings. Laevers' work is strongly echoed in the action research project 'Accounting Early for Life-Long Learning'. Pascal and Bertram claim that emotional well-being is one of four factors seen in children who have the potential to be effective learners (8).

Practitioners warm to messages in national documents which urge them to support children's emotional well-being. The early years framework in England includes this aspect of development as one of three in the prime area of Personal, Social and Emotional Development (9). The guidance document *Social and Emotional Aspects of Development* (SEAD) highlights emotional development as one of the three building blocks for future success in life (10).

References to children's emotional well-being are also evident in early years frameworks in Wales, Northern Ireland and Scotland (11, 12, 13). The Welsh Foundation Phase Framework, which now extends to children aged three to seven years old, states that children begin to express their feelings and understand the feelings of others, and usefully outlines six outcomes showing the expected progression for children's emotional development. In the New Zealand Early Childhood Curriculum document *Te Whariki*, there is a section on well-being which states that two of the entitlements for children are 'an expectation that the early childhood education setting is an enjoyable place to be; a place where they have fun; and to develop a trust that their emotional needs will be responded to' (14). Despite these affirming messages there continue to be strong concerns about children's emotional well-being in England: some concerns are linked to the current thrust on raising standards and pushing young children into a 'hurry along' curriculum rather than allowing them to enjoy an unpressurised childhood. Our education system is increasingly seen as a means of satisfying the demands of industry and commerce, these being mainly interpreted in terms of academic achievement. Many staff, particularly in reception classes, now believe that the downward pressure on attainment has forced them into practices which they know intuitively are counter-productive for children. Practitioners are pressured into teaching early phonics to children, often through rote learning. Reception teachers are urged to document children's progress in detail and ensure that the children achieve a good standard across all of the Early Learning Goals. A current consultation initiated by Ofsted proposes that children should be 'tested' when they arrive in Reception (15). The role of local authorities is marginalised and Ofsted is now seen as the main arbiter for quality. Staff in some private and voluntary settings still feel intimidated by the prospect of inspection, believing that inspectors are mainly interested in children learning to read, write and calculate: this leads them to try to accelerate younger children's attainment in early literacy and numeracy at the expense of attention being given to the other areas of learning or the learning processes outlined in the Characteristics of Effective Learning. Sometimes these fears and practices arise as a consequence of misunderstanding the requirements. Nevertheless, it is a hard and worrying fact that many practitioners continue to feel compelled to act in a way which does not recognise or value how children might feel.

Commonsense and our own experiences tell us that we cannot function properly if we are unhappy, upset or angry. Our behaviour and thinking are heavily influenced by our feelings. Emotional development in young children is rapid and profound. Their feelings affect their self-esteem, the way in which they relate to others, and their grasp of right and wrong. In order to equip them for living now and later, early years practitioners need to understand what influences children's emotional lives, how this unfolds, and what is required to care for it.

Psychological Perspectives

Accepting that young children's emotional well-being can be important for their wider and long-term development, we highlight the following three factors that influence emotional outcomes:

- the environment that surrounds the child;
- the quality of the relationships the child experiences;
- the child's communication and language skills.

The impact of the environment on emotional well-being

The many brain connectors that link and 'fire up' brain cells during the early weeks and months of life are strengthened or weakened by the experiences that are encountered. The young brain's plasticity enables it to adapt to its circumstances or surroundings. And repetition is important. When a baby is exposed to experiences again and again, the connectors are strengthened through use and have a decisive impact on development (16).

Pleasurable play experiences are regarded as very important for young children. Isaacs believed that play was a form of self-expression that helped children release their feelings safely and rehearse ways of dealing with different emotions (17). Winnicott supported this psychoanalytic view, seeing play as offering a safe space for children where they could explore the tensions in their everyday lives, recognise the problems, and face up to difficult and strong emotions (18).

We have already looked at Bronfenbrenner's model of ecological development which described how the four layers of society impacted on a child's social development (see Chapter 3). This model applies equally to emotional well-being:

- *The microsystem* reflects the child's daily experiences at home and in the setting which may stimulate and enrich positive feelings or may induce negative emotions of fear and a lack of confidence.
- *The mesosystem* may mean that the microsystems of home and nursery either reinforce or conflict: the child may encounter similar environments which offer and affirm feelings of being loved and secure; or experience inconsistent and confusing messages when one environment is very controlling and the other has few boundaries.
- *The exosystem* reflects the conditions that affect family life: flexible working hours enable parents to be with their child when most needed; long working hours away from home may restrict time spent with the family.
- *The macrosystem* or wider context can mean a child-friendly society where children feel welcome, valued and respected, or national policies which pay little attention to children's needs and overlook how they may be feeling (19).

Reflection Point

Think of other examples from each of the four systems which may impact on children's emotional well-being.

The quality of relationships

Attachments

Research indicates that where children start their lives having at least one person with whom they have a strong bond or attachment they can develop a resistance to stress in their lives (20). This bond provides a form of protection both for the early years and in their future lives and it is a basic requirement for children to establish wider social attachments as they grow up. If a baby is physically and emotionally close to one person initially (most usually his birth mother), this makes his later separation from her more tolerable rather than less. From birth, every day that this significant person can be with the baby, to discover him, help him to know her, meet his needs, give him pleasure and take pleasure in him, will contribute to a fund of confidence and inner peace. Even a brief few weeks of this relationship will offer the baby a good start. As parents spend time with their new baby they get to know his signals: a hungry or tired cry or sign of discomfort; a prolonged gaze as the baby starts to focus; body movements which suggest his need to play and communicate.

Responsive and loving adults are crucial to all aspects of infant development. And you cannot overdose young infants with attention. Every time a baby receives a response to something she appears to need, the better. Penelope Leach draws attention to historical evidence of the possible consequences of the strict rationing of attention. After the Second World War, thousands of orphaned and refugee babies were kept in institutions where their physical care was excellent but wholly impersonal. Many of these babies failed to thrive – worse, some died without, seemingly, any physical reason for this. In 1990, the same dreadful situation became apparent in the packed orphanages in Romania. Quite early on, researchers concluded that these babies and small children suffered from the lack of maternal care. Later this was amended, recognising that it was not so much the lack of a link with their natural parent, but the deprivation of responsive and loving care. Leach stressed that this lack of attachment can of course occur within the family, for example, where a potentially loving parent becomes clinically depressed and is unable to sustain a loving bond with the child (21).

Very young babies rapidly tune in to a close relationship with their mother or main carer. The baby is already familiar with her mother's voice and starts to recognise her face and smell. When held by her mum or dad a baby's heartbeat calms immediately. The deepest part of the brain is concerned with feelings and its development is fundamental to all other aspects of development. From a safe and secure base the young baby will start to explore her environment and become open to new experiences. A young brain grows through sensory experiences, taste, touch, hearing, seeing and smell. If experiences are repeated often enough, the connections between brain cells are strengthened. When babies are provided with familiar and consistent routines this helps them to start to make sense of what is happening to them and they will begin to build up a predictable mental structure in their lives. Daily routines such as feeding, nappy changing and bath-time allow babies and their carers to enjoy loving exchanges.

Young babies cannot handle their feelings and are dependent on their carer to interpret their signals of distress, e.g. a hungry cry or wriggle of discomfort. Over time, if the baby's signals are recognised and responded to, he will begin to trust that his mum or carer is always there to 'make things better'. The most effective provision is based on 'contingent care' which is a bespoke response to the baby's actual needs rather than what the carer thinks he might need (22). Given this optimal start the baby is helped to be calm and to start to manage his behaviour: for example, an infant, who has been loved, respected and listened to, starts to show care and concern for others.

Importantly, babies' brains also thrive on companionship. Colwyn Trevarthen suggests what this looks like for a child, and this description applies equally to a baby:

> Children do need affection and support and protection and so on but they need a lot more than that. They need company which is interested and curious and affectionate ... Children are very good at private research. They can do it very well, but they don't do it if they are discouraged, if they feel unwanted or lonely then they don't explore. (23)

Although mum or dad are likely to be the most significant carers, a baby may form a bond with other close family members – a sibling or grandparent in particular. However, important attachments will only be made with a small group of people who know the child well. Young children's need for an attachment is also ongoing throughout and beyond the early years phase. For those who have established a secure close relationship as babies the roots of security are already established. However, at times, for example when facing change or stresses, children will need to be reassured that their special person is still there for them.

Figure 7.1   Sharing 'Peek-a-Boo'
© Siren Films

The key person

When babies and small children move into a group setting and come to separate from their parents, the essential need is to appoint a key person with whom the child can make a similar (but not identical) attachment. It is now mandatory in England for all children in the EYFS to have a key person. This section examines the role and looks at implications for the key person when working with children of different ages.

What is a key person?

The young child's need for intimate interaction through close attachment continues when he moves to a childminder or into a group setting and this is where the key person plays a critical role. As we have seen, very young children thrive on familiarity and predictability and these involve ensuring a continuity of attention through a staff member developing a personal relationship with that child. Whether the term 'key worker' or 'key person' is used, the role is based on relationships. The key person forms a special association with both the young child and his parents. When this approach is well established it offers benefits to all concerned, as clearly described by Peter Elfer and colleagues and summarised here:

Babies and young children will experience a close, affectionate and reliable relationship and are helped to feel unique and special.

Parents will have a link with someone who is fully committed to their child and this can offer them 'peace of mind'.

The key person feels that she is really important to the child and family which offers great job satisfaction.

The manager or head recognises some important requirements for quality provision are met: that children are settled and well cared for, parents feel comfortable with the provision, and staff are involved with and committed to their work (24).

The quality of the key person relationship has a direct bearing on a very young child's learning. The chemical cortisol, present in all of us, surges in conditions of stress and can close down functions. When a child is loved and cherished he is relaxed and in the right state of mind to learn. When these conditions are not present, the levels of cortisol rise. Leach and colleagues offer a cautious warning about the effects of full day-care for very young children under two years old when they are in the care of inexperienced and poorly trained staff: in these circumstances staff may care for each child's physical needs but not be aware of the need for close and intimate interactions to foster each child's unique qualities. This approach of treating all children equally can lead to a flatness of affect which is insufficient to support a developing personality (25). A key person approach ensures consistency for a young child and this is particularly necessary in a large, free-flowing nursery setting or Foundation Stage Unit. In a reception class that is usually staffed by a teacher and assistant, it is easier to establish similar interactions and expectations and so the key person role may be shared. Nevertheless, careful thought needs to be given to the organisation of playtimes and lunchtimes when reception children may encounter other adults. At these times new children can be particularly vulnerable and during these early days where possible they should be supported by a key person being there for them.

More detailed guidance on the key person role may be found in *The Social and Emotional Aspects of Development: Guidance for Practitioners Working in the Early Years Foundation Stage* (26).

Children's communication and language skills

Children's experiences and expressions of feelings develop tremendously during the early years of life. Most of their basic emotions are in place by age two years but the process starts long before then. Trevarthen suggests that:

> ... every infant is born with the receptive awareness and expressive body needed to communicate fully with others. They can feel and express curiosity, intention, doubt and anxiety, love and pride in admired accomplishment, shame and jealousy at being misinterpreted. Their manifest need is for expressive contact with sympathetic joy-seeking, generous company. (27)

Young children also quickly develop unique means of expressing their feelings and then use these deliberately to suit the occasion (28).

Case Study 7.1

Maggie's emotions change frequently and rapidly. She can be furious one moment when her block construction collapses, but jump for joy the next moment when her childminder announces they are going out to the shops. By contrast, Kirsty's feelings are more long lasting and even. She rarely shows excitement, but plays equably by herself for most of the time. When Kirsty is upset or angry it is difficult to cheer her up. Her angry feelings (or mood) remain with her, sometimes for a whole day.

Comment

Linda, the childminder, was aware that these two 3-year-old girls had dissimilar emotional styles which required different approaches. Maggie was often easier to deal with, although unpredictable, while Kirsty's feelings were less easy to 'read'.

Reflection Point

What approaches would you take when building close attachments with Maggie and Kirsty?

Whenever we share our throughts and feelings with others we communicate. This can happen through spoken language and also through our gestures, eye gaze, and facial and bodily expressions (29). There is a two-way link between feelings and communication: children who have emotional problems often find it difficult to communicate how they feel, whereas those with limited language may experience emotional and behavioural difficulties which are increasingly evident later in life (30).

Despite important differences in expressive style, young children are full of raw emotion and feel acutely. The power of their emotion is heightened as their feelings are not tempered by experience. Most things are happening for the first time, and as a consequence children can be desolate in their distress, pent up with fury, and over-brimming with joy. They are receptive to all the experiences that are offered to them. The effect of this responsiveness for those children who live turbulent lives is that they may do so on an emotional roller-coaster. In situations like this children can be ruled by their emotions. This is particularly noticeable with those young children who find it hard to express themselves in spoken language. It is difficult for an adult to be fluent and articulate when she is angry or distressed, so how much more so for a 2- or 3-year-old when emotions overwhelm her?

Young children's feelings, positive and negative, will initially be best reflected through their actions. They will dance for the sheer pleasure of twirling their bodies in space, and they will make marks, daub colours, stick materials, make patterns, and build and construct imaginary scenarios to depict pleasures and turmoils which initially they are unable to talk about. Provision of a broad programme allows all children to find appropriate ways to represent what they are feeling; over time they learn the language which describes these feelings. A narrow programme which only allows them to use limited materials, or which places an undue emphasis on representing experiences through just written symbols, is not inclusive. It is only those children who have already benefited from rich active and sensory experiences who will start to make sense of written numbers and letters: at this stage they will enjoy being helped to count, spot the letters of their name in signs and books, and practise writing them. A nursery programme should actively help all children to make this transition to using symbols. However, children's readiness cannot be pre-empted.

Requiring all children to do things for which only some are ready will result in only some of them making any sense of what they are doing.

Using play to communicate

Children will play out what they experience in life and observations of their play will provide rich evidence of their views and feelings.

Play therapy is defined as a way of helping troubled children deal with difficult life events: play is used by a trusted therapist as a means of communication as it helps children to explore, express, and start to understand painful experiences (31).

The three stages common in therapeutic play are:

- *sensory play*: children use a tactile medium such as clay or mud to explore and control through banging, shaping or smearing;
- *projective play*: children use toys and props to tell a story that reflects their inner concerns and fears;
- *symbolic play*: children negotiate roles and play out stories, making it clear where play is starting and stopping.

Young Children's Developing Understanding of Feelings

Young children need to have experience of myriad of emotions before they can begin to understand them. Using puppets with children, Denham found that those who showed both positive and negative feelings in their play were more likely to realise and comprehend what others were feeling in different situations (32). Moreover, using puppets again, Denham suggested that children were beginning to recognise that in a given situation people may feel differently. For example, many children could understand that a puppet could be sad about going to nursery, while they would be happy (33). This tied in with earlier studies which indicated that young children were able to appreciate another viewpoint and were not just focused on themselves (34).

It is much more difficult though for children to understand that emotions can be mixed. When 6-year-olds were asked to predict the feelings of a person who eventually found his lost dog but it was injured, they typically said that the owner would feel totally happy or sad, but not a mixture of both. Children at ten years old acknowledged that it was possible to feel both emotions at the same time (35). Furthermore, although they may show complex feelings, they cannot predict them. However, it seems that social convention plays a part, as from a young age children can be influenced to show feelings which are socially acceptable but not genuine. In one study, 4-year-old girls responded to social pressures by smiling when the researcher presented them with a disappointing toy, although when they examined their toy alone they showed their disappointment. (Interestingly, boys did not attempt to mask their feelings in the same way.)

Questioned later, when they were able to swap their disappointing gift for a more exciting one, the little girls admitted to being disappointed, but thought that this would not have been recognised because of their polite words of thanks. These children made no reference to their smiling faces or the control of their real emotions, and despite their behaviour were unaware of how their displayed emotion could beguile observers (36). As children grow older they begin to understand that the feelings they show to others may not be the same as their true feelings.

This lesson is a necessary one as part of becoming socialised. Nevertheless, where young children are pressurised or coerced into constantly masking their true feelings and substituting socially acceptable responses, this could lead to them misunderstanding the function of emotions in life.

Case Study 7.2

Emily settled at her pre-school, seemingly without difficulty. However, she was overly polite in her responses to adults. When greeted in the morning by the nursery assistant, Emily would respond to advances with, 'I'm extremely well, thank you very much'. She would thank individual staff when they supplied paper on the easel and after she had listened to a story. Emily made no advances towards other children – when they took apparatus from her and refused to allow her a turn on their wheeled toys outside she appeared to be at a loss. One day Danny took her beloved teddy from her. Emily did not protest but was later found in the cloakroom curled up in a ball. When the nursery assistant tried to talk through that matter with her, Emily repeatedly chanted, 'I'm very well, thank you', and refused to acknowledge her loss.

Comment

Emily had been heavily conditioned into controlling her feelings and being polite. The effect of this was that some of her behaviour was inappropriate and was regarded as bizarre by other children. When Emily experienced the loss of her teddy she was unable to give vent to her feelings, although her body language demonstrated her great distress.

The nursery worked closely with Emily's parents, encouraging them to help her understand more about her feelings and be able to express them. She left the nursery after one year, still effusively and indiscriminately thanking adults but more able to express her feelings of anger and frustration where appropriate.

Reflection Point

How would you convey Emily's progress in managing her feelings to the receiving teacher in Reception?

Practical Suggestions

Listen and observe

- Listen for and carefully observe any signs of distress in a young baby and learn to identify the reason, e.g. hunger, discomfort, boredom, tiredness.
- Try to catch children's responses during different parts of the day.
- Observe how they cope with the challenges of new activities or a new member of staff.
- Observe the body language of those children who cannot easily verbalise their feelings, particularly those with English as an additional language.

Plan clear expectations and support for the role of the key person

Provide guidance based on the following requirements:

Responsibilities

Relationships/Links

- Establish an initial trusting relationship with parents/carers, e.g. through home visits, a pre-arranged initial meeting, introduction to the setting.
- Maintain close, ongoing working links with parents through clear professional boundaries.
- Develop good communication links with parents to exchange information about the child and circumstances which affect him, e.g. through friendly face-to-face contact, daily link book, diaries, photographs, telephone calls (where a family is given two key persons, parents to be aware of the work rota and know which member of staff is working).
- Establish close personal links with each child to ensure that they feel special, and experience an affectionate and reliable bond.
- Liaise frequently and regularly with staff, e.g. to exchange information about your key children, provide a voice for each child, over time, to encourage the children to establish relationships with a wider circle of adults.
- Link with other agencies, e.g. in order to provide the family with additional support/expertise, to ensure that the family experience a well managed transition to and from the setting.

Knowledge and understanding

- Clearly understand the need for confidentiality in regard to each family's circumstances.
- Become informed about each child's family background in order to understand more about that child's behaviour and be better equipped to deal with it.
- Develop knowledge of each child's home language, e.g. to use this to greet the child and parent each day.

- Develop an understanding of child development from birth to age five.
- Tune in to each family when communicating important messages, e.g. early attachment, the central role of parents in the child's ongoing development, the expectations for and of parents during their child's time in the setting.
- Become familiar with:
  - o the EYFS and internal documentation, and understand how these might best be used to support the progress and wellbeing of very young children, e.g. through the use of observation sheets, developmental charts etc.;
  - o internal policies and procedures relating to the Safeguarding and Welfare requirements;
  - o the daily routines which ensure that children start to recognise a predictable pattern to the day.

Key attributes of the role

- Secure self-esteem.
- Emotionally mature and able to cope with complexity.
- Willingness to learn from parents.
- Comfortable with diversity and a respectful attitude towards different family situations.
- Strong interpersonal skills, e.g. friendly, open, discrete, patient, tolerant.
- Good communication (verbal and non-verbal) and listening and negotiating skills.
- Ability to de-centre and empathise with children and their parents.
- Genuine interest in each family and the child's developing story.
- A reflective approach to practice.
- The motivation to develop professionally and so increase expertise and skills.

Recruitment, induction and ongoing support for the key person

- Recruitment procedures to involve staff and parent representation.
- A warm welcome from friendly, approachable staff who demonstrate solidarity as a team.
- Links to a trained mentor and an opportunity to continue to shadow aspects of the work.
- Provision of a 'buddy' to share the key children and ensure cover when the key person is absent.
- Access to a staff handbook which provides details of the daily routines and procedures.
- Access to a library of professional books/articles.
- Observation by and feedback from line manager to establish any strengths and areas to develop.

(Continued)

(Continued)

- Initial training in key aspects of the work, e.g. attachment theory.
- Effective supervision to provide for confidential shared discussion, coaching to develop effectiveness and regular opportunities for in-house training, e.g. staff meetings, training days to develop communication and counselling skills.

Provide an environment which enables children to acknowledge and express their feelings

- Affirm a baby's distress by gentle rocking and gently telling him that you know he is hungry or tired.
- Share a toddler's enjoyment of a game, e.g. peek-a-boo, and encourage him to repeat it again and again.
- Organise a broad range of experiences which enable children to express their feelings in different ways.
- Provide resources: a punch bag on which to vent angry feelings; a large soft animal or soft woolly scarves for lonely/upset children to cuddle; a large stuffed figure of a granddad sat in an armchair to whom children can confide their worries.
- Have regular displays of adults and children expressing different emotions. Use these in discussions with small groups and encourage children to identify with the feelings and to share their own experiences.
- Introduce a worry bag (a drawstring bag) and display a selection of shells (worry shells) nearby. If a child is worried, he can be encouraged to select a shell and take it to an adult to share his concern. After the worry has been discussed (and hopefully resolved) the child visibly gets rid of the worry shell by placing it in the drawstring bag.

Help children to acquire a clear and understandable picture of life in the setting/class

- Make clear the daily sequence of events by using a pictorial timeline.
- Have a large clock and make clear the times when certain activities begin and end (with practice, many 4-year-olds will learn to use the clock as a reference point).

Professional Practice Questions

1. How well do I read the signals of various feelings expressed by the babies in my key group?
2. How do my feelings (impatience, frustration, pleasure, sympathy) affect how I interact with individual children?
3. How well do we support our less experienced colleagues in their key person roles?

Work with Parents

- Ask parents to share with you the events/situations that excite their child, and make him happy, worried, frightened, angry and/or frustrated.
- Suggest that parents anticipate and try to avoid contexts that cause their child's negative feelings, e.g. provide a torch/nightlite/favourite soft toy to help alleviate his fear of the dark.

References

1. Denham, S.A. (2007) 'Dealing with feelings: how children negotiate the worlds of emotion and social relationships'. Invited Article in *Cognition, Brain Behaviour*, X1 (1) (March 1–48).
2. Allen, G. (2011) *Early Intervention: The Next Steps: Independent Report to HM Government*. Cabinet Office, London SW1A 2WH.
3. The Children's Society (2012) *Promoting Positive Well-being for Children: A Report for Decision Makers, in Parliament, Central Government and Local Areas*. Available at www.childrenssociety.org.uk, p. 4.
4. Goleman, D. (1998) *Working with Emotional Intelligence*. London: Bloomsbury, p. 4.
5. Damasio, A. (1994) *Descartes' Error: Emotion, Reason and the Human Brain*, quoted in D. Goleman (1996) *Emotional Intelligence*. London: Bloomsbury, p. 19.
6. Goleman, D. (1998) *Working with Emotional Intelligence*. London: Bloomsbury, p. 239.
7. Laevers, F. (1999) 'The Experiential Education project: well-being and involvement make the difference', *Early Education*, 27 (Spring).
8. Pascal, C. and Bertram, T. (1998) 'Accounting Early for Life-Long Learning'. Keynote talk at Early Years Conference, Dorchester, July.
9. Department for Education (DfE) (2012) *Statutory Framework for the EYFS*. London: HMSO, p. 1.6.
10. Department for Children, Schools and Families (DCSF) (2008) *Social and Emotional Aspects of Development (SEAD)*. London: DCSF.
11. Department for Education, Lifelong Learning and Skills (2008) *Foundation Phase: Framework for Children's Learning*. Cardiff: Welsh Assembly Government. Available at www.wales.gov.uk
12. Northern Ireland Council for the Curriculum Examinations and Assessment (2006) *Understanding the Foundation Stage*. Belfast: Council for the Curriculum, Examinations and Assessment. Available at www.nicurriculum.org.uk/foundationstage
13. Scottish Government Publication (2008) *The Early Years Framework*. Available at www.scotland.gov.uk/earlyyearsframework
14. New Zealand Ministry of Education (1996) *Te Whariki: Early Childhood Curriculum*. Wellington: Learning Media.
15. Gaunt, C. (2013) 'OfSTED chief calls for review of early years assessment', *Nursery World*, 21.6.
16. Shore, R. (1997) *Re-thinking the Brain*. New York: Families and Work Institute, p. 17.
17. Isaacs, S. (1951) *Social Development in Young Children*. London: Routledge, p. 210.

18. Winnicott, D. (1971) *Playing and Reality*. London: Tavistock.
19. Bronfenbrenner, U. (1979) *The Ecology of Human Development*. Cambridge, MA: Harvard University Press.
20. David, T., Gooch, K., Powell, S. and Abbot, L. (2003) *Birth to Three Matters: A Review of the Literature*. London: DfES, p. 46.
21. Leach, P. (1994) *Children First*. London: Michael Joseph, p. 85.
22. Gerhardt, S. (2004) *Why Love Matters*. London: Brunner-Routledge.
23. Trevarthen, C. (2003) quoted in P. Elfer, E. Goldschmied and D. Selleck (eds), *Key Persons in the Nursery*. London: David Fulton, p. 11. (Originally published 1988.)
24. Elfer, P., Goldschmied, E. and Selleck, D. (2003) op.cit. (see note 23), pp. 18–19.
25. Leach, P., Stein, A. and Sylva, K. (2005) *Families, Children and Child Care Study*. Available at Institute of Children, Families and Social Issues, Birkbeck University of London, 7 Bedford Square, London WC1B 3RA.
26. Department for Children, Schools and Families (DCSF) (2008) *Social and Emotional Aspects of Development: Guidance for Practitioners Working in the Early Years Foundation Stage*, Appendix 1. London: DCSF.
27. Trevarthen, C. (2006) '"Doing" education – to know what others know', *Early Education*, 49 (Summer), p. 12.
28. Denham, S. (1998) *Emotional Development in Young Children*. New York: Guilford Press.
29. Doherty-Sneddon, G. (2003) *Children's Unspoken Language*, London: Jessica Kingsley.
30. Cross, M. (2004) *Children with Emotional and Behavioural Difficulties and Communication Problems: There is Always a Problem*. London: Jessica Kingsley.
31. Cattanach, A. (2003) *Introduction to Play Therapy*. Hove: Brunner-Routledge.
32. Denham, S.A. (1986) 'Social cognition, social behaviour, and emotion in pre-schoolers: contextual validation', *Child Development*, 57: 194–201.
33. Denham, S.A. and Couchard, E.A. (1990) 'Young pre-schoolers' understanding of emotion', *Child Study Journal*, 20: 171–92.
34. Borke, H. (1983) 'Piaget's mountains revisited: changes in the egocentric landscape', in M. Donaldson (ed.), *Early Childhood Development and Education*. Oxford: Blackwell.
35. Harris, R.L. (1983) 'Children's understanding of the link between situation and emotion', *Journal of Experimental Child Psychology*, 36: 490–509.
36. Cole, P.M. (1986) 'Children's spontaneous control of facial expression', *Child Development*, 57: 1309–21.

EIGHT Influences on Young Children's Well-being

- Young children learn about feelings through close family contacts.
- Moving to new environments, for children who have recently moved from another country, and coping with loss can cause complex feelings.
- To achieve emotional health children must experience and express a range of feelings; they need to convey negative emotions particularly during times of stress.
- Practitioners and parents help children to regulate their feelings.

The Influence of the Family

Young children's understandings and use of their feelings will be heavily influenced by the significant people around them, initially their parents. An important part of knowing about ourselves is to be able to recognise the various feelings that we have and that other people experience. Elfer suggests that this empathetic behaviour is dependent on children having experienced good attachment where their own feelings have been understood (1). Judy Dunn also reminds us that once children can talk they will show their understanding of others' minds, for instance in the language they use with younger children or adults (2). By stark contrast, there is evidence of how less fortunate children learn different lessons. Goleman provides case studies of the dire emotional effects on small children who have been repeatedly physically abused (3). The most noticeable result is that these children who have suffered so much completely lack any care and concern for others. At two and three years of age they typically ignore any distress shown by other children, and often their responses may be violent. All they are doing however is mirroring the behaviour that they have received themselves.

In families where feelings are not only expressed but are openly discussed, young children are helped to recognise and accept their emotions and those of others. In these circumstances children are also more likely to talk freely about what they feel. These intimate contacts between parents and children involve shared experiences and loving attention over a period of time. Some parents do not provide this as a result of the busy lives they lead. Charles Handy points out how those adults who are under pressure in full-time employment start to realise that their work is beginning to interfere with the relationships they have with those closest to them (4). At the other extreme are parents who, because they are unemployed, have time, but the effects of overcrowded and poor housing and all the other attendant problems of poverty drain them of the resources and patience they could offer to their small children. While a setting would never claim to be able to replace these family interactions, practitioners can work closely with parents and share the task of helping children understand what they feel (see Chapter 15).

Case Study 8.1

Karu was an attractive 5-year-old, an only child, very articulate, and already a competent early reader and skilled at construction. Nevertheless, he rarely talked in school and appeared to use his energies in disrupting activities for other children. He would deliberately tip over containers of apparatus while the teacher was talking, or pinch another child while she was answering the teacher. He refused to sit with other children and often tore up his drawings and early writing before his teacher could see them. By his second term in school Karu had no friends as the rest of the children disapproved of his antisocial activities.

Karu's parents admitted to having their own personal difficulties, but said that they saw very little of him at home as he spent most of his time watching TV in his bedroom. His father said that the one regular point of contact was at bedtime when he read Karu a story. On these occasions he gripped his father's hand very tightly.

Ann, his teacher, decided to try to spend more time with Karu in order to establish a closer bond. She suggested to Karu that he might meet her for a chat or a story in the library at lunchtime. (He had recently asked to stay in at lunchtime rather than go out into the playground where he was becoming increasingly isolated.) Ann made these sessions chatty and welcoming. She always took a cup of tea with her and offered Karu a biscuit. Occasionally she would bring in photos of her home and her cat and tell him about things in her own life at weekends. At first Karu said little, but then he opened up.

He expressed his terror of his father leaving home and of never being able to see him again (in fact this never happened as the parents sorted out their marital problems). Karu told Ann he felt very angry when he was made to come to school. He thought that his parents were deliberately leaving him there knowing that school made him sad. Initially Karu's behaviour was unchanged, but after two weeks of meeting daily with Ann he came to sit close beside her at group time. He gripped her skirt while looking directly at her face. Ann bent down and said quietly, 'I won't leave you Karu, I am always here'. After that point his progress was slow but steady. He continued to talk with Ann and sometimes spoke about happy times with his parents. Eventually he made a friend (a shy newcomer to the school). By the end of term Karu was happy to go into the playground with his friend; he was becoming a sociable and equable member of the class and was able to listen and participate as one of a group.

Comment

Because of his huge anxiety about losing his father, Karu was unable to use his mind to learn from the nursery programme. His anger and resentments were not expressed verbally but were shown in his behaviour towards others. Ann's daily link with Karu helped to meet his hunger for love and security. His improved progress and well-being were a consequence of being able to talk through his feelings and trust his teacher.

Reflection Point

How often do I ask parents to share any concerns they may have about changes in their child's behaviour and share my own observations with them?

Children's emotional understandings are dependent not only on the degree of family support but also on what sex they happen to be. Different messages about emotions can be given to boys and girls. In one small study, mothers talked more often to their 18-month-old daughters about feelings than they did to their sons at this age. By the time they were two years old these little girls were seen as more likely to be interested in and articulate about feelings than the boys (5). Other studies offer further evidence. When parents make up stories for their small children they use more emotion words for their daughters than their sons; when mothers play with their children they show a wider range of emotions to girls than to boys. Brody and Hall, who summarised these studies, suggested that as a result of the experiences they have, and because girls become more competent at an early age with language than do boys, this results in the girls being able to use words to explore feelings. By contrast boys are not helped so well to verbalise and so tend to be confrontational with their feelings and become less tuned in to their own and others' emotions (6). These early experiences and consequent emotional differences can very often continue into adulthood and be seen in relationships. Goleman suggests that women are well prepared to cope with the emotional aspects of a relationship; conversely, men are more inclined to minimise emotions and are less aware of the importance of discussing and expressing feelings as a way of sustaining a partnership. He argues that this emotional imbalance between the sexes is a significant factor in the break-up of marriages [7].

Given the importance that most of us attach to a stable and loving relationship in our lives, perhaps early years provision should aim to redress these differences in the emotional lessons that children learn.

The Effect of Transition on Children's Feelings

A young child on familiar territory at home or in a nursery is likely to feel secure and be confident and competent. Any move means that a child is emotionally challenged. The initial effect on young children's confidence and independence when moving from a known setting has already been explored (see Chapters 1 and 5). We have seen that children experience many complex and often conflicting feelings. Excitement and anticipation of the move are tempered by anxiety, distress and confusion about the unknown. In these circumstances children's emotional well-being is not secure and this then affects their ability to learn.

Case Study 8.2

Bimla and Daisy (4 years) were playing with small world resources. Bimla called to Janice her key person, 'Janice will you help us?' Janice cheerfully agreed and asked the two girls what is happening:

Bimla: 'You see Janice, little teddy is going to big school and he's frightened, he's really frightened'.

Daisy: 'Yeh an, an he doesn't want to go does he Bimla, so he shuts himself in this box' (squeezes the bear into a small box), 'oh no he won't fit'.

Bimla: 'His mummy is looking for him' (uses a high pitched voice), 'Teddy, Teddy where are you, come on Teddy'.

Daisy: 'Shhh ... he is hiding from his mum cos he doesn't like big school. It's ... it's too big and the children are big, so Ted won't go'.

Bimla: 'But his mummy is cross Janice, what will happen'?

Janice: 'Poor Teddy, I think that we need to help him and then he might start to like school. Perhaps we might find him a friend'.

Comment

Janice listened carefully to the graphic drama. She had no training in play therapy but quickly realised that the two girls were playing out their own fears about moving to the reception class the following term. Having been invited to join the play, Janice was able to immediately suggest ways to help Ted which she hoped would allay some of their anxiety.

Reflection Point

What further actions might you take to encourage Bimla and Janice to feel more positive about their forthcoming transition?

Working memory is recognised as an important feature for a child's developing self-regulation (8). However, negative feelings can have an effect on children's working memory. This is stressed in research from Western Australia where working memory is described as a measure of the number of things that one can cope with at any one time (9). Adults all have the capacity to keep a number of ideas and skills in their minds at one time. Once these ideas and skills become familiar they become less onerous; in effect, skills which were initially learned individually and laboriously can fuse together and become automatic. Young children who are new to all learning find everything a challenge and there is so much more to remember. For example, a child who is learning to use the painting easel has to learn how to hold her paintbrush, how to apply paint and return the brush to the paint pot, what to do with the painting once it is completed, where to wash her hands and hang her apron. With practice much of this becomes routine and leaves her free to concentrate on the painting itself. However, if a child new to a nursery is worried about getting dirty or is jealous about a younger brother or sister having attention while she is away from home, these feelings can 'block' a working memory; she is literally in turmoil as a result of feeling uprooted and anxious about being abandoned. As a result, a child can become unsure, confused and forgetful about procedures in which she was previously competent.

Although children will initially show their feelings through what they do, we have seen that spoken language is important for them to learn to deal with emotions. In order to cope with such momentous experiences involved when moving from Reception to Year 1, children need to talk to express their feelings and also make sense of what is happening to them. An Oxfordshire project on transition encouraged reception children to say how they felt about the prospective move. Children expressed their worries about facing the big playground and not knowing where to go, and their fears about being bullied and having to write. Staff were able to pick up on these messages and improve their transition procedures accordingly (10). Other children in the project were very positive and relished the prospect of challenges, doing homework and being with their friends. This reinforces the view that children will respond in various ways to a transition (see Chapter 5).

The recent influx of immigrant families into this country has meant that their children have been forced to make enormous adjustments very rapidly, being faced for a start with a new country, new neighbours and an unfamiliar language. On top of this, family circumstances can mean that both parents need to find work quickly while their children are expected to adapt to a strange setting or school.

Case Study 8.3

Irma, at three-and-a-half years old, was a new arrival at the Children's Centre. She had recently moved from Lithuania with her young parents. Both mum and dad worked shifts at a local hotel and were accommodated in a mobile home which they shared with another Lithuanian couple. Only Irma's dad could speak a few words of English, and all conversations at home were in their mother tongue.

Irma's father stayed to settle Irma in at the centre for the first day but after that was forced to return to work. Irma attended extended hours, but because mum and dad started work very early an elderly Lithuanian lady brought her to the breakfast club and one of her parents collected her in the evening.

During the first four days at the centre Irma appeared stunned. She made no protest when left in the morning, but she refused to take off her coat and sat by the wall hugging a scruffy toy rabbit called Dong. No gentle persuasion could get her to participate in any of the nursery experiences.

There was no dual language assistant who spoke Lithuanian and so Irma's key person, Gay, approached Irma's dad and asked for help to learn a very basic vocabulary. He returned the next day with a list of words and Gay practised these with him.

On Monday morning Gay approached Irma holding another toy rabbit. She pulled two large carrots out of her pocket. Gay smiled encouragingly, and using her newly acquired language she said very haltingly, 'Hello Irma, this is Paulo and he wants a rabbit friend. Would you and Dong like to take care of Paulo? Here are some carrots for breakfast'. Gay repeated her message again and suddenly Irma shot out her arms to hold Paulo. Gay withdrew and observed. Irma cuddled the two rabbits tightly; she picked up a carrot and offered it to each one in turn, crooning quietly.

Comment

Irma's resistance to settling in to the centre was unsurprising given the massive changes involved in moving to a new country. Gay recognised that

Irma would only be approached through something familiar. Irma's dad really appreciated Gay's readiness to talk with his daughter in Lithuanian and proved a useful resource. She observed Irma's attachment to the rabbit and thought that this might be a way to link with her. She also built on Irma's receptive language.

Following the initial breakthrough, a day later Irma moved with the rabbits into the book corner where she shared some picture books with them. A week later, on entering the centre she took off her coat and looked to Gay to show her where to hang it.

Reflection Point

How well do you ensure that you are able to communicate in a mother tongue (using basic vocabulary) with children new to your setting who have English as an additional language?

Young children and bereavement

In certain situations young children may cope with and communicate their feelings in ways which are puzzling to adults. Infants probably have little understanding of death, and on experiencing the loss of a parent or loved relative will show the same anxiety that is evoked by any separation from an attachment figure. This may take the form of anger or denial and eventually detachment and withdrawal. Very young children can mourn the loss of a parent and this may be through physical reactions such as feeding and sleeping difficulties, bed-wetting and constipation (11). Paula Alexander, a parent at the Pen Green Centre of Excellence, describes how her 3-year-old son went back to bed-wetting at home after being told that his father had died:

> At nursery he kept taking things to the sandpit, burying them and digging them up to bring them back to life again. Then he'd say out of the blue 'My daddy's dead'. You have to pay close attention to what they are trying to express. The nursery did a lot of work with him through play. (12)

Adults are usually very prepared to cope with a child's grief in the short term but may not understand that the impact of bereavement is not always immediate. In the same article, Woolfson, a child psychologist, suggests that while adults feel the need to recover from their grief:

> ... there is no urgency in children. You tell them the news and their immediate reaction is to go and play, but it all takes time to work through. One minute a three-year-old will say 'Granny's dead' and the next minute will ask you not to forget to set a place at the table for her.

By around five years most children will understand the difference between a temporary separation and death. They start to accept that death is irreversible and that dead people are different from the living: they cannot move, speak, hear, see, smell or speak (13).

It is important for adults not to have any preconceptions about how children will react to grief. However, there is likely to be a time, once children have absorbed the news, when they will want to talk about their loss and, like Mrs Alexander's small son, recreate their understanding through play. Early years practitioners can play a vital role in responding to each child's needs at a time when a child's family members are likely to be distressed and vulnerable themselves.

Case Study 8.4

Four-year-old Dale's mother had been killed in a car crash the previous evening. His auntie brought him to the nursery the following morning, explaining that she had told Dale the news but the family wanted to keep things as normal as possible for him. The nursery team had little time to prepare how they would respond, but agreed that although they would not try to discuss the sad news with Dale they would communicate their love and care in every way possible. During the session Dale, normally lively and ebullient, was very quiet and withdrawn. He usually loved stories but that morning was only prepared to join the group when invited to sit on his key person's knee. He did not want to choose the story but cuddled up to Rosa and stroked her.

Rosa later found Dale hiding in the cloakroom when others played outside. She brought the pet rabbit Inky to him, invited him to hold it, and then to help her clean out his cage. Dale nuzzled Inky for some time and then suddenly said, 'My mum liked rabbits and now she's dead you know'. He carefully carried the rabbit outside to its cage and then held Rosa's hand tightly for the rest of the morning, only reluctantly relinquishing it when his auntie arrived. On the way home Dale told his auntie that his teachers knew that he was sad and they loved him. However, the following day Dale refused to attend nursery and only reappeared reluctantly after two weeks.

Comment

Rosa played a key role in staying close to Dale at this sad time. She offered him the rabbit knowing that he had often taken it home in the holidays and rightly thought that it would provide a link to his mum.

Reflection Point

How might Rosa help Dale settle back to the nursery and work through his grieving?

Seizing Opportunities for Emotional Learning

We see and hear a great deal about how those adults with emotional problems can track them back to some difficulties in childhood. Because early childhood is one of the very critical times for nurturing emotional growth, if this opportunity is missed, or the nurturing becomes abuse, it becomes progressively harder to compensate for this at a later date. If practitioners aim to prevent these problems emerging in adulthood they must take advantage of the receptive nature of young children and positively help them to achieve emotional health. This means looking at a climate in the early years setting which helps children to feel, think, and talk about feelings. They will think carefully about how to organise this climate.

Encouraging delayed gratification

One major challenge is to help children gradually rein in their impulses, which is another factor which contributes to self-regulation. Goleman quotes an interesting long-term study carried out in the 1960s at Stamford University. A group of 4-year-olds were each offered a marshmallow as a treat. If they were willing to wait for the adult to run an errand they would be allowed two marshmallows when he returned. Goleman reports that some children were unable to wait and grabbed one marshmallow almost immediately after the researcher had left the room. Other children though were able to wait for 15 to 20 minutes for the adult to return. Some however found this discipline really difficult:

> ... to sustain themselves in their struggle they covered their eyes so they wouldn't have to stare at temptation, or rested their heads in their arms, talked to themselves, sang, played games with their hands and feet, even tried to go to sleep. These plucky pre-schoolers got the two marshmallow reward.

This group of 4-year-olds were tracked down at the end of their high school career and the differences between them were starkly clear. The study found that the group who had been prepared to postpone their gratification early in life were as young adults more socially competent, self-assertive, personally effective, and better able to cope with life's problems (14).

Young children are naturally impulsive and this is particularly so for the under threes. Older children can learn to wait, pause and reflect, but it is a very hard lesson for some and slow progress for many. A programme of turn-taking games and activities will help to develop these skills, as will a displayed timeline of routines where children can be encouraged to wait for something special to happen at the end of the session. Above all, if adults regularly share stories and model scenarios which show the benefits of resisting impulse this will influence children over time.

Encouraging children to deal with their feelings

Circle time has become a common means of encouraging children to converse about things that matter to them. In the hands of a sensitive practitioner, and used with older children, this can be very effective. However, there is a danger of circle time being accepted as a blanket method for dealing with many personal, social and emotional matters: unfortunately, there are no mechanical teaching methods which automatically give us insights or answers. Circle times with young children can come adrift if they are managed for large groups, if they are not carefully planned and prepared, if they are not conducted by a known and trusted adult, if the adult is not already tuned in to some of the children's needs and concerns, or if they become a dull and predictable routine.

Children, like adults, are more likely to talk about things that affect them with people who show that they are genuinely interested, who are prepared to give them the time to listen, and who reciprocate some of their experiences. Children's feelings will be stirred by sensory experiences such as listening to music, looking at and touching beautiful things, and tasting and smelling. If they can talk about their reactions to these positive experiences, it will alert them to recognise similar feelings on another occasion. In the same way they need to recognise negative emotions. Anger and fury which results in a loss of control can be extremely frightening for a 3- or 4-year-old. Sensitive adults can provide safety and reassurance and encourage children to try to see patterns in their behaviour and the reasons for their strong reactions. In this way children will come to accept and regulate their feelings. Those who are encouraged to feel free to express their ideas and their feelings, such as joy, sadness, frustration and fear, can develop strategies and adapt their behaviour to cope with various events or stressful situations (15).

Adults respond to children's expressed feelings in different ways. While positive feelings are always acknowledged and welcomed, negative emotions are regarded differently in ways that can validate or dismiss them (16). When Stefan showed that he was afraid of being left in the dark, his mum tried to reassure him by saying that there was nothing to be afraid of and that he would always be safe when she was nearby. While this response was well intentioned it only gave two messages: that Stefan had a reason to have this feeling, and that he was safe only so long as his mum was around. By taking this further to validate fears and worries, adults can encourage young children to explore and try to understand what they are feeling. They may do this through:

empathy i.e. trying to understand and identify with the child's fear;

explanation and discussion i.e. encouraging the child to explain the fear and then discussing together how it might be dealt with;

exploration and expression i.e. enabling the child to represent the fear through talking, drawing, painting, or movement and role play;

confronting the fear i.e. taking action by facing a fear together, for example, overcoming a fear of dogs by looking at pictures of them, stroking a furry toy dog, observing the behaviour of a puppy, and looking at a dog from a distance and gradually moving closer to it.

Adults as role models

Children who are emotionally vulnerable desperately need a calm and safe environment. However, occasionally a setting that emphasises calm therapy can be in danger of repressing emotions. Children have the right both to witness and to experience different feelings. Living in a calm, bland atmosphere can produce dull people. Children's feelings should also be respected. It is questionable whether adults should attempt to jolly children along when they are bereft at being left in the nursery, or when their friend will not play with them. This sorrow and desolation is more devastating than that experienced by an adult in a comparable situation, for the simple reason that the child does not have the life experience which tells her that the cause of the distress is only temporary. A simple acknowledgement of sympathy will at least show the child that she is being taken seriously. As always, practitioners play a crucial role as models. A strong relationship between adults and children is founded on feeling. Young children should be helped to label their feelings and need to observe adults showing emotions (17, 18). In such a setting children understand that the adults care for them, laugh with them, and share their tragedies and excitements, and also become angry when the boundaries for behaviour are broken. So long as love and care are prevalent, children will flourish and grow given this healthy emotional repertoire.

Practical Suggestions

Help children to develop coping strategies

- Use the language of feelings: suggest labels to describe children's emotions, e.g. bubbly, excited, fizzy, gloomy; encourage them to use the vocabulary in relation to their own and others' feelings.
- Help self-contained and cautious children to recognise and open up to excitement, joy and wonder in the safe knowledge that these feelings are acceptable and can be controlled.
- Provide ways of talking to meet needs, e.g. instead of pushing a child off a bike in anger, suggest that the child requests to have her turn.

(Continued)

(Continued)

Demonstrate that everyone has feelings

- Talk about how you feel, and what makes you angry, excited or worried.
- Use situation stories to help children understand why people feel differently.

Professional Practice Questions

1. How well have new children come to terms with their feelings on admission to the nursery? How do I know?
2. What have I done today (this week) to help children be more aware of their feelings?
3. How do I help some of my older children to become less impulsive?

Work with Parents

- Suggest that parents help their older children to delay gratification and to point out the benefits of doing so, e.g. keep some sweets until tomorrow, wait until the baby has woken up if you want to hold him.
- Suggest that parents use the language of feelings at home and encourage their child to do so.

References

1. Elfer, P. (2007) *Life at Two: Attachments, Key People and Development* (user notes). Siren Films Ltd, 5 Charlotte Square, Newcastle upon Tyne, NE1 4XF. www.sirenfilms.co.uk
2. Dunn, J. (1999) 'Mindreading and social relationships', in M. Bennett (ed.), *Developmental Psychology*. London: Taylor and Francis, pp. 55–71.
3. Goleman, D. (1996) *Emotional Intelligence*. London: Bloomsbury.
4. Handy, C. (1994) *The Empty Raincoat*. London: Hutchinson.
5. Dunn, J., Bretherton, I. and Munn, P. (1987) 'Conversations about feeling states between mothers and their young children', *Developmental Psychology*, 23: 1–8.
6. Brody, L.R. and Hall, J.A. (1993) 'Gender and emotion', in M. Lewis and J. Haviland (eds), *Handbook of Emotions*. New York: Guilford Press.
7. Goleman, D. (1996) op.cit. (see note 3).
8. Garon, D.N., Bryson, S.E. and Smith, I.M. (2008) 'Executive function in pre-schoolers: a review using an integrative framework', *Psychology Bulletin*, Jan: 134 (1) 31–60 doi:10.1037/0033-2909. 134. 1.31.

9. Rees, D. and Shortland-Jones, B. (1996) *Reading Developmental Continuum: First Steps Project*. Department of Western Australia: Rigby Heinemann.
10. Oxfordshire County Council (2006) *Transition Foundation Stage to Year One*. Oxfordshire County Council. Available at www.oxfordshire.gov.uk
11. Black, D. (1998) 'Bereavement in children', *British Medical Journal*, 21 March, 316 (7135): 931–5.
12. Williams, E. (1997) 'It's not bad to be sad', *TES Primary*, 12 September, p. 13.
13. Black, D. (1998) op.cit. (see note 11).
14. Goleman, D. (1996) op.cit. (see note 3), pp. 60–83.
15. Early Education (2012) *Development Matters in the Early Years Framework*, www.early-education.org.uk, p. 13.
16. Sorin, R. (2003) 'Validating young children's feelings and experiences of fear', *Contemporary Issues in Early Childhood*, 4 (1): 80–6.
17. Strain, J.D. and Ostrosky, M.M. (2008) 'Fostering emotional literacy in young children: Labelling and emotions', *What Works Brief 21*, Child Care and Head Start Bureau in the US Department of Health and Human Services.
18. Early Education (2012) *Development Matters in the Early Years Framework*, op.cit. (see note 15).

NINE Dispositions for Learning

- Dispositions to learn are stable patterns of behaviour, which emerge from babyhood and are affected by feelings and influenced by family life.
- In order to learn, babies and young children must want to do so.
- On entry to a group setting the child's inclination to learn is strengthened through a secure attachment with a key person.
- Positive dispositions for learning are further reinforced by opportunities to practise these in varied experiences, which take account of children's interests.

We hear a great deal today about the problem of disaffection in society. Many adults become disaffected with their partners, hence the high rate of family break-up. People in all walks of life grow to be dissatisfied with their employment. Disaffected adolescents are accused of being demotivated towards study, and lacking in persistence and initiative. There is also a worrying trend of children being excluded from, and truanting from, primary schools. Yet as the term 'disaffection' implies, at one time there was a positive attitude towards what is now being rejected. All partnerships start on an optimistic note: most people feel positive when starting a new job, and at one point in their lives children are strongly disposed to learn and most view starting school as an exciting venture.

This chapter does not intend to attempt to tease out why people become dissatisfied with their lot, as there are many books and courses which offer advice and support for living positive and satisfying lives. However, all the literature and counselling courses emphasise that whatever the circumstances, the key to living and learning successfully lies within ourselves: it is to do with our views and attitudes and what we make from what we are given. In the previous chapter we looked at the inextricable link between the emotions and other aspects of our development. We saw how receptive young children are towards emotional learning. The same messages apply to attitudes or dispositions. We know that the young brain is very alert, that the mechanisms are all present to promote powerful learning. Nevertheless, unless young children are disposed or inclined to use what they know, the mechanisms will not function.

What are Dispositions?

Lillian Katz makes a useful distinction between attitudes and dispositions. She states that whereas an attitude consists of a set of beliefs, a disposition demonstrates those beliefs in behaviour. It is possible to have a positive or negative attitude towards something but not be disposed to take any action about it. Katz suggests that young children are not assumed to have attitudes because they are too young to think evaluatively. However, all we are learning about the impressionable young brain indicates that beliefs, attitudes and dispositions are being shaped in infancy. Katz further differentiates between feelings and dispositions. The former are emotional states, while the latter are habits of mind which result in patterns of behaviour (1). As we saw in the previous chapter, feelings can be powerful, but with young children they can be transitory, while dispositions are likely to be more stable and long-lasting. Nevertheless, feelings will significantly affect dispositions.

Case Study 9.1

Tony was constantly anxious when faced with anything new or a different routine. He looked worried and clearly felt insecure when presented with the opportunity of climbing on a new climbing frame. He was persuaded to climb onto the first rung but was not prepared to persist with the challenge of the new equipment. Tony's anxious feelings had led him to adopt a very cautious disposition.

Comment

Tony's parents had encouraged his cautious approach to new experiences. His mother urged him continually to 'be careful' and 'watch out'. Her over-protective manner stemmed from the cot death of Tony's younger brother and the need to keep her remaining child safe. Tony's key person understood the reasons for his behaviour and initially encouraged him to play within his comfort zone.

Reflection Point

How would you work with Tony to encourage a 'have a go' approach to new experiences?

Katz also points up the difference between predispositions (that is, the genetic gifts that are present at conception) and dispositions which are learned. Moreover, dispositions do not automatically follow on from predispositions. It is easy to believe of a friendly and outgoing baby who is bursting with curiosity that these qualities will remain with her for life. Given supportive experiences and guidance that baby will strengthen her predispositions to socialise and learn, however, if she is not given these opportunities the early positive traits are in danger of weakening.

Attention is given to attitudes and dispositions in other chapters. For example, in Chapters 3 and 12 we see how children develop sociable and moral dispositions, and in Chapter 14 how attitudes of interest and tolerance towards difference are fostered. This chapter looks particularly at dispositions for learning and the messages for practitioners who work with young children.

Babies are born with a passion to find out. Gopnik and colleagues suggest that 2-year-olds have a particular drive to make sense of everything around them as can be seen in their boundless energy to investigate and starting to ask questions (2). They lack experience of the world but their physical, intellectual, social and emotional antennae are tuned to make sense of it. This is a common endowment given to all healthy children and it happens without any formal education. However, the effects of their environment influence this heritage. Children's early investigations may be strengthened or restricted and by three and four years of age the impact of their early life experiences are already evident. It is easy to spot those individuals who show signs of a positive disposition to learn, such as high levels of motivation and perseverance, as well as those who are more passive or distractible.

Practitioners now have some national pointers for the dispositions that they should strengthen in young children. The Foundation Phase Curriculum in Wales emphasises how play can be a serious business for children and aid their disposition to learn through perseverance, concentration and attention to detail (3). In Northern Ireland the Foundation Stage Curriculum includes a theme of 'Learning to Learn'. This links an intention for children to develop a positive attitude to learning with a capability to manage it (4). The Early Years Foundation Stage in England highlights the characteristics of effective teaching and learning. The three characteristics identify how children develop aptitudes to learn through:

playing and exploring i.e. children investigate and experience things and 'have a go';

active learning i.e. children concentrate and keep on trying if they encounter difficulties and enjoy achievements;

creating and thinking critically i.e. children have and develop their own ideas, making links between those ideas, and develop strategies for doing so (5).

The characteristics are closely aligned to Margaret Carr's five aspects of dispositions, namely taking an interest, being involved, persisting with

Figure 9.1   Flora Ready, Willing and Able to Climb a Tree

difficulty or uncertainty, communicating with others, and taking increasing responsibility. Carr usefully suggests that these aspects or domains can be analysed in three parts:

> *being ready* i.e. when children see themselves as learners;
>
> *being willing* i.e. when they recognise that the environment offers them scope for learning;
>
> *being able* i.e. when they have the knowledge, skills and understanding that will enable them to be ready and willing (6).

Developing Dispositions at Home

Once again, dispositions to learn are grown in family life. Bronfenbrenner's ecological theory suggests that a main influencing factor is the family's response to their child (7). Close family members may delight in their child's enthusiasms and interests, or they may ignore them and be irritated when their infant persists in repeating a pre-occupation with enclosing or covering things up. Children who live in well-organised households will observe and become accustomed to daily routines: they will learn to predict the pattern of each day, organise their personal belongings, and value order. The effect on a small child may, of course, differ according to the impact and strength of the daily messages, the way in which parents help the child to make sense of what is happening, and the child's own personality. Some children may use these early lessons to develop systematic and orderly habits of learning. Others may be dominated by and become dependent upon that routine which can lead to them becoming rigid and inflexible.

Case Study 9.2

Chloe at 18 months loved to draw. The crayons that she used were stored in a large biscuit tin. She would carefully choose her crayon, use it, and then replace it in the tin, saying 'back, back' before selecting another. She clearly enjoyed not only making marks but also selecting and replacing the tools.

Three-year-old Amy spent most of her time in the nursery tidying books. She smacked children's hands when they came to the book area to browse through books and use them. As soon as a book was removed from the shelf Amy replaced it. She was unable to concentrate on a group story if any books were lying around and would dart off to tidy them up. Amy disliked any change in the nursery regime. One sunny morning the nursery teacher announced that children could have their snack outside. Amy refused to go out. When gently encouraged to do so, she shouted, 'I don't like this, we don't do this'.

Comment

Chloe's mother had encouraged her to be independent and to tidy away her toys as part of a game. The toddler was already enjoying the mastery of managing her drawing tools as well as the magic effects of using them. For Amy, tidiness and routine had assumed an undue importance, and so great was her need to be in control that this meant she was unable to relate to other children or to enjoy different curriculum activities.

Reflection Point

How might Amy be helped to strengthen a disposition to enjoy experiences and relax her controlling attitudes?

Learning is not Compulsory

Although a very young child's learning and progress is influenced both positively and negatively by the care, stimulus, neglect or indifference of the family, ultimately they are hinged to the child's own motivation. The same applies when the child moves to a group setting. His inner drive to learn remains the key factor in his subsequent achievement. This suggests that above all else practitioners need to reflect on how their provision strengthens this drive. Martha Bronson describes how motivation helps children to control their learning by getting their physical, social and cognitive activities started, and then providing the direction and the force necessary to keep these going. Bronson states that motivation is at the centre of self-regulation (8).

One of the major tasks for any early years practitioner is to identify what learning has occurred before a child starts in a group setting. Fisher (9) likens the 'composition' of each child's learning to a jigsaw puzzle, with individual pieces gradually fitting into place, thereby casting light on wider and deeper understandings. Following this analogy, the practitioner needs to recognise the pieces of cognition already in place and support each child in adding to their personal cognitive jigsaw. This approach to assessment and teaching respects the child's initiatives and places the practitioner in the position of a tutor. Conversely, if the practitioner ignores previous learning and attempts to 'take over' the construction of the cognitive puzzle, this damages the disposition to learn. The child is confused, the puzzle is no longer under his control, and his motivation to know more is diminished.

The key person once again plays a significant role in bonding with each baby and child as rapidly as possible. An attachment grows as the key person carefully observes her new charge and so finds out what he likes and dislikes and what really interests him. The more the key person can identify how each child 'ticks' the greater the chance of her providing for children's needs and fuelling their curiosity.

Learning is hard work for anyone: very young children have so much to learn and they must feel energised to do so. Much will be achieved through their own natural curiosity, but babies and young children also need warm support and encouragement from close adults who share their own enthusiasms. This support should stem from a clear understanding of the significant steps in a child's natural development and the signals that these give for future learning. These are usefully outlined by Bruce and Spratt in regard to developing children's essential literacy skills. Some of the steps they include are:

relating to others – engaging in social interactions such as eye contact, turn taking and imitation;

movement – being aware that a baby's gross and fine motor co-ordination are closely linked to reading and writing later on;

making and using symbols – recognising the personal symbols that children make and use through singing, dancing, drawing, painting, constructing and other ways of communicating without words;

conversations – having interactions with children which are based on the tenets of easy and reciprocal verbal and non-verbal exchanges;

listening to sounds in language – encouraging recognition of matching sounds;

rhythm, rhyme, intonation, alliteration – all of these help children to later learn about syllables in words, understand punctuation, hear patterns in sound, and recognise a repetition of sounds at the beginning of words: enjoyable opportunities for this learning are through action rhymes and songs and stories;

well-being – preserving the child's enthusiasm for literacy learning by offering support at the right pace and in the right way for each child (10).

It is now well understood that young children learn more effectively when they are active, having fun, and having regular and frequent access to adults. Many children under the age of five years find it difficult to sit still even for short periods or to understand new knowledge or concepts when they are taught to a group. Although reception practice is changing radically to meet the requirements of the EYFS, these are still standard procedures from the time that children enter many reception classes. The best literacy and numeracy sessions are creatively adapted to meet individual needs through flexible timings, good staffing ratios which allow some children to have individual attention, and regular use of enjoyable play methods to allow children to practise new skills and ideas. In these sessions all children are supported in their learning, and are likely to want to learn more. Without giving this attention to young children's diverse learning needs, routine and prescriptive programmes may not reach some children and not challenge others. Confusion and boredom result in demotivation: in extreme cases the result could be putting children off reading for leisure or delighting in numeracy patterns and problems for life. In short, we could end up with children who are able to read, write and calculate, but who have no desire to use these competencies. Lillian Katz points out that 'it is not much use to have the skills if the process of acquiring them is so painful that the learner never wants to use them' (11).

Even young children can show signs of disaffection towards their schooling. Gill Barratt, in her arresting study of young children starting school in reception classes, shows how they can be turned against school by a curriculum and organisation that do not take account of their interests, what they know already, or the ways in which they have learned it. At this age they do not have open to them the options of older children who may try to avoid attending school. At four and five years old children have little choice as they accompany their parents. However, as Gill Barrett says, they do have the power to withdraw their goodwill (12). Any knowledgeable early years practitioner will recognise the body language of a 3- or 4-year-old who does not wish to comply with a request or take part in an activity. We may insist on attendance but we cannot require children to learn.

However, practitioners who know their children well can entice them by drawing on their enthusiasms, provoking their curiosity, and building on their natural drive to learn.

Case Study 9.3

Kane, at four years old, was excited about starting school. His nursery had served him well for two years, helping him to become confident and independent, but for the last term it had not offered him sufficient challenge, particularly to match his deep interest in numbers. At home his dad played cards with him regularly and Kane was very able to see number patterns and do simple number calculations. He was visibly bored with the nursery and very keen to go to 'big school'.

Kane learned the school routines quickly. He was eager to show his ability in numeracy but was daunted when his responses were sometimes ignored in order for other children to contribute. He had little interest in sorting and matching activities and found the early practical recording of numbers easy and routine. After three weeks Kane's teacher, Sue, was concerned about him. He was restless and inattentive for much of the day and no longer volunteered answers in group times. In contradiction to the picture that Kane's mum had provided of his abilities, he appeared to have no interest in mathematical activities and his baseline assessment score for maths was low. Sue arranged for a Year 6 boy who was interested in maths to work with Kane for 20 minutes a day for a trial period of two weeks. Initially the boy played similar games to the ones that Kane played at home with his dad. This developed into a programme of number problems, mental arithmetic and logic. After one week Kane's behaviour had changed noticeably. He continued to look forward to sessions with his Year 6 friend (which were reduced to weekly occasions) but was now enthusiastic about other activities, particularly construction and design technology. He developed and applied his abilities in numeracy, shape and space and produced some exciting models. Kane was also pleased to help other children with their work.

Comment

Before Kane was admitted to school Sue had fortunately taken the time to listen to his parents, gaining a clear picture of his interests and capabilities. She rapidly noted the mismatch between Kane's reported abilities at home and what he demonstrated in the reception class. She recognised that he was not being challenged and her prompt and imaginative action helped to reverse his early disaffection.

Reflection Point

What are the key things you need to find out from parents about their child when they are about to start school?

How best could you gain this information?

Practical Suggestions

Observe

- Notice items that interest babies when they are lying on their backs or tummies, and then ensure that these items are part of continuous provision and where possible are accessible to touch.
- Note how far a mobile baby is prepared to move to reach an object; over time move the object to encourage and challenge further mobility.
- Jot down the number of investigations that a mobile baby makes during one day.
- Notice when a child shows that he is ready, willing and able to do something, e.g. readiness (an eagerness to climb); willingness (noticing a low branched tree that he feels able to climb); and ability (demonstrating measured movement and careful balance when climbing).
- Observe how intentional a young child is when approaching an activity, e.g. collecting materials together before constructing a den.

Encourage organised approaches to learning

- Provide boundaries for using equipment/apparatus. Use circles and squares of material (small rugs can be used for larger construction) which can be laid out on a surface to provide the area on which to work.
- Help older children to think sequentially when they set up, work at, or clear away an activity. Ask them, 'What will you do first?', 'What next?'

Professional Practice Questions

1. How does our environment provoke a 2-year-old to extend his interests?
2. How well do I demonstrate and share my own interests and enthusiasms to learn?
3. How do I ensure that older children are keen to use and apply their new literacy and mathematical skills?
4. How rapidly do we notice signs of children's lack of enthusiasm for learning and what do we do about it?

Work with Parents

- Suggest that parents recognise and encourage young children's natural keenness to 'help', e.g. allowing them to wash and wipe up dishes, clean vegetables, fold clothes, and pair up socks that have been washed.

References

1. Katz, L. (1995) *Talks with Teachers of Young Children*. Norwood, NJ: Ablex.
2. Gopnik, A., Melzoff, A. and Kuhl, P. (1999) *How Babies Think: The Science of Childhood*. London: Weidenfeld & Nicholson.
3. Department for Lifelong Learning and Skills (2008) *Foundation Phase Framework for Children's Learning 3–7 in Wales*. Cardiff: Welsh Assembly Government, p. 6.
4. Northern Ireland Council for the Curriculum, Examinations and Assessment (2006) *Understanding the Foundation Stage: Progression in Personal Development and Mutual Understanding*. Available at www.nicurriculum.org.uk/foundation-stage, p. 4.
5. Department for Education (DfE) (2012) *Statutory Framework for the EYFS*. London: DfE, 1.10.
6. Carr, M. (2001) *Assessment in Early Childhood Settings: Learning Stories*. London: Paul Chapman, p. 23.
7. Bronfenbrenner, U. (1979) *The Ecology of Human Development*. Cambridge, MA: Harvard University Press.
8. Bronson, M. (2000) *Self-regulation in Early Childhood: Nature and Nurture*. New York: Guilford Press.
9. Fisher, J. (2013) *Starting from the Child* (fourth edition). Buckingham: Open University Press, p. 14.
10. Bruce, T. and Spratt, J. (2008) *The Essentials of Literacy from 0–7*. London: Sage, pp. 14–18.
11. Katz, L. (2011) 'Current perspectives on the Early Childhood Curriculum', in *Too Much too Soon?* Stroud: Hawthorne Press, p. 122.
12. Barrett, G. (1989) 'Introduction', in G. Barrett (ed.), *Disaffection from School? The Early Years*. Lewes: Falmer.

TEN   Nurturing Dispositions to Learn

- Practitioners play an important role in identifying, encouraging and strengthening children's disposition to learn.
- Practitioners can help children by making their own learning traits explicit.
- The curriculum builds on children's positive learning inclinations.
- Children need the freedom to create and make meaning with support from practitioners.
- Assessment needs to incorporate children's dispositions as well as their achievements.

All healthy babies are born ready and eager to learn (1, 2). The EYFS summarises this as 'Every child is a competent learner from birth who can be resilient, capable, confident and self-assured' (3). This drive to learn will not survive however unless it is fostered. Studies show the potential to enhance learning dispositions when they encounter challenge and become resilient (4, 5). Recognising and strengthening children's inclinations to learn is at the heart of good practice. If this is lacking a practitioner will not succeed in motivating children and they will not flourish.

Dispositions are Caught rather than Taught

Lillian Katz makes it clear that while skills can be taught directly, dispositions are learned in a more subtle way (6). Any visitor to a nursery setting will immediately be aware how readily most young children are inclined to learn and how engrossed they can be. Indeed, for the lay person this can appear deceptively simple: young children can appear to co-operate naturally, persevere, think carefully, and be well organised in what they do. However, practitioners know only too well that these positive dispositions do not just occur, and that the seeds are sown at home, while in the nursery setting and early school days positive learning traits are developed through interesting experiences and practitioner involvement.

Real learning is not something that other people can do for us. However well-constructed a curriculum programme may be, it cannot ensure that young children learn. It may, of course, result in children performing. Children can be taught the alphabet song and how to recite rhymes and numbers. This is not necessarily a bad thing in itself as a measure of rote learning (which is what this is) will aid children's working memory (see Chapter 8), however, the dangerous thing here is that a demonstration of rote learning can seduce lay people into believing that a great deal more has been achieved than is actually the case. In a hierarchy, rote learning is lower order learning. Higher order learning requires children to have the inner drive to learn for themselves. It is more than just tacking new learning onto what they already know. In order for children to make true progress in learning they need to make sense of new information by using what they know already and modifying, updating and rethinking their ideas in the light of new knowledge. This learning is creative, active and personal. It is also very hard work. Young children must feel that it is worthwhile investing their considerable energies.

The High Scope method of working is well known for emphasising an active approach to learning. The High Scope study tracked children from the age of five years old to adulthood. It found that those children who had experienced an early education from five to seven years that encouraged a mastery orientation (see Chapter 2) became significantly more effective learners in the long term. The study concluded that helping children to develop a sense of 'personal control' is a key factor in enabling their progress in learning and subsequent success (7).

Children's schemas

Any programme which supports children's inclinations to learn will do so by showing regard for their interests. This means being aware of their schemes of thought (see Chapter 1). If schemas are recognised and supported they help young children to make links in their learning and so provide for continuity. Craig, at 12 months old, repeatedly spilt his food onto the tray of his feeding chair and traced up-and-down lines in the liquid. When he started at toddler group he drew mainly vertical lines when finger painting. Later at a pre-school Craig constantly referred to the tall trees surrounding the building. His mum had discussed this with him and had taken a photograph of him standing by the side of one of the trees.

Craig observed that, in the photograph, 'here is my head but you can't see the head of the tree'. He enjoyed drawing, i.e. mainly a series of vertical lines to represent the trees. In the reception class he practised his own writing which was largely composed of vertical marks of a broadly standard size. In physical play and in conversation he showed a good understanding of positional language, particularly 'up and down' and 'taller and shorter'. This small boy was also interested in other aspects of life, but here we can see how an early pattern of behaviour persisted and was strengthened to support further learning.

Case Study 10.1

As a baby and toddler Evan had been readily interested in picture books and later he had happily occupied himself making marks with large crayons on sheets of scrap paper. His mum was delighted in these early signs of interest in literacy, and when he was three years old she sent him to a nursery which stated that children's early development of reading and writing was a priority. Evan was required to spend some part of each day completing a workbook where he learned to copy his name and other simple words. He learned to recognise flash cards of common words and came home with lists of these words to practise. Positive reports were given of his progress.

Evan made a sound transition to his reception class at four years of age but his teacher reported that he was very reluctant to spend any time engaged in reading and writing activities. He refused to take part in any 'play writing' in role play, claiming that he did not know the words. This attitude persisted throughout the first two terms in school despite his teacher's constant efforts and encouragement. It changed significantly when a new teaching assistant arrived. Despite many demands on her time, she agreed with the teacher to spend 15 minutes a day with Evan, playing word games, sharing writing activities in role play, and writing him a special card each day for him to take home to 'read'. She introduced Evan to a soft toy panda who 'lived' in a cardboard box. She said that the panda was lonely and suggested that Evan write to him. His numerous written communications with the panda were reciprocated on 'panda-headed' notepaper.

By the end of the year Evan was very keen to share books: he often 'wrote' at length, using many of the words he had learned previously in the nursery, and he particularly enjoyed writing and illustrating cards for the teaching assistant.

Comment

Evan's initial motivation towards literacy was probably 'force-fed' at nursery. By the end of his nursery career he had developed certain reading and writing skills but his enthusiasm was dampened. Positive dispositions are not easy to reignite once they are extinguished. On starting school, because of his reluctance to enjoy books and seeming lack of confidence to practise and apply what he knew, Evan initially made slow progress in literacy. He required a one-to-one relationship with a sympathetic practitioner to help restore his positive attitudes to learning. Without this prompt support Evan might well have lost his urge for learning more about literacy for a much longer period.

Reflection Point

Consider if the teaching assistant has, by the nature of her work with Evan, become his key person.

During the early stages in their life, young children will have experiences that will begin to form their own rich mental environment. James Flynn, writing in the *eJournal* for the Royal Society of Arts, suggests that this unique environment can be 'caught':

> ... the things parents do at present for their children are all worth doing; reading stories, good diet and exercise, good schooling. But somewhere along the line children must fall in love with ideas ... so they will ... seek out friends who are alert, earn their living doing something cognitively complex, develop leisure interests that are challenging. And the best way to get them to fall in love with ideas is to fall in love with ideas yourselves. (8)

Lillian Katz echoes this:

> If teachers want their young pupils to have robust dispositions to investigate, hypothesise, experiment, conjecture and so forth, they might consider making their own such intellectual dispositions more visible to the children. (9)

The role of adults

Adults play a powerful role in supporting children's learning dispositions. Over the years we have experienced doubts about where the practitioner featured in nursery settings. The understandable fear of not following the hard line of prescriptive teaching has led some settings to adopt the mistaken assumption that warm relationships are an end in themselves, i.e. that adults' main role is to be friendly, encouraging and loving. Clearly, warm and positive relationships have to be the foundation for any effective work with young children, but we realise now that that it is not enough. If young children are praised frequently and indiscriminately, if everything they do is always regarded as intrinsically clever, then how are they going to learn? Our young children deserve more than this benign environment because it does nothing to challenge their intellectual development. The best work by practitioners, epitomised by the approach in Reggio Emilia, is three-pronged, i.e. based on relationships, observations and support. The central idea in the Reggio schools is of the rich child who is, on his own initiative, capable of making meaning from experience (10). The key person will provide the conditions for this by:

- encouraging children to access and select from a broad range of experiences;
- giving children time to make sense of what they experience;
- having their eyes and ears open to the multiplicity of ways in which children convey their thoughts and understandings;
- acknowledging and respecting children's quiet times of absorbed activity;
- being responsive to each child's differing need for the key person to be present, attentive and available as a co-player and partner in conversation;
- knowing when to contribute to children's ideas and when to allow them to build new understandings unaided (11).

The EEL Project provides an additional and similar emphasis on the role of the adult. It includes an instrument for assessing how well practitioners nurture learning, namely the Adult Engagement Scale (12). This refers to three core elements:

Sensitivity: how well the adult is 'tuned in' and the degree of response to the feelings and well-being of the child.

Stimulation: how effective the adult is when taking part in the child's learning.

Autonomy: the degree of freedom which the adult provides to allow the child to experiment, make judgements, choose activities and express ideas. It also includes the boundaries established to deal with conflict and behaviour.

This useful set of descriptors is further endorsed in the introduction to *Excellence and Enjoyment* (13) and in the EPPE project (14). The clear and united message which emerges is that practitioners should and do impact on the ways in which children approach learning. Early years staff understand that, by taking their cues from babies and children, they are more likely to be going with the tide of their motivation.

Case Study 10.2

The staff at Tachbrook Nursery School deliberately develop children's experience of and capacity for sustained, imaginative play; they encourage story play to develop over lengthy periods of time, i.e. often a term and sometimes longer.

In a move to deepen children's super-hero play, the headteacher, Tess, shared informally with a small group illustrations and stories of some characters from myths. The Russian story of the witch Baba Yaga Boneylegs particularly captured the children's interest and this was the start of a play theme which lasted for two terms. The play was always situated outside; children were provided with open-ended props, boxes and fabrics, and the freedom to use these as they wished. Different strands to the play included hunting Baba Yaga and other monsters such as the Minotaur and Medusa. Children also explored ideas about power and the usefulness of magic charms and potions. During the play, staff saw children coping with their fears, supporting friends, and developing an understanding of cause and effect and ways to represent things through signs and symbols. They internalised the story and, using their own mark-making, were able to narrate the plot onto large sheets of paper.

Comment

The children's high level of commitment to their play is self-evident, together with tremendous benefits to their personal development. In particular it helped them delve into their deepest fears and concerns. The 'teaching' which made this possible is subtle and sensitive. Staff provide a daily time for story play and initially set the ground rules. However, importantly, adults do not dominate but 'pump-prime', encourage and help to embellish and lift children's ideas. The headteacher refers to the adult's role being to 'supply nuggets of inspiration to take the play forward' (15).

Clearly it is not possible to make learning fun all of the time but methods of teaching with young children must, above all, ensure that they strengthen positive attitudes towards what is being learned. Those positive attitudes will be needed when the learning becomes difficult.

Reflection Point

How successfully do you offer 'nuggets of inspiration' to support and extend children's play?

A curriculum that supports positive learning dispositions

The way in which something is taught may either strengthen positive attitudes or damage them (16). For many years now, early years practitioners have become concerned that the 'paper and pencil culture' evident in some settings and primary schools has had a negative influence on practice with younger children. However, the Characteristics of Teaching and Learning, with its emphasis on play, active learning and creating and thinking critically, is tailor-made for babies and young children and conducive to them enjoying learning (17).

A play-based curriculum

The receptiveness of young children to all influences means that there is just as much potential to develop unhelpful or even harmful inclinations to learning (passive, inflexible, distractible) as there is to promote the positive. A baby is likely to be well inclined to learn if there are items readily available which intrigue him and if his key person takes an interest in how he explores them using his senses. Although children mature in learning, 4-year-olds are still very concerned with themselves, the people closest to them, and the environment in which they live. They continue to gain information through touching, tasting, smelling, listening and observing, and by using their bodies. They can concentrate really well when things make sense to them. They need to try things out for themselves, practise what they have learned, and be helped to clarify their thoughts through discussion. A play-based programme which pays attention to these characteristics is likely to feed children's urge to want to learn more and think more.

An attainment-based curriculum

Conversely, in settings where the mandatory curriculum for 0–5-year-olds is interpreted narrowly, practitioners may provide a programme more concerned with attainment and focused towards teaching a particular range of concepts and skills which are regarded as essential for children to attain high standards at a later stage in their schooling. Typically this includes instructing children to learn about sounds, letters, numbers and shapes, often through limited pencil and paper exercises where attainment is easily noted and recorded. Physical skills of cutting and sticking may be taught, but with few opportunities for children to use these for their own purposes. In these circumstances children learn certain things but only on adult terms. Prescriptive activities may set a ceiling on attainment and so some children may not be challenged sufficiently. Bored children are also likely to switch off any enthusiasm to learn and many will become distractible and inattentive. Even more disturbing is when children are conditioned to this type of regime; they simply comply with what is being offered. Compliant behaviour, unlike restlessness, will not provide the sharp signals of disaffection. Nevertheless, compliancy is not a mark of active learning. Young children may comply simply in order to please the adult. This then becomes an easy route to 'learning' and as a consequence other more active learning channels will diminish when they are not used.

Some babies and children may, of course, arrive at a nursery setting with negative inclinations towards learning. For many different reasons they may not be confident or willing to try new experiences. In these cases the key person needs time to establish a trusting relationship with the child and then gently encourage small steps towards a mastery approach. However, it is important to distinguish between a negative disposition and developmentally appropriate behaviour. For example, it is perfectly acceptable for a young 3-year-old to 'flit' between activities and be easily distracted in a small group activity, but this same behaviour in a child of five may need to be considered more seriously, and by age seven such an attitude would seriously inhibit a child's progress.

A focus on learning

As children mature their enthusiasm for work is prompted in different ways. Those who are focused on learning are interested in it for its own sake. They are keen to gain new skills and understandings in order to improve. They are attentive and believe that their efforts in learning will pay off.

A focus on achievement

Other children become more concerned about their performance and how competent others judge them to be. This group depends on comparing their achievements with those of others, and test and examination results matter more than the satisfaction achieved from learning. Although these patterns are more noticeable in older children their seeds are sown in early childhood, one example being a tendency to shower extrinsic rewards such as stickers and badges on a child which, over time, become meaningless. Katz rejects this approach, suggesting that if young children are regularly exposed to experiences that are intrinsically interesting and absorb their energies, this exposure is more likely to support a future positive disposition for learning.

The statutory framework in England recognises that a play-based curriculum is essential for children's development and states that 'children learn by leading their own play and by taking part in play which is guided by adults' (18). However, it is not clear how practitioners would make a judgement about the balance between these two approaches. Helpful guidance is available in two publications from Early Education and the National Strategies (19, 20). By the same token, those young children who are exhorted to compete with others and complete tasks in order to gain adult approval are not likely to be so disposed towards learning but rather to perform and succeed against others.

Case Study 10.3

Kieran, a much loved only child, attended a kindergarten from two years old. He appeared settled and his parents were very pleased with his apparent progress. From three years onwards, Kieran completed a page a day in his numeracy and English books and learned words to prepare him for entry to

(Continued)

(Continued)

a reading scheme. His teacher reported to Kieran's mother that, at times, he was reluctant to 'get down to work', but they had found ways of persuading him by offering lots of praise, including large Mickey Mouse stickers in his book. By age four Kieran's record showed that he could write two sentences and tackle addition and subtraction equations. He had completed all the books in the first level of a reading scheme.

On transfer to a nursery reception class Kieran was given a choice of activities and was captivated by the construction apparatus. He spent every available moment building. He talked about the constructions that he had made but told his teacher Clara that he did not like reading and that he could not write. He appeared to have no interest in numbers and actively avoided any questions to do with calculations. Kieran was keen to attend school but his parents were very dissatisfied with the teacher's comment that after one term he appeared to have made little progress in reading, writing and numeracy. When asked why Kieran had received no stickers for his work, Clara explained that the school did not use extrinsic rewards but aimed for children to be motivated by their own efforts and achievements. Clara made great efforts with Kieran and suggested that he needed time to work through his fascination with construction. Despite this, at the end of the year Kieran's parents removed him to a private school, which had a good 'academic' reputation. His parents explained that they felt that their son needed a further challenge. At seven years old Kieran was refusing to go to school and was attending a therapy clinic at the local child development centre.

Comment

Kieran's parents genuinely believed that their child was having a head start by being taught formal knowledge and skills early in life. Although he appeared to respond to the rewards offered in the kindergarten, Kieran had realised that learning to read, write and become numerate involved dull repetition. Given the option to do more interesting things in school, Kieran was not prepared to use up his time and energy on activities that had become a chore: his reception teacher was unable to repair his damaged motivation to learn to record formally. Kieran's negative dispositions towards learning probably strengthened when he faced the additional stress of starting at the new private school. Within one year, faced with a curriculum that emphasised the very aspects of work that he disliked, his negative attitudes had spread to an aversion to school.

Reflection Point

What were the main factors which resulted in Kieran becoming a school refuser?

What needed to happen to ensure that he had a happy and successful early years career?

Supporting children to create

Sustained imaginative play is a sure way to build on children's interests; practice must give scope for young children to demonstrate their imaginative and creative powers. The 5X5X5 arts-based action research project, which started in 2000, collects information on and gives support to developing children's creative capacities. This wonderful venture recognises children as creative meaning makers, and practitioners and artists as enablers of their explorations. It was inspired initially by approaches in Reggio Emilia. The project works with children, educational settings and artists, and consistently observes and documents the dispositions and behaviours demonstrated by young children when they are participating in creative experiences. For example, the practitioner at Longvernal Nursery reported 'concentration developed in all children and was particularly noticeable in children who had shorter concentration spans. In addition, children's independence has grown with children selecting and using resources more without adult direction. Their imaginative play developed at a deeper level due to space and freedom ... mixing resources ... concentration ... independence in relation to using materials/resources ... extended language and partnership with peers' (21).

Well-planned adult stimulus which follows children's interests will encourage them to dig deep into experiences and strengthen their interests. At Longvernal Nursery, observing that children (two to five years old) became interested in pirates, the artist introduced them to treasure maps. The adults then stood back and noticed how the children explored and used the materials and resources to communicate their ideas. The group made a map together and then the children worked on scorched materials to create their own maps: 'The results were unique, creative and purely magical! Treasure ... treasure!' (22).

The enterprises in the 5X5X5 project involve time for children to explore their ideas. In his classic, thought-provoking book, *Hare Brain, Tortoise Mind* (23), Guy Claxton suggests that there is a very important place for allowing thoughts to incubate. In work with young children, we so often emphasise the need for rapid answers, for working at a brisk pace, for keeping busy. There is undoubtedly good reason for encouraging young children to keep mentally alert. However, there is also a different and more creative way of thinking which is only achieved through consideration and mulling things over. Claxton acknowledges the importance of the fast and focused thinking of the hare brain in certain circumstances; he is, though, more interested in the slower processes of the mind where reflection is central. He suggests that play is significant for the tortoise mind in that it involves 'messing about' and figuring things out. This book makes a strong case for time for day-dreaming, for toying with thoughts, for sleeping on a problem and returning to it. In Reggio Emilia and in the many good quality settings in this country, practitioners believe that young children should have opportunities to allow ideas to arise slowly and naturally and they therefore make provision for this.

Assessing dispositions

Although there is increasing acknowledgement of the important role of dispositions in early education, making sure that they are in place is more difficult. It is quite easy to misconstrue young children's behaviour. Mechanical compliance when completing a task, or a child's attraction towards a novel activity, can be misinterpreted as evidence of genuine concentration and interest. Measuring these aspects of personal development is a very different matter from measuring the acquisition of skills and concepts.

There is a particular danger in using simplistic methods to gather information about children's dispositions. For example, children may be asked to record their attitudes to aspects of daily life in a nursery through highlighting happy or sad faces. Who is to say what factors may influence the recording? The chances are that young children may guess what will please the adult and act accordingly, copy their neighbour, or record their decision impulsively, without having a clear understanding of the issues. Some of the most effective methods of finding out about children's thoughts and feelings, which underlie dispositions, are through listening, conversing with and observing the child in action. Gill Barrett's approach (see Chapter 1), using pictures depicting children's different actions, encouraged children to describe their own thoughts and feelings which they recognised and identified with some of the behaviours shown. Susan Denham likewise used puppets effectively to gain similar information about children's emotions (see Chapter 8).

Assessment requirements

Assessment and evaluation of early years practice and children's outcomes have emerged as government initiatives largely as a consequence of public money being used to fund 2- to 5-year-olds in nursery settings. Major initiatives have been developed to provide a means of quality control and quality improvement, and now include a much greater focus on children's learning dispositions as well as their achievements. The statutory framework requires information from both (in)formative, ongoing assessment and summative (summary) assessment. Formative assessments take place regularly and frequently and are based on close observations and conversations with children. Summative assessments are required at two points, namely at age two and at the end of the EYFS (24). The progress check at two years old suggests that practitioners may choose to include how a child is disposed to learn by referring to the learning characteristics. The Early Years Foundation Profile, completed at the end of the reception year, makes it mandatory for practitioners to include a short written commentary on the three characteristics of learning. Year 1 teachers then receive information on each child which outlines not only what she knows and understands but also what type of a learner she is. Evidence for the Profile is based on observations and formative assessments and also takes account of comments from parents and carers, other adults, and the child. The Profile Handbook emphasises that the environment required to reveal dispositions and aptitudes for learning should offer 'rich opportunities to initiate ideas and activities' (25). This approach is exemplified clearly in the well-established project work in Reggio Emilia. There are Helpful Possible Lines of Enquiry to follow when teasing out evidence for each of the learning characteristics, for example investigating whether a child demonstrates persistence, curiosity or inventiveness (26). The Profile Exemplications helpfully show some inspiring examples of children learning actively through play, sharing thoughts and ideas, and enjoying learning (27).

Examples from research

Margaret Carr's approach to assessment is particularly geared towards children's dispositions, and she asks the crucial question 'How can eager learning be described and encouraged?' (28). Carr responds to her own question through introducing the notion of Learning Stories as a way of assessing dispositions. A Learning Story is a structured narrative which includes the context and relationships with adults and other children: it highlights the activity and includes an interpretation from the author who knows the child well. The story concentrates on the five aspects of dispositions and gives evidence of new or sustained interest, involvement, challenge, communication and responsibility. Carr gives an example of a Learning Story for 4-year-old Sean in which he perseveres with a difficult task even when he gets 'stuck'. Attached to the story is a photo of Sean using the carpentry drill. The teacher, Annette, writes: 'The bit's too small, Annette, get a bigger one.' We do, drill a hole and then use a drill to put in the screw. 'What screwdriver do we need?' 'The flat one.' Sean chooses the correct one and tries to use it. 'It's stuck.' He kept on trying even when it was difficult. Carr explains that this Learning Story will provide a focus for a discussion between Annette and Sean and, together with other Learning Stories, help both adult and child to see how well he is progressing in persisting with difficulty (29). In a later publication Carr and Lee consider further how we might assess children as learners. They pinpoint when children:

- construct their own opportunities to learn;
- make learning connections from one place to another;
- recognise the learning journey that they are on;
- explore their understandings in a range of increasingly complex ways (30).

These four themes focus on learning dispositions and resonate closely with the learning characteristics.

Other research studies have also played a key role in assessment. The Effective Early Learning (EEL), Accounting for Life-Long Learning (AcE) and the Baby Effective Early Learning (BEEL) programmes are projects from the Centre for Research in Early Childhood in Birmingham. These projects are immensely valuable because they help early years practitioners to look closely at children and become aware of aspects of their behaviour. The EEL project introduced practitioners to a valuable observation instrument for identifying and measuring children's involvement. The Child Involvement Scale is based on the work of Ferre Laevers who studied how a child might be involved in deep learning as opposed to just being occupied and busy. Laevers defines the concept of Involvement as 'a quality of human activity, characterised by concentration and persistence, a high level of motivation, intense perceptions and experiencing of meaning, a strong flow of energy – a high degree of satisfaction, and based on the exploratory drive and basic development of schemes' (31).

Laevers suggests that when children are involved in this way they show certain characteristics or signals, which can be graded to show the level at which they are working. These signals include:

concentration;

energy;

creativity;

facial expression and posture;

persistence;

precision;

reaction time;

language;

satisfaction.

The EEL Project very usefully adopted Laevers' work. The Child Involvement Scale enables practitioners in different settings to look closely at children and assess their level of involvement in activities through the absence or presence of the above signals (32).

The Involvement Scale which features in the EEL Project has helped practitioners measure how well children are involved in learning as it concentrates on the process. The ongoing AcE Project is concerned with the outcomes or results of effective early learning. The project recognises children's dispositions to learn as one of four important indicators of effective learning. Part of the project is to help early years practitioners identify and nurture those characteristics which appear to be linked with dispositions to learn (33). The BEEL project highlights the behaviour of children less than three years old linked to three concepts, i.e. how infants demonstrate:

social and emotional 'connectedness';

exploration;

meaning making.

Practitioners are encouraged to discuss how their own approaches and provision support these behaviours (34). The projects have helped to make learning dispositions more visible and indicated ways of observing and assessing them.

Figure 10.1   Ruby Exploring a Treasure Bag

Practical Suggestions

Help children to concentrate and persevere

- Where possible, provide a quiet area where children can work without distraction. Provide notices for them to use, such as 'Please do not disturb'.

(Continued)

(Continued)

- Encourage older children to make stand-up signs, such as 'Please leave', which they can place on an unfinished piece of work to which they wish to return.
- Note when a child's perseverance is flagging. Offer practical help yourself or encourage another child to support the completion of an activity.
- Make clearing up tasks manageable by sharing the work and asking children to choose a specific area of responsibility to keep tidy. Encourage children to congratulate each other when they have completed their task.
- Introduce a vacant post in a reception class for an 'inspector to check clearing up': a new appointee can then be selected on a weekly basis.

Develop memory skills

- *Kim's Game*: place four objects on a tray, remove one object in turn, and then invite children to identify what is missing. Gradually increase the number of objects over a period of time.
- *Pelmanism*: make a giant game with matching pictures which link to the characters and objects in a favourite storybook, e.g. *The Three Bears*. These are placed face down on a table; children in turn select a card and aim to collect a matching pair. Introduce the game with four matching pairs of pictures; increase this number over time.
- Regularly change an item of display in your room. Encourage children to spot the change. Give individual children responsibility for changing the display.

Encourage enquiry and help children to learn through their senses

- Take children on a sensory walk (wear old clothes!). Visit a quiet location; ask children to: crawl on the ground and describe what they can see; close their eyes and describe what they can feel; close their eyes and open their ears and describe what they can hear; close their eyes and open their noses and sniff and describe what they can smell.
- Provide a 'feely' bag with objects made in different shapes and textiles which are changed each week. Play a guessing game when children in turn close their eyes and try to describe and identify the object.
- Play a listening game: children form a circle and a child is chosen/ volunteers to be 'Peter'. 'Peter' goes into the centre of the circle and closes his eyes; the children pass a bell around and chant 'Peter, Peter, listen well. Peter, Peter who rings the bell?' When the chanting stops a child rings the bell. 'Peter' must point to the direction of the ringing.

Encourage organised approaches to learning

- Provide boundaries for using equipment/apparatus. Use circles and squares of material (small rugs can be used for larger construction) which can be laid out on a surface to provide the area on which to work.
- Help children to think sequentially when they set up, work at, or clear away an activity. Ask them 'What will you do first?' and 'What next?'

Encourage reflection

Young children need lots of opportunities to be spontaneous and share thoughts and experiences immediately. While adults should be available to allow this immediacy, it is also useful to encourage children to mull things over and to take time to think:

- Provide a thinking area in a quiet corner of the room; provide a couple of comfy chairs, interesting pictures/photographs, strange shaped stones/pieces of driftwood. Make it clear that this place is available for quietly growing thoughts; establish a culture which encourages children to share their thoughts regularly and informally.
- Help children learn to visualise, e.g. when reading a story, stop from time to time and ask children to close their eyes and 'see the picture in their mind'.

Make your own positive learning traits explicit

Use comments in easy conversations:

- 'I'm really curious about ...'
- 'I want to explore this; it looks exciting'.
- 'I just had to finish my book last night to find out the end'.

Professional Practice Questions

1. How far does our sensory room (area) nurture or bombard a baby's sensory explorations?
2. How effectively do I act as a co-player to encourage babies' and children's interests?
3. What areas of learning do I most enjoy and what do I enjoy least? How does this affect the children's dispositions to learn?
4. How well do I show my key children that I am 'in love' with ideas?
5. What scope is there for children to persevere and follow through their ideas and discoveries?
6. How does our daily timetable help children to concentrate and persist?
7. How does the layout of my environment encourage children to reflect?

> **Work with Parents**
>
> • Ask parents to observe and share with you any signals of their child's deep-level involvement in activities at home.
> • Encourage parents to help their children sustain their interests by:
>   ○ giving them time;
>   ○ offering additional resources;
>   ○ showing an interest and playing alongside them.

References

1. David, T., Gouch, K., Powell, S. and Abbott, L. (2003) *Birth to Three Matters: A Review of the Literature*. London: DfES.
2. Wilford, S. (2009) *Nurturing Young Children's Dispositions to Learn*. St Paul, MN: Redleaf Press.
3. Department for Education and Skills (DfES) (2007) *The Early Years Foundation Stage*. London: DfES, para 1.4.
4. Claxton, G. and Carr, M. (2002) Tracking the development of learning dispositions, *Assessment in Education: Principles, Policy and Practice*, 9 (1) March: 9–37.
5. Ouvry, M. (2003) *Exercising Muscles and Minds*. London: National Children's Bureau Enterprises Ltd.
6. Katz, L. (2011) 'Current perspectives on the early childhood curriculum', in R. House, *Too Much too Soon*. Stroud: Hawthorn Press, pp. 121–2.
7. Schweinhart, L.J. and Weikhart, D. (1993) A *Summary of Significant Benefit: The High Scope Perry Pre-school Study through Age* 27. Ypsilanti, MI: High Scope UK.
8. Flynn, J. (2008) 'How to enhance your intelligence', RSA *eJournal*, April, p. 3. Available at www.thersa.org.uk/journal
9. Katz, L.G. (1995) *Talks with Teachers of Young Chidren*. Norwood, NJ: Ablex, p. 65.
10. Edwards, C., Gandini, L. and Forman, G. (1993) *The Hundred Languages of Children: The Reggio Emilia Approach in Early Childhood Education*. Norwood, NJ: Ablex, p. 78.
11. Dowling, M. (2012) *Young Children's Thinking*. London: Sage, p. 107.
12. Pascal, C. and Bertram, T. (1997) *Effective Early Learning*. London: Hodder & Stoughton, p. 13.
13. Department for Education and Skills (DfES) (2003) *Excellence and Enjoyment: A Strategy for Primary Schools*. London: DfES, p. 9, para 3.1.
14. Sylva, K., Melhuish, M., Sammons, P., Siraj-Blatchford, I., Taggart, B. and Elliot, K. (2003) *The Effective Provision of Pre-school Education* (EPPE) *Project: Summary of Findings*. London: Institute of Education, University of London.
15. Bunting, J. (2004) *Learning through Sustained Imaginative Play at Tachbrook Nursery School*, Floor 13, Westminster City Hall, London SW1E 6QP.
16. Katz, L. (1995) op.cit. (see note 9).
17. Department for Education (DfE) (2012) *Statutory Framework for the EYFS*. London: HMSO, 1.9.
18. Department for Education (DfE) (2012) op.cit. (see note 17), 11.9.

19. Moylett, H. and Stewart, N. (2012) *Understanding the Revised Early Years Foundation Stage*. London: Early Education, pp. 30–3.
20. Department for Children, Schools and Families (2009) *Learning, Playing and Interacting: Good Practice in the EYFS*. Available at www.foundationyears.org.uk
21. Bancroft, S., Fawcett, H. and Hay, M.P. (2007) 5X5X5 *Researching Children Researching the World*. 5X55X5 = creativity, PO Box 3236, Chippenham SN15 9DE, Bath Spa University/Arts Council England, p. 20.
22. 5X5X5 (2007) *100 Words*. 5X55X5 = creativity, PO Box 3236, Chippenham SN15 9DE.
23. Claxton, G. (1997) *Hare Brain, Tortoise Mind*. London: Fourth Estate.
24. Department for Education (DfE) (2012) op.cit. (see note 17), 2.3, 2.6.
25. Department for Education (DfE) Standards and Testing Agency (2013) *EYFS Profile Handbook*. London: HMSO, p. 10.
26. Department for Education (DfE) Standards and Testing Agency (2013) op.cit (see note 25), pp. 56/57.
27. Department for Education (DfE) Standards and Testing Agency (2012) *EYFS Profile Exemplifications for the Level of Learning and Development expected at the end of the EYFS*. London: HMSO.
28. Carr, M. (2001) *Assessment in Early Childhood Settings: Learning Stories*, London: Paul Chapman, p. 21.
29. Carr, M. (2001) op.cit. (see note 28), p. 96.
30. Carr, M. and Lee, W. (2012) *Learning Stories: Constructing Learner Identities in Early Education*. London: Sage, p. 1.
31. Laevers, F. (1994) *The Leuven Involvement Scale for Young Children* (video and manual). Experiential Education Series No. 1. Leuven, Belgium: Centre for Experiential Education.
32. Pascal, C. and Bertram, T. (1997) *Effective Early Learning*: *Case Studies in Improvement*. London: Hodder & Stoughton, p. 12.
33. Pascal, C. and Bertram, T. (2008) *Accounting Early for Life Long Learning* (AcE) *Programme Pilot*, Amber Publications and Training. Available at www.amber publications.org.uk
34. Pascal, C. and Bertram, T. (2007) 'Quality and the under 3s: introducing the Baby Effective Early Learning (BEEL) programme', *Early Education*, 52 (Summer): 12–14.

ELEVEN Young Children's Behaviour

- Theorists recognise that children should be supported to regulate their behaviour.
- Young children should be helped to understand about right and wrong and to eventually develop their own moral code, rather than simply be encouraged to comply with adult requirements to behave properly.
- Babies and infants become aware of behaviour in the home and start to tune in to the feelings of others.
- Parents and practitioners set boundaries in line with their own beliefs about how far children should learn to develop a conscience for themselves or be directed to behave.
- Children's behaviour is influenced by their temperament, through their observations of others and through their feelings and physical needs.

Close adults recognise that in the process of growing up children will adopt different ways of behaving. However, views about what constitutes acceptable behaviour and how it is acquired have evolved as a result of increased knowledge and understanding about child development. Educational thinkers have held widely differing views about young children's moral development. In the fourth and fifth centuries, philosophers and theologians such as St Augustine supported the view of the child as a creature of original sin, i.e. small children were regarded as innately wicked and in need of careful moulding to lure them away from the devil. The most obvious way of suppressing the inborn tendency to sin appeared to be the use of corporal punishment. Portraits of medieval and Elizabethan schoolmasters usually show them with the birch, described as 'God's instrument to cure the evils of their condition' (1). This doctrine of original sin was widely subscribed to until the eighteenth century, when Rousseau took an opposite view. He portrayed young children as innocents, i.e. children were seen to be naturally good and in need of rescue from a bad world. He believed that children could be disciplined through natural circumstances. In some cases his suggestions are rather extreme. For example, in his most famous work, *Émile* (1762), Rousseau suggests that if Émile broke his bedroom window, he would have to sleep in a draughty room and the cold which followed would alert him to his wrong action. This suggestion ignores the fact that the consequence might also be that Émile catches his death of cold (2)! However, Rousseau's denial of original sin, and his statement that all is good as it comes from nature, did have the effect of bringing about a kinder and more sympathetic way of dealing with children's misbehaviour. Modern thinking has moved forward to recognise small children as powerful learners who are beginning to make sense of situations from babyhood and to develop their own moral stances from an early age. By the end of the Early Years Foundation Stage (EYFS) children are expected to talk about their own and others' behaviour and its consequences, and know that some behaviour is unacceptable. They should be able to adjust their behaviour to different situations and take changes of routine in their stride (3).

Psychological Perspectives

The Tickell review recognises that self-regulation is a significant influence on becoming an effective lifelong learner (4), and we have seen in previous chapters that development starts very early. Some of the theories that support self-regulated behaviour are described below.

Social constructivism

Vygotsky (see Chapter 3) believed that social contacts lead young children to adopt the values and behaviour that they have observed in daily life. He cites the development of rules that children adopt in play when they assume different roles.

Psychoanalytic

As we have seen (in Chapter 5), Isaacs believed in giving children scope to be responsible. She was also a great proponent of play, particularly when this was chosen by the child. Isaacs emphasises the therapeutic value of play, arguing that free dramatic play lessens tensions and anxiety in children and allows them to control (i.e. regulate) their behaviour (5).

Environmental

Bronfenbrenner's ecological approach (see Chapter 3) reminds us how various aspects of the environment can support or restrict a child's propensity to adopt mindful behaviour:

- *The microsystem* may mean that the child is influenced by observing positive models of close adults caring and acting responsibly towards one another, or negative examples of adults showing feckless and selfish attitudes in the way they conduct their lives.
- *The exosystem* can have negative or positive effects on a child's behaviour when family life is altered by the arrival of a new baby or by a parent suddenly leaving the family home.
- *The macrosystem* refers to the wider context-national policies when social and cultural services are provided to enrich young children's lives, or when valued and much used family services such as local pre-school provision and public transport are suddenly stopped.

Motivational

Albert Bandura's perspective connects children's behaviour to their delight and motivation in achieving mastery (see Chapter 2). Their motivation to make things happen leads to self-efficacy and allows them to develop control over their behaviour.

Carol Dweck similarly agrees that motivation plays a large part in controlling behaviour and links this to a child's self-belief and positive mindset (see Chapter 2).

Martha Bronson, who has written extensively on self-regulation, believes that even infants can recognise that they have control, both over their bodies, by making things happen, and later by adopting certain behaviours, clearly seen in 2-year-olds' determination to do things for themselves. This recognition is a powerful motivator towards becoming self-regulated. Bronson stresses that young children must have the scope to take decisions. She argues that a regimented classroom climate, in which all children are required to act in the same way, reduces children's feelings of control and discourages them from regulating their behaviour (6).

Factors which Affect Young Children's Behaviour

Newborn babies are not disposed to behave in a particular way but once exposed to the world they learn rapidly. Jenny Lindon gives a comprehensive outline of the major influences on early behaviour (7). Drawing on this work, four of these influences are examined below: family experiences, individual temperament, the ways in which children think, and their emotional needs.

Family experiences

The first steps in learning about behaviour are in the home. A young baby's main concern is for survival and his behaviour is heavily geared towards ensuring that he isn't abandoned (8). During his first year he forms close attachments and learns to trust a few special people and needs their comfort and support. He also starts to manage his own feelings, for example, he manages to soothe himself and get himself to sleep. In the family very young children begin to see how people whom they love behave and they then try to copy aspects of this behaviour. Judy Dunn's early work (see Chapter 3) shows how aware a baby and young child are about how family members act. In this way, through what she terms 'affective tuning', a 1-year-old baby begins to learn about other people's feelings. A 2-year-old child has a good idea of what annoys, distresses or pleases others who are close to him: this is apparent when they use this knowledge as a source of power in challenging and teasing behaviour during the 'terrible twos' phase. However, although a young child will learn a lot through simply observing family conduct, he will learn a great deal more if he is helped to understand it. Dunn's studies suggest that in families where arguments are followed by discussions about what went wrong and resolutions, all of this helps a young child to grasp moral issues (9). Where young children have family members who demonstrate consistent and reasonable expectations about how to behave, it is easier for children to respond.

As well as watching and learning from the behaviour of others, young children start to find out what they are allowed to do, i.e. what is acceptable behaviour and what is not. In early infancy children are dependent on older family members, and later, practitioners, to provide this information. Towards the end of the first year a baby looks to his mum or key person to see how he should respond (this is called social referencing). The information he receives is a crucial part of bringing up children in the home and setting, and it includes establishing the boundaries for behaviour. These boundaries should be few, explicit, and always in a child's interest. A 1-year-old starts to understand what 'no' means. Around 18 months temper tantrums emerge as the child tests the ground rules and wants to assert his independence. Frustrations emerge when the child is unable to complete something that he has chosen to do, commonly trying to dress himself, or where he does not yet have the language to express his needs or is over restricted. The way in which boundaries are set will determine how children learn about rules and, eventually, how they are able to regulate their own behaviour. If a child is encouraged to understand the reason for a rule there is more chance of him respecting it. Moreover, given that he has a secure and strong relationship with an adult he will be willing to please. Isabel's mum, for example, had an easy relationship with her small daughter; she responded to Isabel's questions carefully and tended to share some of her views and thinking with her. At two-and-a-half years old, although Isabel had no real grasp of cause and effect, she trusted her mother's rule about always wearing a seatbelt in the car. The different beliefs that parents and practitioners have about how to raise children will include what they expect as regards their behaviour and how they intend to help their children achieve this.

Adults' views of what constitutes acceptable behaviour from young children will be influenced according to their own, cultural and social and moral beliefs. For some parents, the main goal will be for their children to follow religious precepts such as a Christian or Muslim code of conduct. Others may want their children to work out their own way of behaving based on care and respect for others. Yet other families' beliefs might cause them to want their children to become aggressive and defend themselves, to develop prejudices and acquire dishonest traits as a way of coping with the world.

Approaches to bringing up children

Parents may have given a great deal of thought to how they intend to bring up their children. In practice, however, emotions such as fatigue, anger and love will sometimes hijack the best thought-out strategies. Parents' approaches are also often influenced by memories of how they were brought up. Young mothers may admit to hearing themselves repeat what their mothers said when responding to their own children. Although the management of behaviour takes many forms, it is likely to reflect three different approaches which can be crudely categorised as the permissive, the negotiated, and the directed.

Permissive

Following Rousseau's philosophy, some parents and practitioners believe firmly that children should be allowed to be 'free spirits'. They feel strongly that the best way for children to achieve this 'freedom' is for them to be unfettered by adult requirements. Adults who follow this approach are fearful of crushing a child's personality; they hold the view that it may be unnecessarily repressive to require good behaviour. Children raised in such an environment may be encouraged from a very young age to make their own decisions about matters of daily life such as what to eat and when to go to bed. Even antisocial actions may go unreprimanded as adults believe that a policy of laissez-faire will allow children to eventually come to sort out right from wrong actions for themselves.

Negotiated

Other families and settings may adopt negotiated approaches to managing behaviour in the belief that young children need authoritative guidance with this aspect of learning as with any other. Adults explain the reasons for rules and offer loving support to help children achieve them. This helps young children to understand how to try to control their behaviour. Moreover, in an easy and loving relationship, young children will want to behave in a way which pleases the adults who care for them. As they practise this behaviour they grow to internalise it and, as they grow older, the behaviour stems from self-regulation.

Directed

Adults who direct young children's behaviour share the beliefs of the early thinkers who viewed children as being in need of strong moral exhortation. Strict external rules are imposed and threats of punishment used as a way of influencing how children behave. The need to control and require obedience stems from an authoritarian rather than authoritative approach. Adults may also adopt more subtle ways of directing behaviour by using emotional blackmail. In these cases young children are compelled to behave well because they are afraid of being punished or losing affection. Adults may also direct or control behaviour through heavy use of rewards. While young children need praise and encouragement to support good behaviour, too many tangible inducements will dampen children's own motivation to behave well.

It is useful for staff to gain insights into parents' views and approaches as well as making clear the approach that is adopted in the setting. Even where parents have different views about handling behaviour, they may respect a clearly argued counter-view from practitioners which is based on the child's interests.

Temperament

We may understand a child's temperament as her nature or personality which is the outcome of inherited traits and nurture. Lindon suggests that temperament influences the way in which a child reacts to her early experiences. She gives the following examples of different types of temperament and how these can impact on behaviour (10):

- *Active-passive*: some children will take initiatives for themselves, will search for a new stimulus and be physically robust; others will wait for things to happen to them.
- *Sociable-withdrawn*: some children are very gregarious and need other children around them; others may be more self-contained, less outgoing, or may find it difficult to make friends (see Chapter 3).

- *Wary-impetuous*: children vary in how they deal with new situations; some may be cautious and circumspect, others unheeding.
- *Negative-positive attitude*: while all children have to deal with irritations and upsets at some time, their capacity to cope and handle feelings differs; some children will have a low threshold of tolerance.
- *Disinterested-involved*: some children appear to have a very brief attention span and are very easily distracted while others, given interesting activities, are able to focus and become involved.

Case Study 11.1

On admission to the nursery it was immediately obvious that Gemma (four years old) was fastidious about her clothes. She always arrived dressed in pristine outfits. Gemma refused to play with any messy materials and even after handling books she would wash her hands. On one occasion in the cloakroom, a faulty tap resulted in water being sprayed onto her dress. The little girl was inconsolable. She said that only naughty children dirtied their clothes and that naughty children were not allowed to come to the nursery. The nursery supervisor related this incident to Gemma's mum and suggested that they might work together to help her have a more relaxed attitude towards keeping clean. Gemma arrived at nursery the next day, smiling and enveloped in a pretty protective smock.

Comment

Gemma had taken very seriously her mother's strong cautions to keep her clothes clean at nursery. She clearly linked notions of right and wrong with cleanliness. Provision of a smock allowed Gemma to relax and gave her the confidence to take part in painting and water play (where she was very careful to wear additional protective clothing). However, early home influences remained. Gemma continued to disapprove of mess and was often in tears when sand or water was spilt. After two terms at the nursery, staff still needed to reassure her that a mark on her clothes was acceptable and did not constitute naughty behaviour.

Reflection Point

How might you have liaised with Gemma's parents to enlist their support in helping to change her behaviour?

Thinking

Building on the social intelligence that they have gained from observing and experiencing the outcomes of family behaviour, on entry to a setting young children will watch, listen and think. They will note not only what adults say but also what they do. They will very quickly pick up on adults' expectations and the overall atmosphere in a setting. Children listen not only to words, but to the way in which a request is phrased or a tone of voice: they also observe what happens if a request is not responded to (for example, what an adult does if the children do respond to a request to tidy up). Generally, young children are very keen to please and a warm, consistent and harmonious ethos supports adults and children to behave well towards each other. However, they are very sensitive to underlying currents, for example of friction between adults or a lack of interest in the children. Thankfully these are rare occurrences, but where they exist young children can feel adrift and become anxious and demanding.

Case Study 11.2

Four-year-old Marcus had twin baby brothers and one older sister, Rose. Rose was very caring towards her young brothers; she helped to dress and feed the twins and read them all stories when she returned home from school. Her mum had told Rose on a number of occasions that she was a good older sister. When Marcus started school he insisted that he shared this caring role. He carefully put on the twins' socks and shoes and cleared up their toys. Sometimes, however, Marcus found this role difficult. On these occasions he wanted sole attention from Rose and his mum. On one of these days when mum rebuked Marcus about his demanding behaviour, he said that he only wanted a sister, he did not want brothers.

Comment

Marcus had learned a great deal from Rose about caring behaviour. However, understandably because of his own need for love and attention, he sometimes found it difficult to put others first.

Reflection Point

This is a natural and common response from young children who have a new baby in the family. What can nursery staff do to support Marcus?

Emotional and physical needs

All of us are affected by the way we feel and this is shown in our behaviour for good or ill. Many young children are emotionally robust and show the effects of positive feelings in their joyous and vigorous approach to all that they do. Others however are more needy and, even given the support of a loving family, they may still show helpless and dependent behaviour. We can also recognise that children's feelings will change and this is reflected in their behaviour. Often the reason for the change is obvious and it is a temporary episode. For example, we would expect a child to show mixed behaviour when faced with the excitement, but also the threat, of a new baby in the family. Moving to a new house, having an illness or bereavement in the family or, perhaps even worse for a child, parents separating, pose huge disruptions and may cause children to regress and adopt babyish behaviour until they have adjusted to the change. Once the cause of the new behaviour is recognised, often a watchful eye, patience, understanding and additional attention from the practitioner are sufficient to 'tide the child over' during this difficult and turbulent period.

Physical factors also impact on behaviour. Deprivation of opportunities for frequent and regular exercise will show in all aspects of children's well-being and learning. Lack of proper sleep can lead children to misbehave, underachieve, become restless and overactive. A newborn baby sleeps for around 16 hours in every 24 hours; this reduces over time so that a child of three to six years old requires on average between 11 to 13 hours of sleep every night. Kati Hajibagheri from Imperial College London produced a review of research into sleep, and concluded that 'if children are sleep deprived on a regular basis, it interferes with the processing of knowledge acquired during the day. And that has an impact on development and learning' (11). The type and amount of food given can also influence behaviour. Research studies continue to confirm that certain artificial colourings can cause an increased level of hyper-active behaviour, particularly in 3-year-olds (12). Moreover there is plenty of anecdotal evidence to show that hungry children can become restless and irritable.

Common Types of Behaviour

Most very young children are not fluent in spoken language and the way they behave is their means of giving us messages. In a high-quality early years setting, children's joy and zest for life, their interest and involvement displayed in activities, are evidence of them feeling in harmony with their surroundings. Equally, if things go wrong for them or they feel bad within themselves, this will be reflected through their actions. We would accept that most young children are still at an early stage of learning social behaviour and that support for them to achieve positive social behaviour is a standard part of early years practice. It is also important to recognise when children's behaviour may be difficult to cope with but is entirely appropriate for their age. Temper tantrums are a good example. They may emerge around 18 months and be violent and explosive. The cause may simply be frustration; the young child feels restricted and unable to achieve what he wants to do. Alternatively he may be tired or over-stimulated. Temper tantrums should be seen as reassuringly 'normal' around this age. Nevertheless, certain worrying behaviours are increasingly evident in settings and require more understanding and attention. Emotional and Behavioural Difficulties is one of the four broad areas of special educational needs outlined in the 2002 SEN Code of Practice (currently under review), and may include some of the following behaviours (13):

1. *Distressed behaviour* Some children appear to be overwhelmed by emotional distress and so are unable to control the way in which they behave. In extreme cases this may show itself in screaming and crying or aggressive behaviour towards other children or adults. Some very young babies struggle to adjust and regulate their reactions, they may cry persistently, resist being fed and going to sleep, and be unable to soothe themselves (14). One possible cause may be that the child has 'missed out' on having continuous care and love from birth and so has no strong attachment: this is most commonly seen in children who have had different placements in care or where there are turbulent family relationships (15).

2. *Attention-seeking behaviour* Some children constantly seek attention by exhibiting behaviour which is difficult to ignore. Attention-seeking behaviour has negative connotations when it is probably more accurate to describe it as 'attention-needing'. For some young children (and older ones for that matter) any attention is better than no attention. And by four years old a child may have learned that the one sure way of gaining attention is through negative behaviour. Demanding attention in this way may not be a conscious decision for a child, but it is what that child has learned.

3. *Attention-deficit behaviours and sleeplessness* Young children are exuberant and active; this is a normal aspect of their development. However, we hear increasingly of those who are extremely fidgety, unable to concentrate, and who do not sleep well. We should be aware of changes in children's lifestyles and their responses that cause this to be highlighted. In their world there is much more going on today to assault the senses and so practitioners have a more difficult task to hold their attention. Moreover, there have always been those young children who have found it difficult to listen; the difference was that, in former days, these children were compliant but quietly switched off, but now the signs of a lack of concentration are much more overt and noticeable. Whatever the reason, the effects of continual distractible behaviour and an inability to sleep can be hard to deal with both at home and in a setting. Worryingly though there seems to be a need to label this troublesome behaviour as a first step to control it. Hence, the increasing use of the terms 'Attention Deficit Disorder' (ADD) and 'Attention Deficit with Hyperactivity Disorder' (ADHD). It is important to understand the different behaviours of children with ADD and ADHD. The former disorder may cause children to be inattentive and 'flit' from one activity to another, but they may be relatively unobtrusive doing this. Those children with ADHD are much more noticeable; they are often demanding and disruptive to others. Rather than look at the underlying reasons for the problem, too often the response has been an over-ready prescription of medication, notably Ritalin, to control the symptoms. Although these drugs can help to calm behaviour, they can also produce negative side effects such as mentioned below.

4. *Depressed behaviour* Chapter 7 drew attention to increased signs of some young children showing constant anxiety, depression and withdrawal. They may persistently fret about things or appear to find life a burden: this behaviour is particularly sad when shown at such an early stage in

life. It is also easy to overlook in a busy early years setting but a key person should be aware of any body language and expressions which indicate 'sadness'. One apparent signal may be when a child regresses and returns to the comforts of being a baby. Children who are prescribed drugs to control hyperactivity may have a negative 'spin off' and become lethargic and depressed: it can be a matter of exchanging one disorder for another. Disturbingly, depression early in life may be long term and re-emerge in adolescence (16).

The above behaviours signal that all is not well in the child's life and this is being communicated. We have outlined some of the contributory factors but we should also be mindful of the impact of a child's experiences in an early years setting. For example, it may simply be that behaviour problems are compounded by a lack of physical activity in the programme. The most highly developed level of movement for young children is to stay still: prolonged sitting can cause undeveloped muscles to become cramped and painful, and they need to use their bodies in order to focus and think (17). The lack of a strong play-based curriculum is still too evident, despite current actions from the government. In her insightful, classic study entitled *Listening to Four-Year-Olds*, Jacqui Cousins found that children talked of being 'too hurried to play'. When play is permitted, reception teachers admit to adopting a more controlling role: 'We cut it short ... stop them ... interrupt ... it must be irritating for the children ...' One little girl's comments from the study poignantly sum up children's confusion about the pressure: 'Hurry up! Hurry up! It time! What it time for?' (18). Fifteen years since this study was completed, government directives for curriculum coverage and outcomes mean that teachers still struggle to adopt a relaxed pace with plenty of time available for children's own initiatives.

Practical Suggestions

Listen and observe

- Be alert to signs of depression and anxiety in babies and young children, e.g. listlessness, withdrawal.
- Observe children in role play in order to gain insights into their positive behaviour with others, e.g. able to share, include and praise others, give way, and consider how these children influence others.

Be a step ahead

- Help children to think about their behaviour before the event; give a gentle reminder, call the child's name, and make eye contact.

- Provide a special signal for a child who finds it particularly difficult to maintain social behaviour, e.g. 'Joe, your teddy wants you to do this really well', or 'Here is the flag, Joe'.

Reinforcing rules

- Introduce the children to a puppet who has recently joined the group; explain to them that the puppet does not know how to behave and will need to be told about the agreed rules in the nursery.
- Use puppets to play out scenarios involving different aspects of behaviour, e.g. arguments about whose turn it is to have a toy/ride a tricycle. Ask children to offer the puppets possible solutions.
- Discuss how everyone needs to behave in the nursery. Agree two or three key rules and display them pictorially in the nursery. Encourage children to remind one another of what has been agreed.

Provide a supportive environment

- Avoid temper tantrums, e.g. provide time and encouragement for an infant to dress and feed himself.
- Create a programme which makes it practically possible for children to share and take turns, e.g. ensure that there is sufficient apparatus for all members of a group to have regular access; provide a 'pit-stop' and a means for children to 'sign up' (make their mark) to have a turn on a wheeled toy outside.
- Provide a substitute for very young children to release their aggression, e.g. suggest that, whenever they are angry, they pummel a cushion or some dough rather than a child.
- Help older children in the Foundation Stage to express their needs in words rather than physically. For example, Janine wants a turn on the rocking horse and is likely to push off Emma who is having a very long ride. Suggest that instead she goes to Emma and politely says that it is her turn now. Support Janine's request in order to reinforce that she has acted properly.

Professional Practice Questions

1. How well do we use our observations to: gain an accurate and balanced picture of young children's antisocial behaviour; plan effective action?
2. How often do we 'catch' children behaving well and report this to parents?
3. How many boundaries that we set are totally in the interests of children's well-being?
4. How many boundaries are for the convenience of adults?

> ## Work with Parents
> * Encourage parents to consider their style of parenting (permissive, negotiated, directed) and understand how this impacts on their child's behaviour.
> * Suggest that parents consider possible physical reasons for their child's difficult behaviour (a lack of exercise, sleep, food), plan action, and note if there is improvement.

References

1. Curtis, S.J. and Boultwood, M.E. (1961) *A Short History of Educational Ideas.* London: University Tutorial Press, p. 278.
2. Ibid.
3. Department for Education (DfE) (2012) *Statutory Framework for The Early Years Foundation Stage*: London: DfE, p. 8, 1.13.
4. Tickell, C. (2011) *The Early Years: Foundations for Life, Health and Learning. An Independent Report to H Government on the Early Years Foundation Stage.* London: Department for Education.
5. Isaacs, S. (1933) *The Social Development of Young Children: A Study of Beginnings.* London: Routledge and Kegan Paul.
6. Bronson, M.B. (2000) *Self-regulation in Early Childhood: Nature and Nurture.* New York: The Guilford Press.
7. Lindon, J. (2003) *Childcare and Early Education.* London: Thompson, pp. 475–87.
8. Thomas, S. (2007) *Nurturing Babies and Children Under Four.* London: Heinemann, p. 15.
9. Dunn, J. (1988) *The Beginnings of Social Understanding.* Oxford: Blackwell.
10. Lindon, J. (2003) op.cit. (see note 7), p. 200.
11. Hajibagheri, K. (2008) quoted in 'Why we must wake up to sleepy pupils', *The Times Educational Supplement*, Research, 25 April, p. 38.
12. Committee on Toxicity of Chemicals in Food, Consumer Products and the Environment (COT) (2007) *Investigation of the Effect of Mixtures of Certain Food Colours and Preservatives on Behaviour in Children.* Available at www.cot.food.gov.uk
13. Department for Education and Skills (DfES) (2002) *Promoting Children's Mental Health within Early Years and School Settings.* London: HMSO.
14. Barton, M.L. and Robins, D. (2000) 'Regulatory disorders', in C. Zeenah (ed.), *Handbook of Infant Mental Health* (second edition). New York: Guilford Press, pp. 311–25.
15. Pryor, V. and Glaser, D. (2006) *Understanding Attachment and Attachment Disorders.* London: Jessica Kingsley.
16. Nauert, R. (2010) 'Depression in young children', *PsychCentral News*. Available at psychcentral.com/news, 20.5.
17. Goddard Blythe, S. (2000) 'Mind and body', *Nursery World*, 15 June.
18. Cousins, J. (1999) *Listening to Four-Year-Olds.* London: National Early Years Network/National Children's Bureau.

TWELVE Achieving Self-regulated Behaviour

- In order for children to develop their own code of behaviour they must learn about cause and effect and motives for actions, and develop empathy.
- Practitioners should be aware of the factors which shape children's behaviour, listen to the messages that the behaviour conveys, and always offer a positive example.

Although, as the early thinkers showed, it is possible to coerce children into 'good' behaviour, this has little to do with sound moral development. The ultimate aim must be to enable children to understand about right and wrong and so behave morally from their own motives. If we want children eventually to develop a strong moral code for themselves, then we must be concerned with more than them doing as they are told and parroting good manners. Their behaviour must come from the pull of their own conscience rather than from simply complying with instruction. Mia Kelmer-Pringle (1) describes this by referring to behaviour being inner or outer directed. Of course, inner-directed behaviour is a tall order for a 3- or 4-year-old, but it is then that the seeds are sown which are reflected in beliefs and behaviour in later life.

Most children under three years old are not yet able to appreciate another perspective. Thomas suggests that a useful way of assessing this is to play 'hide and seek' or 'hunt the thimble'. If the child hides himself or the thimble in the same place that an adult selected this indicates that he can't yet grasp that he can think differently from the adult (2). However, the 3-year-old is beginning to recognise that other people or animals can be hurt or harmed; these empathetic understandings will grow when for example adults read and discuss situation stories with children. In order to start to regulate their behaviour children must begin to learn about cause and effect and intentions. The latter is a very difficult concept at such a young age and will only emerge over a period of time. A child starts to learn about cause and effect quite early on when he is able to project: 'If I throw that cup it will smash' or 'If I hit Carl it will hurt him.' Gradually he starts to understand about the consequences of his actions. In time, he will come to recognise intention. Sometimes we mean to act wrongly and what we do is deliberate. At other times we do not intend to do anything wrong although the result is not good. We may not intend to drop a beautiful vase, i.e. it was an accident. Piaget's work showed that only children over eight years old understood about intention (3). However, as Bruce points out, more recent work with children, particularly by Donaldson, shows that these understandings can develop earlier when children are helped to learn in familiar circumstances (4).

Dreikurs and Soltz describe how adults might redirect children's behaviour by ensuring that they experience the consequences of their actions:

- Natural consequences may follow an action. For instance a child who has deliberately torn her dress may be upset that she is no longer able to wear it.
- Logical consequences will be determined by the adult but they need to make sense to the child. If he persistently knocks down another child's construction he needs a clear but friendly warning that he will be moved from the area, and if the behaviour continues it is important that the warning is carried out.

The authors emphasise that the consequence must be recognised as relevant to the behaviour. An artificial consequence, such as being deprived of time outside, has nothing to do with an anti-social action: it becomes a punishment and is likely to be regarded by children as unfair (5).

As part of understanding another perspective, young children need to be able to empathise, namely to understand how others feel and put themselves in their shoes. As we saw earlier, Dunn shows that feelings of empathy develop very early in close family contexts. Here, babies and toddlers have had opportunities to be in close communication with the people who care for them and have been with adults who share, explain and discuss feelings with them. By coming to understand about the feelings of the people they love, children can later extend these understandings to empathise with others with whom they are less familiar.

Case Study 12.1

Ibu, three years old, loved bathtime at home. He often came home from the nursery with specks of paint or clay on him and liked to wash them off in the bath. On getting out, Ibu would look at himself approvingly and say, 'all clean'.

Ibu made friends with a new Traveller boy who had arrived at the nursery. Walter settled quickly into nursery life, but often when the two boys played, Walter would appear uncomfortable and complain of feeling itchy. On one occasion, Ibu looked at his friend and lovingly suggested 'Walt needs bath to feel nice'.

Comment

From his limited experience of being dirty, Ibu understood the reason for Walter's discomfort. He was already placing himself in Walter's position and wanted his friend to experience the same pleasures from washing that he did.

Reflection Point

How do you help young children at different stages of development to show genuine empathetic behaviour to others?

However, before children can have regard for others they have to feel secure and loved themselves. Laevers' emphasis on the importance of personal well-being (6) is echoed by a group of primary teachers; in the context of their daily work, they recognised that the children who have positive self-esteem and a feeling of well-being will naturally recognise the work of others and praise them for it (7). This applies equally to adults. People are not likely to show this generous and caring behaviour when they lack the certainty of their own worth and so are hungry for recognition for themselves.

Case Study 12.2

Three-year-old Toby was collected from playgroup by his mum who picked him up and gave him a hug. Toby looked over to where Sean was still waiting for his mum who was late arriving. 'Hug Sean as well', Toby asked his mum.

Comment

Toby knew how much he was loved by his mum. He showed immense sensitivity in noting Sean's 'aloneness' and could afford to be generous in offering to share his mum's affection with the other little boy.

Reflection Point

How clearly do you identify those children who lack positive self-regard?
What practical steps do you take to improve each child's view of herself?

Making it Possible for Children to Behave Well

Having realistic expectations

Young children will only be able to behave in a way which is appropriate for their stage of development. As we have seen, if a 2- or 3-year-old has a temper tantrum, that is perfectly acceptable; at this age, emotions are powerful and difficult to control. Again, children under five years old find it difficult to mask feelings of frustration and boredom. Expectations both at home and in the nursery can be unrealistic. Adults may become upset or frustrated because 3- and 4-year olds find it difficult to be quiet when adults converse, or to sit and listen to instructions or a story in large groups. It is important to recognise that children's social skills and powers of concentration will grow as they mature. At five and six years old they may manage these things, but fidgety behaviour and interruptions before then are not necessarily signs of poor behaviour. Although a 4-year-old can be encouraged to recognise that at times other people do need to talk without her, occasionally her own need for attention will be stronger.

Providing for movement

Young children are naturally active and need to feel comfortable and confident in their bodies. Goddard Blythe suggests that a child's experience of movement will play a central part in shaping his personality, feelings and achievements (8). Two sensory systems are particularly important in this respect.

The *vestibular system* is situated in the inner ear; it develops a few weeks after birth and is essential for healthy development. It is the most influential of the sensory systems and modifies and co-ordinates messages received from other systems. If the vestibular activity is working well it helps young children to maintain balance, posture and co-ordination. By linking head movements with eye movement children can track an image and later follow a word on a page. Importantly, if children experience plenty of motion through space it helps their senses to work better and enables them to focus and pay attention. Many Montessori settings encourage children to start the day with vigorous vestibular activity in order to help them settle to quieter activities.

The *proprioceptive system* uses information from the muscles and joints to make us aware of our body position. When working well it allows children to move parts of their bodies without watching them. It can influence activity such as sitting on a chair and balancing on one foot. White describes proprioception as 'internal eyes' (9). Children with a poor proprioceptive system will have difficultly doing anything they cannot see: they may appear clumsy, poorly co-ordinated, and restless. Encouraging activity that causes muscles and joints to work against resistance has a calming effect as it helps to decrease the over-reaction to sensations.

When practitioners ensure that both of these systems are working effectively they help to protect children from being over aroused and hyper-
active or under-aroused, lethargic and passive. Having regular and frequent
opportunities to exercise balance, co-ordination and body movements will
assist with regulating the senses, reducing frustration, and allowing children
to feel happily in control. These opportunities are better organised outdoors
and should always happen at the child's discretion in a play context.

Being consistent

One of the most confusing things for a young child must be to have contact
with a number of adults who expect different things, or who require one
thing on one occasion and something different on another. The former can
happen when home and setting have markedly different expectations, or
when adults at home or in the setting are not of one mind. The latter is
most likely to arise when adults act pragmatically rather than considering
what sense a child will make of their requirement. It is all too easy, when
harassed under the pressure of time, to give in to a child's insistent
demand for sweets or to overlook one child hitting another; in less stressful
circumstances close adults might be more able to consider the consequences of their response for children's future behaviour.

Inconsistent expectations also occur commonly in a setting where a
young child experiences being in different groups during the course of a
day. A 2-year-old attending a breakfast club with older children may be
expected to comply with what is expected of others in terms of table manners, or may be over-indulged, fed and treated as a baby. Moving on into
the nursery that child may then encounter entirely different expectations
in making choices and acting independently. Early years practitioners must
work as a team to ensure that, as far as possible, children encounter similar treatment; they should also be alert to children's understandings of how
they should behave. For example, where they have been used to directive
language, e.g. 'Do this', 'Stop that', they may find it difficult to cope with
indirect requests such as 'Would you mind clearing up please?'

In cases where there is no single clear message about what is acceptable
behaviour, children may eventually develop double standards as they learn
to use the different behaviours approved in each situation. This, however,
provides no basis for children to start to internalise a moral code for themselves. This internalisation is more likely to develop if young children learn
that there is one constant expectation for how they should behave.

Encouraging conflict resolution

Until children learn to see another's perspective and to use language to
express their feelings and needs they will use physical action to protect
their rights. McTavish points out that 'Fighting and arguing help children

to practise dealing with conflict and power and to develop social skills. This may also be the only way they know how to deal with anger' (10). Sometimes violent exchanges can lead children to resolve issues; we should be careful not to intervene too quickly and so deprive them of learning how to deal with these situations themselves. However, at times most children will benefit from learning ways of dealing with conflicts which include the adult:

asking each child to describe or show what happened and to listen carefully to the other's point of view;

recognising and reflecting back what has caused the anger to erupt for each child, for example 'You are cross Alma because Ana pushed you and took the red bike you were waiting for'. 'You are angry Ana because you had been waiting a long time for the bike and Alma wouldn't let you ride it';

encouraging the children to suggest what they could do now to make things better;

discussing the options with them in order to decide on the best suggestion.

Requiring children to say sorry is not helpful, as the sentiment is often meaningless to a young child and McTavish suggests that it can detract from the source of the conflict (11).

Providing positive role models

Behaviour and the development of moral values, like dispositions, can be heavily influenced by what children observe from adults who are close to them. Small children learn a great deal through imitation. If they love their parents and key persons they will want to be like them. This, of course, places a heavy responsibility on all of us who live and work with children. As Kelmer-Pringle pointed out, it is what we really are and how we behave which matter, not what we say or believe we say (12).

Case Study 12.3

Carl found that the cake in his lunchbox had disappeared. He discovered that James had taken it; James was hungry because his au pair had forgotten to pack his lunch-box properly. The teacher took both upset children aside. She gently asked James to think if there might have been any other solution to the problem. Together they agreed that a better line of action would have been for James to have told an adult that he was hungry. James himself suggested that in recompense he would bring Carl a cake from home tomorrow. At the end of the day (with the permission of James and Carl) the teacher shared this episode with the other children. Everyone agreed that taking things without permission was not good and should not happen in the nursery.

Comment

Later, when sharing this episode on a training course, Jane, the teacher, admitted that, although she was very aware that different standards were often accepted at home, she considered that her first task was to establish a clear moral code of conduct in the nursery. At the same time she worked with parents, using examples of children's behaviour such as this one, to emphasise the need for the setting's code to be reinforced at home.

Reflection Point

Consider the basic rules(code) for behaviour in the nursery:

- How well are the rules understood by the children?
- How far have children contributed to the code?
- How clear are parents about the code?

In order for young children to strengthen their understandings about the behaviour of other people, they need to practise roles for themselves. This is possible in play where children can explore being a powerful adult and try out different relationships in total safety. Role play can help moral development in three ways:

- It can enable children to sort out their own feelings.
- It can help them to stand in other people's shoes (to decentre) and explore how they might feel.
- It places them in practical situations where they need to negotiate ways of behaving and treating other children.

Providing a programme which gives insights into behaviour

In a setting which has developed a positive ethos or climate for children's moral development, the adults will have considered carefully the types of experiences that will both introduce and help to reinforce notions of right and wrong. Although first-hand experience of behaviour is the most powerful way of influencing young children's actions, stories are also very helpful in introducing moral dilemmas and giving moral messages.

We know now that children learn all sorts of things better in situations that they understand. It follows then that any nursery programme should make the most of those situations that occur in daily activities and routines. It is through helping to comfort a child who has fallen and has grazed knees, or being generous to a younger child who has interrupted an activity, that moral behaviour is practised. Discussion also plays an important key role. Insightful practitioners will skilfully turn a minor catastrophe into a moral lesson.

Case Study 12.4

Patri (at three-and-a-half years old) had few toys at home and the nursery staff were aware that he regularly hid small items and took them home. His key worker had discussed this issue generally in her small group. She explained that although everyone was tempted, it was not right for individuals to take things for themselves as this would mean that there were not enough things to play with in the nursery. She also suggested that anyone, including herself, could store things in their pockets and forget them, so it was a good idea to check each day to see if this had happened. Patri did not respond to these messages and continued to take equipment home. Soon after the discussion, however, Patri was observed stuffing items under a teddy bear's blanket and whispering to teddy to hide them. Another discussion followed along the same lines. Approximately a week after this, Patri was observed again with the teddy. Using a similar tone and manner to that adopted by his key worker, Patri counselled the teddy to 'be a good boy and put things [again hidden under the blanket] back for the children to play with'. During the next month Patri was less and less inclined to take things home. He was keen to 'find' items in his pocket and share these with the staff, and was always warmly praised for his discovery.

Comment

Patri used role play with the teddy bear to work through his behaviour. Over a period of time he was able to overcome his temptation to take things without loss of face.

Reflection Point

Parents can become very concerned if their children persistently bring things home from the nursery. How might you enlist their support in dealing with the issue?

Supporting Children Who Show Challenging Behaviour

Challenging behaviour is behaviour that:

- interferes with a child's cognitive, social or emotional development;
- is harmful to the child, other children or adults;
- puts a child at risk for later social problems or school failure (13).

Collette Drift, writing about children's behaviour, reminds us of the SEN Code of Practice which states that children with emotional and behavioural difficulties have an equal entitlement to positive, inclusive praise as any other (14). Around the same time she was writing her book in 2007 there were more than 4,000 suspensions of children aged five years and under in England. Of the 400 suspensions of children aged two and three years old from nurseries, 310 involved accusations of physical assault or threatening behaviour against another child or an adult (15). It is surely an indictment on society that this should have occurred and it remains important to support settings against taking such drastic action. Gender can influence identifying and labelling children's behaviour. The Ofsted report, *Managing Challenging Behaviour* (2005), praised early years settings for their sensitive support, but found that in some settings up to 40 per cent of children had challenging behaviour. It noted that:

> Boys are more likely than girls to be defiant and both physically and verbally abusive ... Loud raucous behaviour by boys is often the focus of teacher attention, while inappropriate behaviour by girls is sometimes unnoticed or ignored ... A significant proportion of children with challenging behaviour have poor language and social skills and limited concentration spans. This association is evident in all the early years settings and in three-quarters of the primary schools. (16)

In these circumstances, practitioners will find it helpful to:

> consider the reasons for some children showing low-level disruptive behaviour: look out for 'trigger points' that spark off troublesome altercations;
>
> be aware that even though some boys' antisocial behaviour may be particularly noticeable, this should not mean gender stereotyping which can in turn lead to self-fulfilling prophecies.

It is imperative that all practitioners should have the skills to deal with more severe behaviour in order to support a young child having this experience of failure.

The Camden Early Years Intervention Team is experienced in taking positive action in this regard. They offer training to practitioners on strategies to lessen the likelihood of a child's behaviour becoming a crisis. The team points out that very challenging behaviour is complex and it is only too easy and not helpful to attribute blame to the child, parents or early years staff: this can be exacerbated when other parents complain about the behaviour. In fact there are always a number of factors which influence behaviour, and so it is both necessary to identify the underlying reasons for the child's actions and at the same time use skilled strategies to reduce the incidents. The basic rules require that all adults keep calm and reassure parents that the behaviour is acknowledged and the staff are supporting the child. Recorded observations will show the pattern and frequency of incidents of the behaviour. It may be necessary to carry out a nursery risk assessment and, if the child is aggressive, for staff to position themselves between the child and other children. Sometimes children will use their own methods of coping: for example, the Camden team refer to a little girl who, in the build-up to a tantrum, would withdraw to sit on the floor in a toilet cubicle in order to calm down (17).

Supporting positive behaviour, loving the child

It is unfortunate to use the term 'management' in relation to children's behaviour as it implies control and supervision and reduces the child's contribution to the problem. It can be quite an effort for adults learning to behave well in difficult circumstances and is a huge challenge for some young children who are still trying to regulate their behaviour. Episodes of critical behaviour result from a child who is flooded with emotion and who is probably incapable of listening. The priority is to ensure that everyone is kept safe. Once the child has calmed down the behaviour can be discussed. The child may recognise that adults are listening to her and respond to being asked what she could do to avoid the difficult behaviour. She also needs guidance in the form of a few clear boundaries, which should help her to understand what behaviour is wanted: despite this, she will often fail to meet expectations. If these expectations have been clear and constant, and communicated in a loving way, children usually know when they have transgressed and this is accompanied by a feeling of personal disappointment and letdown. Rather than simply rebuke the misbehaviour, it is important to help children recover to a point where they can try again. Clearly, deliberate and persistent misbehaviour should be reprimanded but it should be the act that is disapproved of rather than the child. Children must be secure in the knowledge that they are loved, despite their wrong actions.

Practical Suggestions

Listen and observe

- Note those children who find it difficult to concentrate and consider the reasons for this, e.g. over long periods sitting, a lack of opportunity to play outside, story not pitched to their level of understanding.

Provide a supportive environment

- Help children to settle conflicts: listen carefully to both parties and show your interest and concern in what the children say and do.
- Provide children with many tangible examples of moral behaviour, e.g. discuss kind behaviour and encourage children to report their own and examples of others' kind actions.

Support strong vestibular development

- By rocking a baby and playing rocking games.
- By providing:
  - low jumping off points (slopes, steps, slides);
  - things to twist and turn around;
  - surfaces at different angles and heights (twisting paths, hillocks for climbing and rolling down);
  - resources such as swings, tyres, hammocks, rockers.

Support a strong proprioceptive system by providing:

- dough and clay activities to work hands and fingers;
- facilities for rolling in different ways, in a barrel, tyre or rolling their bodies down a slope;
- scope for jumping on a trampoline, onto cushions, off a low wall;
- scope for pushing and pulling, a trolley full of bricks, tug of war.

Professional Practice Questions

1. Which aspects of my behaviour offer a positive model for young children?
2. How well is our environment equipped to support children's vestibular and proprioceptive development?
3. How far do we as a staff show common and consistent expectations of children's behaviour based on shared values?
4. How well is our team supported through training and supervision to deal with children's challenging behaviour?

Work with Parents

- Encourage parents to help their child see the consequences of his actions and start to understand the difference between a mistaken and deliberate act.
- Help parents to recognise their child's need for unconditional love even when he shows challenging behaviour.
- Explain how regular physical activity may help to calm their child's behaviour.

References

1. Kelmer-Pringle, M. (1974) *The Needs of Children.* London: Hutchinson.
2. Thomas, S. (2007) *Nurturing Babies and Children Under Four.* London: Heinemann, p. 114.

3. Piaget, J. (1932) *The Moral Judgement of the Child.* Harmondsworth: Penguin.
4. Bruce, T. (2005) *Early Childhood Education* (third edition). London: Hodder & Stoughton.
5. Dreikurs, R. and Soltz, V. (2012) 'Happy children: a challenge to parents', in J. Lindon (ed.) (third edition), *Understanding Child Development 0–8 Years.* London: Hodder Education. (Originally published 1995.)
6. Laevers, F. (ed.) (1996) *An Exploration of the Concept of Involvement as an Indicator of Quality in Early Childhood Education.* Dundee: Scottish Consultative Council on the Curriculum.
7. Fountain, S. (1990) *Learning Together: Global Education 407.* Cheltenham: Stanley Thornes.
8. Goddard-Blythe, S. (2004) *The Well Balanced Child.* Stroud: Hawthorn Press.
9. White, J. (2007) *Playing and Learning Outdoors.* London: Routledge, p. 71.
10. McTavish, A. (2007) *Feelings and Behaviour: A Creative Approach.* The British Association for Early Childhood Education, Early Education. Available at www.earlyeducation.org.uk, p. 9.
11. McTavish, A. (2007) op.cit. (see note 10).
12. Kelmer-Pringle, M. (1974) op.cit. (see note 1).
13. Klass, C.S., Guskin, K. and Thomas, M. (1995) 'The early childhood program: promoting children's development through and within relationships', *Zero to Three*, 16: 9–17.
14. Drifte, C. (2008) *Encouraging Positive Behaviour in the Early Years.* London: Sage, p. 3.
15. *The Times* (2008) *Nursery schools struggle with troubled and violent children*, 7 November, p. 5.
16. Ofsted (2005) *Managing Challenging Behaviour.* London: Ofsted, pp. 8–9.
17. Camden Early Years Intervention Team (2004) 'Warning signs', *Nursery World*, 22 July, p. 13.

THIRTEEN   Young Children's Spirituality

- Aspects of today's society severely constrain children's spiritual growth and contribute to the danger of disenchantment with the wonder of childhood.
- And yet young children have great potential to develop spiritually because of being open to new thoughts and ideas.
- Although many children are assailed by sophisticated experiences, most are very impressionable to everyday events and search for meaning in their lives.
- Children learn to self-regulate their behaviour through concentrating their minds and bodies.
- Young children will grow in spirit if they are supported by warmth, order and consistency, guided to appreciate the non-materialistic aspects of life, and encouraged to develop their creativity.

At a time when many churches are facing diminished congregations, interest in a spiritual dimension to life has strengthened in recent years. As the moral doctrines set down by organised religion appear to have less impact on people, many are struggling to find new meanings and guidance to the ways in which they should conduct their lives. Despite this there have been very few studies of young children's spiritual development, few insights as to what it comprises, and little guidance on how it should be fostered. There are now no references to spiritual development in the Framework for the Early Years Foundation Stage or the National Curriculum Key Stage 1. However, within the 2014 Ofsted Inspection Framework which includes maintained nursery schools, children's spiritual growth is visible. Spiritual, moral, social and cultural development (SMSC) is considered under achievement, the quality of teaching, behaviour, leadership and management of the school, and over-all effectiveness. In other words, there is an expectation that SMSC will be woven throughout whole school (and nursery) provision. Moreover, the new requirements mean that providing evidence is now more than a paper exer-cise as children will also be asked about their experiences in these areas (1). The curriculum for the Foundation Stage in Northern Ireland also makes brief reference to spiritual development as part of SMSC, and the Welsh Framework for the Foundation Stage goes further and has a section on spir-itual and moral development. This includes requirements for children to have opportunities to reflect and experience quiet and creative times (2). Reflection and quietness do not come naturally to young children; they are such physical beings and so full of life and vitality that the term 'spiritual' does not appear to fit. Spiritual development can seem remote from the ten-ets of early education, which stress the importance of activity and 'being'. And yet during the early years of life children are not naturally weighed down by materialism (although some are in danger of being so, as described below) and are very receptive to thoughts and ideas. Clearly this is a good basis for beginning to recognise the things of quality and significance in life.

The emphasis for early years non-maintained provision in England now appears overwhelmingly secular, but it is both possible and desirable to be aware of spiritual elements if we look carefully at some standards. One of the Teacher's Standards (early years) requires staff to 'demonstrate and model the positive values, attitudes and behaviours expected from children' (3). Previous chapters have already highlighted some of these attitudes which are basic to children's personal, social and emotional development. This chapter draws attention to those which contribute to a spiritual dimension.

What is Spirituality?

There is a tendency to confuse the spiritual with the religious, although all religions share a sense of the sacred which is surely something worthwhile and precious to pass on to young children. In this chapter it is proposed that spiritual values can stand by themselves.

Elaine McCreery offers a straightforward definition of spirituality as awareness that there is something 'Other, something greater than the course of everyday events' (4).

We need to know how this definition is seen in practice. Generic guid-ance from the Office for Standards in Education (Ofsted) suggests that children's spiritual development is demonstrated by their:

- beliefs, religious or otherwise, which inform their perspectives on life and their interest and respect for other people's feelings and values;
- sense of enjoyment and fascination in learning about themselves, others and the world around them;

- use of imagination and creativity in their learning;
- willingness to reflect on their experiences (5).

The Ofsted guidance includes some of the topics already covered in this book. Trying to narrow the meaning down I would suggest that, for the purposes of this chapter, spirituality is about appreciating the journey through life in the deepest sense, particularly special moments, and recognising our own inner resources to help us cope with the journey. This is probably the most challenging aspect of development to promote when working with young children, but one of the most important, given that they are growing up in an increasingly soulless society. It is illustrated by three trends.

Consumerism

The first significant example is the huge emphasis on consumerism which can massively distract children from recognising and enjoying the less tangible aspects of life. Mother Teresa, when visiting North America, observed that the whole society seemed to have an abundance of possessions (6), and Joanne Christolph Arnold, a passionate advocate for children, argues that our rich, Western society has enslaved children to consumerism:

> As advertisers tap the bottomless pockets of adults whose money is fueling the most prosperous economy in the history of the world, they are discovering the most lucrative market of all: their little (and not so little) boys and girls. At once the easiest targets and the most persuasive wheedlers, today's children and teens have been successfully harnessed to pull their parents back to the mall week after week, month after month and year after year. (7)

The Archbishop of Canterbury, Rowan Williams, backed up this view. In his powerful book *Lost Icons* Williams attacks the Disney empire which, he claims, is turning children into consumers by its marketing strategies (8). Despite some notable exceptions of poverty in every country, there is no doubt that most young children in Western Europe and the USA have far more things than they need. Parents seem to work longer and harder to provide children with more and more luxuries. This reaches a peak at birthday and Christmas celebrations. Amanda Craig, a journalist and parent, describes vividly the orgy of pre-Christmas spending:

> Going into any high street now is like walking into Toy Story: shiny boxes piled high with Barbies in fluffy tinsel-pink or Smash and Crush Hulks in flak-jacket khaki. There are multi-coloured buttons, buzzers, clashing lights and remote-controlled flights; there are bells, yells, singing fish and howling owls. Crazed by greed and ignorance, children race about in a frenzy of indiscriminate desperation or log onto web-sites such as iwantoneofthose. com. The whole enterprise is a vision of hell. (9)

But as we know too well, material wealth does not necessarily feed the spirit. Having witnessed affluent lifestyles in North America, Mother Teresa offered a stark message. She commented that she also had never seen 'such a poverty of the spirit, of loneliness and of being unwanted, that is the worst disease in the world today, not tuberculosis or leprosy. It is a poverty born of a lack of love' (10). As for young children, by giving them so much and making it so easy to replace and replenish things, we are denying them the need to really cherish and value what they have.

An emphasis on achievement in early education

The second trend is linked to education. Williams also points the finger at the priorities of our early educational system. He suggests that current ideas about the purpose of childhood education are to give children the skills they will need to survive and succeed in a competitive and even dangerously cut-throat world (11). By implication, the archbishop suggests that this means an emphasis on a relentless programme designed to improve children rather than one which understands and gently steers and strengthens their natural development. Although the EYFS appears to support a relaxed, play-based curriculum, many practitioners feel under pressure to provide children with a heavy diet of literacy and numeracy too soon, and some parents become too easily caught up with the need for their children to achieve as much as possible as early as possible.

The 'loss of childhood'

This emphasis for children to acquire formal skills early is a small part of the third trend which is the move to rush them prematurely into the adult world. We hear a great deal nowadays about the 'loss of childhood' and this reflects a view that inevitably children are 'growing up' too quickly and become too knowing about the ways of the world at an early age. The media are quick to exploit this, particularly for small girls, and make-up, jewellery and sexually provocative clothes are heavily marketed. This perception of children as miniature adults becomes a vicious circle as it can affect the ways in which they are treated by parents and carers. The move has been slow and insidious. Thirty years ago Marie Winn identified this in her valuable book *Children without Childhoods*:

> ... as today's children impress adults with their sophisticated ways, adults begin to change their ideas about children and their needs; that is they form new ideas about childhood as adults act less protectively and as they expose children to the underside of their lives, adult sexuality, suffering, fear of death, these former innocents grow tougher perforce, less playful and trusting, more sceptical, in short more like adults. (12)

The above trends paint a grim picture which continues, as do issues that were highlighted in The Good Childhood Enquiry which added that a culture of individualism is causing a range of problems for children. The report suggests that the over-riding belief that you need to take care of yourself is flawed, as evidence shows that unselfish people are happier. There is also a clear message for parents in the report who are urged to help their children develop spiritual qualities (13). These messages indicate important factors that we should face and try to combat if we are to protect and strengthen children's inner lives. In highlighting some of these factors I draw on two sources:

The current guidance from Ofsted mentioned earlier in the chapter (14).

Selected points in David Hay's thoughtful book *The Spirit of the Child* (15).

The headings below have been interpreted in a way relevant for young children's spiritual growth.

Awareness

Although young babies rapidly recognise their mother's milk, voice and smell, for the most part they live in the moment, having no sense of the past or future. Margaret Donaldson suggests that this 'living in the moment', which she calls 'the point mode', is also apparent in older children (16). Hay describes a vivid, immediate experience in his family:

One morning when he was very young our son Simon called excitedly for me to run to the window. When I hurried over he pointed triumphantly out of the window and ecstatically cried out, 'Grass!' One only has to think of how frequently small children are transfixed by the moment in this way to realize how natural and universal the point mode is to childhood. (17)

Young children use their bodies and sensory experiences in order to focus on and sense situations. They find it difficult to describe what they experience but their awareness springs from listening to the messages that spring from within them. Truly absorbed awareness is described by the social psychologist Mihaly Csikszentmihalyi as 'flow'. He suggests that this occurs when you are totally immersed in something that interests you and experience a liberating feeling of mastery (18). Young children's lives are filled with new challenges to conquer, most of which will require their undivided attention: some joyous experiences of achievement may also be linked to spirituality.

Beliefs

As we have seen, children will already have some firm beliefs by the time they enter the reception class. These may include religious beliefs, including some hazy notions of deity, and they will almost certainly include some values, for example, about how to treat people. Rebecca Nye's fascinating interviews with children about their spirituality included responses from 6-year-old Freddie as he discussed the importance of friendships and his difficulties in maintaining friends. His comment about God reflects core values: 'God's the kindest person I know, I think ... because he never shouts or tells you off, because he never even speaks to you apart from perhaps when you're dead' (19). It is important that we listen to children talking about their beliefs and values; in so doing they will start to recognise that not everyone thinks alike or attaches the same importance to particular issues.

Early childhood is a time when understandings of difference are formed (20). Parents and practitioners should give young children opportunities to explore spirituality and different beliefs (21). Whatever the belief of parents children should be encouraged to respect all views and values. One way to do this is to read them simple stories from different cultures. Over time these will help them to understand that even if children from other countries and cultures eat different food and have different customs we all share love and respect. Informal conversations with individuals or in small groups are most appropriate where a good and trusting relationship has been established between the practitioner and children.

Case Study 13.1

Staff in a Children's Centre invited kindergarten children to share their own and others' understandings of spiritual issues. They drew pictures of their beliefs, had discussions with leaders of different religions and an atheist philosopher, and transformed their play area into some of the children's views of heaven. Parents fully supported the project and marvelled at their children's abilities to have deep conversations about beliefs. The teachers learned that, given the opportunity, children can engage in real discussions about beliefs. Max, one of the children, summed it up: 'The fun thing about studying different beliefs is that they are all different' (22).

Comment

Factors which support this impressive exploration included: staff who had high expectations of the children and were prepared to listen to them; opportunities for children to portray their beliefs in different ways; and support from parents.

Reflection Point

Consider the attributes and skills that these children had which enabled them to gain so much from this project.

Children know when their thoughts and beliefs are acknowledged and respected. This can sometimes be difficult when the beliefs do not accord with those of the practitioner. However, insisting that 'You don't really mean that do you?' can easily undermine the child and will not necessarily change her way of thinking. The child should at least feel that she has been given a voice and that voice is respected. As Kahil Gibran says when talking of children, 'You may house their bodies but not their souls, for their souls dwell in the house of tomorrow, which you cannot visit, not even in your dreams' (23).

A Sense of Awe, Wonder and Mystery

The roots of spirituality are founded in early experiences of awe, wonder and mystery. This is certainly the easiest aspect of spiritual development to foster, as young children are so very impressionable. They have lived for a very short time and to them most of life is still a mystery. Young children wonder at the mundane and constantly remind us more jaundiced adults of the joy of being alive. And yet the very process of growing up and experiencing more formal education can stifle the curiosity that leads to wonder and the exploration of the world. Wordsworth described this beautifully:

> Heaven lies about us in our infancy!
>
> Shades of the prison-house begin to close
>
> Upon the growing boy (24).

The most successful examples of encouraging awe and wonder at all ages can occur when adults themselves are open to the miracles and mysteries of life.

Case Study 13.2

Alice, a pre-school worker, had planned to encourage children to observe and share thoughts about growing things. She also wanted to impress the group with the power and beauty of nature. Alice passed around some sunflower seeds for each child to look at closely through a magnifying glass. They talked about the shape and feel of the seeds and what might be inside the hard shell. Alice then asked the children to close their eyes and think hard about the little seed growing. When they opened their eyes, in front of the children were two huge sunflower plants growing in pots. Jamie gazed in amazement and whispered, 'It's grown into the sun!'

(Continued)

(Continued)

Comment

This is a good example of adult-directed learning. The topic was planned and resourced well and children were encouraged to observe, discuss, predict and visualise, as well as have sensory experiences to help them understand 'growth'. The wonder that the children experience when they view the huge plants provides a spiritual dimension.

Reflection Point

How might you extend this experience and add a further spiritual dimension?

Experiencing Feelings of Transcendence

The word 'transcendence' derives from the Latin word *transcendere* which means 'to climb over'. Young children do 'climb over' and reach out to the limits of their world as part of growing up. A child experiences her inner strengths when she summons up courage to venture into the playground alone for the first time. When Ahmed lay on the carpet, closed his eyes and listened to a brief extract of Beethoven, he said softly afterwards, 'The music burst out of me'. Children also go beyond everyday events in their imaginative play where they explore possibilities.

In our materialistic part of the world, children are bombarded with stimuli and invitations to expand their lives. They have sophisticated experiences at a very early age and these can lead them to look always for answers outside of themselves. We can offer young children something of infinite value if we help them to look for resources within.

Although most young children are naturally noisy and exuberant, like all of us they can also thrive on peace and tranquillity. However, even if they need peace, not all will find it easy to quieten themselves; some will find silence threatening and not all will be as prepared as Ahmed was to close their eyes in a group. Practitioners can help children learn ways to relax, contemplate and concentrate, but these habits will only be acquired over a period of time and in an atmosphere of trust. Many settings and schools now recognise the benefits of encouraging children to lie still and listen to music when they come into class following a noisy lunch break. Other settings teach simple yoga techniques to help relaxation. Observing these sessions it is striking to see how well young children respond, as if they crave these moments of calm. Joanna Haynes, who writes about children as philosophers, uses stilling techniques to help children focus. Describing how she uses the phrase 'Make your bodies still and ready to listen' as a settling phrase, she says that one child commented that in order to really listen you have to be still both inside your body as well as outside. Haynes goes on to say that this led to children discussing what this comment might mean and a decision to alter the original phrase to 'Make yourselves still, outside and inside' (25).

Helping children to meditate takes them a step forward to transcendence. At the Maharishi school in Lancashire, children aged four are introduced to meditation and breathing exercises. Five-year-old children learn their Word of Wisdom and repeat this word as they walk to school or play with construction. At this age they do it for five minutes twice a day and after that they add one minute for every year in school (26). Caroline Sherwood in her book on meditation aptly describes it as 'making friends with ourselves' (27).

Encouraging children in these ways to control and concentrate their minds and bodies is an important step towards them regulating their behaviour.

Searching for Meaning and Purpose

Bruno Bettelheim writes: 'Today, as in times past, the most important and also the most difficult task in raising a child is helping him to find meaning in life. Many growth experiences are needed to achieve this' (28).

And yet young children constantly search for meaning through their questions, many of which confront the big issues in life. Some of these may be related to the child's personal circumstances, e.g. 'Why doesn't my mummy live with us any more?' Others may be of a more philosophical nature, e.g. 'Why does the moon look at me?' Yet others may deal with more imponderable issues, e.g. 'Where do you go when you die?' or 'Who is God?' These last questions are the most difficult to deal with and there are no set answers. However, some basic principles are helpful. The first is to keep responses simple and honest, e.g. 'God is very special to a lot of people who believe that God made the world and all the things living in it.' That should be quite sufficient to satisfy an initial question and the child will probably move on to the next burning issue such as a request to play outside. The second is to admit when you do not have an answer but that you are really thinking about it. A child will be satisfied if you show that it is a very important question and that you are interested in discussing possibilities and finding out what he thinks.

Those who work with young children are frequently pained by the traumas faced by so many during their early years of life. It is amazing how some children do appear to withstand huge disruptions, as well as selfish and sometimes cruel behaviour that is shown towards them. Other children are, sadly, noticeably damaged and life is a confusion to them. Sometimes early years staff can help children deal with, and even come to terms with, aspects of suffering, e.g. a friend who is hurt or upset can be comforted and reassured, or a pet dies and can be buried with suitable rituals. However, at times staff can feel inadequate to deal with some hardships that children face outside the nursery. On these occasions, all that is possible is to draw on trusting relationships, to encourage children to talk, and try to point out any good and positive aspects that arise from pain. On all occasions it is helpful for children to recognise and share good memories and see them as one of life's gifts.

Creativity

Bernadette Duffy reminds us of the universal human desire to be creative throughout history. She refers to how creation myths from religious and cultural groups express the profound need, satisfaction and pleasure in generating something new (29). Conversations with young children and observations of their models, drawings and paintings are a testimony to their original thinking and creativity. All but the most damaged children enter the nursery with creative talents, but it is during the early years that these talents blossom or wither. Practitioners know that, as with any learning, growth in creativity does not just happen, but is crucially dependent on key factors which include the curriculum and the role of the adult.

Children under five are now entitled to creative development as one of the seven areas of learning. This area involves exploring and using media and materials and imaginative use of media to represent ideas, thoughts and feelings (30). However, in the government document *All Our Futures* the breadth of creative thinking is recognised: 'Creativity is not unique to the arts' (31). The Characteristic of Learning 'Creating and Thinking Critically' acknowledges this statement and is concerned with children using their minds to be original, creative thinkers and apply this across all areas (32). Good nursery settings and schools have always recognised that young children need a multiplicity of ways to represent their understandings. This is expressed beautifully in the title *The Hundred Languages of Children*, which describes the work of the pre-primary schools in Reggio Emilia (33). These Italian schools emphasise the ways in which young children use what the schools term 'graphic languages' to record their observations, ideas, memories and feelings. This type of curriculum is inclusive. It is worth remembering that a programme which only offers children narrow opportunities to record, perhaps simply to write or crayon, is necessarily reducing opportunities for those who may need to show their learning in different ways.

Being creative involves emotions. The 5X5X5 Project (see Chapter 5), which encompasses many elements of spirituality, built much of its creative work with children on Ferre Laevers' research which highlights the need for a learning environment to focus on children's well-being. This includes offering children the chance to feel easy, spontaneous, safe, competent and satisfied. They should experience tenderness and warmth, social recognition, meaning in life, and moral value (34). Young children can release powerful feelings and extend their emotional repertoire in dancing, stamping, twisting, role play, and mark-making (see Chapter 7). Robert Sternberg also suggests that negative feelings, such as anxiety, can inhibit imaginative and creative thoughts and actions (35).

Creativity cannot be forced. Lesley Webb, a wise and informed educator of young children, once described the process of compost-making in the mind. Good compost, like ideas, needs time to ripen and mature. Claxton echoes this when he argues that creativity is helped when people slow down and reflect, and he suggests that deep and creative thinking is enhanced by serendipity (36). Probably all of us would relate to this, recognising, for example, the regenerative effect of a relaxing holiday in the midst of a busy life. The notion is particularly applicable to young children. During the early years when so much learning takes place children need to have plenty of opportunities to use and apply new ideas. In this way they become secure and confident with new information. In our current culture of targets and achievements, we are in danger of promoting a 'hurry along' curriculum. The result of this can be that children hang on by their fingertips to new knowledge without any chance to use what they know.

Given a broad and rich curriculum, the right emotional climate and time, children can become totally absorbed in creative activity. Csikszentmihalyi and colleagues observed artists, athletes, musicians and others who showed intense involvement in what they were doing. There appeared to be no extrinsic reasons for their involvement but the 'flow' of their energy or motivation. Whenever we are fully functioning, involved in a challenging activity that requires all our skills and more, we feel a great sense of exhilaration. Because of this we want to repeat the experience. But to feel the same exhilaration again it is necessary to take on a slightly greater challenge and develop slightly greater skills (37). When young children experience this flow they are tapping into their inner resources.

Once again the adult is the most precious resource as she has a direct role in helping children to be creative: this role can best be described by using Bruner's term 'scaffolding' which implies support without constriction. Successful scaffolding requires the adult to make a sound judgement of what the child knows now, an accurate diagnosis of the next step in learning, and provision of suitable support to help the child achieve this. That support could include:

offering appropriate stimulus; this may be through the provision of sensory experiences, aiding memory skills, fostering imagination, or the provision of materials;

teaching the subskills of handling tools, and mixing and managing materials;

listening, questioning and commenting, encouraging the child to bounce ideas or talk through the activity;

encouraging the child to combine materials and link different ways of representing experiences (38).

As with all talents, some children will prove to be more creative than others. Nevertheless, all have potential. Given the time and resources, access to informed adults and some good quality stimulus, these will free young children's creative abilities in, to use Robin Tanner's words, 'making the ordinary and trivial arresting, moving and memorable' (39).

The Contribution of Steiner Schools

Although many early years settings both plan and seize opportunities which support children's spirituality, some provisions make this a keystone for their work. Telling examples are seen in the Rudolph Steiner schools. Around 800 Steiner schools exist around the world. They are very child-centred and the aim is for the spirit of the school to be created by the mutual co-operation of everyone. There is a heavy accent on the use of natural materials and learning about natural crafts. Imaginative play has a high profile (typically children use very simple props, such as drapes and blocks). The sense of community is tangible, through the ritual gathering around a lighted candle at the start and end of the day. Other rituals recognise and celebrate the natural cycle of life; children regularly bake their own bread and work in the garden and observe living things. The practitioner is not there to explicitly teach, but to demonstrate or model certain behaviours. According to Freya Jaffke, a renowned Steiner kindergarten teacher, these behaviours include a sense of order and rhythm, good habits and loving consistency. Jaffke suggests that when the adult exemplifies these behaviours she creates a 'mantle of warmth' which protects children from the outside world and strengthens their inner resources (40).

Caroline Von Heydebrand was a distinguished teacher trainer and supporter of the Steiner philosophy in the early part of the twentieth century. Her words capture overwhelming reverence and respect for the child and the need to trust in the power of the spirit:

> Compulsion in the life of the spirit is unendurable. If the child is given the nourishment proper to him, one which does not constrain but nurtures, then in later life, his soul will have power to investigate and discern and come to find the spiritual foundations of the world through his own reasoning and insight – the means suited to his nature and stage of development. (41)

This belief remains fundamental to Steiner practice. It also has relevance for all practitioners today who are trying to balance the dictates of planning and adult-directed activities with providing space for the child.

Practical Suggestions

Observe and respond

- Be alert to times when very young children delight in the moment.

Nurture children's inner resources

- Help young children to appreciate stillness. Establish a few moments daily when children can close their eyes and be totally quiet. Help them to recognise silence as a gift of life. Encourage them to relax: to lie on the floor and breathe deeply; to make their bodies like flippy, floppy scarecrows. Suggest that they think of beautiful things which they might share afterwards (it is always important to respect all responses, even non-contingent ones!).

Provide places for quiet reflection

- Make spaces available inside and outside for children to withdraw from activity and be alone. It can be a tent or curtained-off area indoors, or simply a bench near some flowering shrubs or underneath a tree. It needs few resources – some comfy cushions as a minimum, but can be enhanced by a vase of flowers, scented herbs, soft lighting and music, all of which can provide a calming atmosphere. The purpose of this space needs to be made clear to children – it is there for each one of them if they want to think or just to be quiet by themselves.

Share precious memories

- The adult shows a small group of children her memory box. She pulls out one or two items: a photo of a dog she had when she was a little girl, or a fir cone that her own child had given her some years ago as a gift. The adult talks about why these things are valuable for her although they do not cost much, or any, money. She introduces a memory box for the nursery. Children are invited to bring in an item that reminds them of a special time. These items are then placed in the memory box and shared at a certain time each week. A sense of occasion can help set the tone for the gathering, e.g. quiet music, lighting a candle, the box placed on a piece of carpet, the child sharing the memory sitting on a particular cushion. If the item is passed around it should be handled with respect and care. It is important that each child presents her 'memory' as she wishes. The adult may also continue to share her memory items with the group and share presentations with those less confident individuals.

Encourage a sense of values

- Encourage older children to talk about what are the most important things in life. Start a story about a girl/boy who was able to wish for the three most precious things to have forever in her/his life. S/he could choose from various items (provide a tray with a selection of the following, either portrayed in photographs or the real objects: a large bar of chocolate; a bike; a loving mum/dad/carer; a popular toy; a large ice-cream; good friends; a cat). Ask the children in turn to make their choices and so open a discussion about what sorts of things are important and why. This will also give useful insights into the children's developing values.

(Continued)

(Continued)

Follow the child

- Listen carefully to children's thoughts and views; affirm them when they struggle with ideas, and give them time to respond to stories and daily situations which have some links to spirituality.

Professional Practice Questions

1. What do I do to take care of my own spiritual life?
2. Am I sufficiently aware of the contexts which encourage babies and young children to feel calm and peaceful?
3. How do we best provide for children to reflect?
4. How strongly do beautiful things (music, art, aspects of nature) feature in our setting?
5. How do our environments and interactions with children inspire them to be creative?
6. How well do we encourage children to value the real treasures in life – love, laughter, friendship, giving?

Work with Parents

Encourage parents to:

- help their child appreciate that many of life's gifts are free: suggest that the child chooses one gift to share and chat about each week, e.g. clouds in the sky, people's smiles;
- offer their child ways to calm down, e.g. a special pebble to hold tight, deep breathing, visualising.

REFERENCES

1. Ofsted (2014) *Ofsted Framework for School Inspection*. London: HMSO.
2. Department for Education, Lifelong Learning and Skills (2007) *Foundation Phase: Framework for Children's Learning for 3–7 year olds in Wales*. Cardiff: Welsh Assembly Government.
3. The Teaching Agency (2013) *Teachers' Standards (Early Years)*. London: DfE/National College for Teaching and Leadership.
4. McCreery, E. (2006) quoted in D. Hay and R. Nye, *The Spirit of the Child*. London: Jessica Kingsley, p. 60.

5. Ofsted (2012) *Subsidiary Guidance for the Inspection of SMSC*. London: Ofsted.
6. deBertodano, T. (ed.) (1993) *Daily Readings with Mother Teresa*. London: HarperCollins, pp. 62–3.
7. Arnold, J.C. (2000) *Endangered*. Robertsbridge: Plough Publishing House, p. 16.
8. Williams, R. (2000) *Lost Icons*. London: Continuum.
9. Craig, A. (2003) 'What children really need', *Sunday Times, News Review*, 30 November, p. 5.
10. de Bertodano, T. (1993) op.cit. (see note 6), pp. 62–3.
11. Williams, R. (2000) op.cit. (see note 8).
12. Winn, M. (1984) *Children without Childhoods*. New York: Penguin, p. 6.
13. Layard, R. and Dunn, J. (2009) *A Good Childhood: Searching for Values in a Competitive Age*. London: The Children's Society.
14. Ofsted (2012) op.cit. (see note 5).
15. Hay, D. and Nye, R. (2006) *The Spirit of the Child*. London: Jessica Kingsley.
16. Donaldson, M. (1992) *Human Minds*. London: Allen Lane/Penguin.
17. Hay, D. and Nye, R. (2006) op.cit. (see note 15), p. 66.
18. Hay, D. and Nye, R. (2006) op.cit. (see note 15), p. 68.
19. Hay. D. and Nye, R. (2006) op.cit. (see note 15), p. 105.
20. Derman Sparkes, L. and Edwards, J.O. (2010) *Anti-bias Education for Young Children and Ourselves*. Washington, DC: NAEYC.
21. Baumgartner, J.J. and Buchanan, T. (2010) 'Supporting each child's spirit', *Young Children* (65) 2: 90–5.
22. Mardell, B. and Abo-Zena, M.M. (2010) 'Kindergartners explore', *National Association for the Education of Young Children* (NAEYC), July.
23. Gibran, K. (1927) *The Prophet*. London: Heinemann, p. 20.
24. Hayden, J.O. (ed.) (1990) 'Intimations of Immortality from Recollections of Early Childhood', in *William Wordsworth: The Poems*. London: Penguin.
25. Haynes, J. (2002) *Children as Philosophers*. London: RoutledgeFalmer, p. 69.
26. Selby, A. (1998) 'The little school of calm', *The Times Magazine*, 5 September, pp. 78–80.
27. Sherwood, C. (1997) *Making Friends with Ourselves: Introducing Children to Meditation*, Kidsmed, 10 Edward Street, Bath BA2 4DU.
28. Bettelheim, B. (1975) *The Uses of Enchantment*. New York: Random House, p. 3.
29. Duffy, B. (1998) *Supporting Creativity and the Imagination in the Early Years*. Buckingham: Open University Press, p. 4.s.
30. Department for Education (2012) *Statutory Framework for the Early Years Foundation Stage*. London: HMSO, p. 9.
31. National Advisory Committee on Creativity and Cultural Education (1999) *All Our Futures*. London: Department for Education and Employment and Department for Culture, Media and Sport, p. 27.
32. Department for Education (2012) op.cit. (see note 30), p. 7, 1.10.
33. Edwards, C., Gandini, L. and Forman, G. (1993) *The Hundred Languages of Children*. Norwood, NJ: Ablex.
34. Bancroft, S., Fawcett, M. and Hay, P. (2007) *5X5X5 Researching Children Researching the World*, 5X5X5 = creativity, PO Box 3236, Chippenham SN15 9DE.
35. Goldberg, K. (2003) 'Are we all potential Einsteins?', *TES Primary Campaign*, 2 May, p. 24.
36. Claxton, G. (1998) *Hare Brain, Tortoise Mind*. London: Fourth Estate, p. 52.

37. Csikszentmihalyi, M. (1988) *Optimal Experience: Psychological Studies of Flow in Consciousness*. Cambridge: Cambridge University Press, p. 367.

38. Dowling, M. (1995) *Starting School at Four: A Joint Endeavour*. London: Paul Chapman.

39. Tanner, R. (1985) *The Way We Have Come*. From a talk at the opening of the Arts Centre at Bishop Grosseteste College, Lincoln.

40. Jaffke, F. (1996) *Work and Play in Early Childhood*. London: Floris.

41. Von Heydebrand, C. (1942) *Childhood: A Study of the Growing Soul*. London: Anthroposophical Publishing Company, p. 181.

FOURTEEN   Living in the Wider World

- Young children become aware of their identity within their family and in the wider community and best learn about others from a basis of tolerance, respect and open-mindedness.
- Through exploring the physical world around them they start to recognise different factors in the built and natural environment which are influenced by change.
- Staff provide children with ways of learning which suit them by building on their interests and extending their enquiries.

Babies and toddlers thrive in the love and security of their homes. The earliest environment is intimate and constant. The 3- and 4-year-old continues to need this secure environment, but she is very mindful of and curious about the world around her. She becomes aware of this wider world through what she hears and observes within the family, through books, the media, and being taken on outings to different places. When she joins an early years setting she meets other adults and children. All these experiences contribute to the child's growing understanding about herself in relation to a wider context. This development links closely to understanding about 'People and Communities' and 'The World' highlighted in the EYFS and in early years frameworks and guidance in the other three countries of the United Kingdom (although worded differently and with some variations in emphases) (1, 2, 3, 4).

All of the national documents emphasise the need for active learning and these requirements are clearly laid out in the Characteristics for Learning in the English statutory framework (5). This chapter deals with how settings can encourage young children to start to understand the similarities and differences between people and communities, places, materials and living things in the wider world.

People and Communities

This aspect, People and Communities, relates to Bronfenbrenner's ecological approach showing how children are influenced by various social systems (see Chapter 3). Essentially it is about the child's world and his developing identity through early involvement with others and his personal experiences (6). Children's first encounters are through attachments with significant people who offer them a model of being loved and cared for. Family members and the key person provide rich experiences for children that they hold in their memories and are eager to share with others. Over time they come to recognise that there are other families apart from their own and meeting new people widens their horizons. People and Communities 'acknowledges that children learn first about themselves and the people who are important to them ... and their growing understanding of diversity and difference is informed by the reality of their own and other people's lives and of the different communities they encounter as they engage with the world' (7). Some children will learn these lessons easily and naturally; others, dependent on their early lifestyles, may need a lot more support. Children will have very different personal experiences of diversity: by the time they begin nursery some will have witnessed a rich, cosmopolitan range of lifestyles; others may have only encountered the cultural traditions in their own community. Nevertheless, all children who will be living in the world tomorrow need to develop an understanding of how other people live. It is during the early years when children are naturally curious and receptive to new ideas that these understandings should take root. Some early years settings will have a wide cultural mix of children or a deliberate policy to include children with special educational or physical needs. In these groups the issues of difference are ready to be grasped. Practitioners have a greater challenge in finding ways to raise children's awareness of diversity in settings with a more homogeneous intake, with families from only one culture or from a narrowly defined social class. However, even in these contexts children can be helped to see how others vary from them as well as what they have in common.

Being Open-minded to Difference

Everyone builds up a set of beliefs about others. These beliefs are influenced by personal experiences but also by a fear of strange or different characteristics. Beliefs may also arise from developing fixed views about others and labelling or stereotyping them.

People often fear the unknown and prejudice can flourish in a climate of ignorance. There are tales of 'closed' societies where 'outsiders' are discouraged. I encountered this in an outlying village in East Anglia in the 1960s; the staff in the school were hostile to any new families being admitted other than the locals and termed them 'foreigners'. This belief was based on the outcome of one family who had moved into the village and whose child had some difficulty in making the transition from a large town school. As a result of this experience the teachers had generalised an expectation to cover all new families. They were genuinely worried that standards of discipline in the school would suffer if 'foreign' children with different ways were allowed to contaminate the others. Their intolerance included a fear of dealing with strange parents and children, who they believed would have different values and lifestyles from those of the families they knew intimately in the village. However, they failed to recognise that families with young children are likely to share many things in common no matter where they come from. They also considered the idea of difference in a very negative sense in that it could only disrupt the status quo rather than add to it.

In this instance the staff had built up negative assumptions of others simply based on where they came from. Fears and suspicions can also arise when people look and act differently. This may be because of the colour of their skin, a disability or their behaviour, which is then linked to a cultural identity.

The teachers in the village school had also developed a fixed or stereotyped view of 'outsiders'. Jenny Lindon points out some important characteristics of stereotyping, which are summarised below:

they are usually unfavourable;

even positive stereotyping restricts, e.g. 'Black boys are natural athletes';

stereotyping depends on a belief that other groups are less varied than one's own, e.g. people are more likely to say of another social or ethnic group 'She's a typical ...', but they will say of their own group 'It all depends';

experiences of individuals who do not fit a stereotype are not thought to give any reason to adjust a view, e.g. 'You're my friend, I don't count you' (8).

The extent to which young children will learn to stereotype others and regard them with fear and suspicion will depend on their own experiences and how they see people they know behaving. Children who mix with various people from a wide variety of cultures, and who have encountered disability from a young age, are more likely to be open-minded about differences. However, this will only happen if they see open-mindedness demonstrated by the adults they know and love. If homes do not offer this model then it is all the more important that the early years setting provides it.

Early Influences which Affect Understanding about Being Equal

Children who are clear about who they are and are at ease with this identity will feel comfortable and positive about themselves. This is likely when they have been encouraged from the start to feel proud of themselves, their backgrounds, and their early achievements. However, some children come to develop their self-esteem at the expense of others. Some families may have encouraged their children to feel naturally superior to others who are not from their social or cultural background. Other children may come from families who themselves suffer from a poor self-image. This may be for reasons of unemployment or a lack of social standing. Children from these backgrounds may have been taught to boost their own position by rejecting others deemed less fortunate than themselves. They may have learned particularly to disparage other children who look different or act in a different manner. If practitioners detect any of these signs in young children, they have a responsibility to demonstrate each child's worth and to counterbalance any feelings of superiority.

Case Study 14.1

Ben, a toddler, was regarded as fragile and was physically over-protected by anxious parents. He had fewer opportunities to develop balancing and climbing skills than other children in the neighbourhood who were encouraged to play actively and take physical risks from babyhood. He also grew to be fearful of hurting himself. By the time he started at a nursery, Ben already regarded physical activity as something to avoid; when he saw other children, confident and assured in using their bodies, Ben strengthened his view of himself as physically incompetent.

After falling from a low rung of a climbing frame, for one term Ben flatly refused to use any apparatus or the outside play area in the nursery. By the age of four years Ben had developed a clear picture of his physical limitations which had sprung from his parents' behaviour towards him. His lack of confidence in his body led him to develop a very cautious disposition. Other children initially avoided including him in any boisterous play and then Ben started to exclude himself from any other activities apart from 'safe' pencil and paper work. He became increasingly isolated, showed no interest in other children, and told his mother that the nursery 'was full of nasty people who tried to make him do things'. Ben's mother decided to withdraw her son from the nursery.

Comment

At three and four years old children are very concerned with finding out who they are and what they can do. They need to feel that they matter. Ben's self-esteem was diminished initially by being over-protected and not being encouraged to build up his physical confidence. This led him to withdraw into himself and become negative about others.

Reflection Point

How do you view Ben's mother's decision to withdraw him from nursery?
How might you encourage her to support Ben to remain in the setting?

Despite heightened awareness on the part of many people, prejudice and discrimination are still deep-rooted in British society. The grounds are widespread: they include what sex, race or ethnic group you are; your religion, age, ability/disability, social class; how you speak, what you wear, and the work that you do. Some of these grounds are covered by law, though all contribute to people being regarded and treated in different ways. We are concerned here with equality issues that affect young children. It is not a matter of treating children the same, but rather ensuring that, whatever their inheritance, all children have a similar entitlement in life. It is in the preschool years that children first receive messages about how they are valued and give these messages to others. Some children are particularly vulnerable. Those children who are in a minority in a group will find it difficult if they are labelled or stereotyped by others.

It is a mistake to think that young children are immune from prejudice. Jane Lane points out that 'Just because we hope children will not learn to be racially prejudiced we must not delude ourselves into believing such hopes will be fulfilled and that therefore we need to do nothing about it. Every racist attacker was once a child'. Lane quotes a case study of a 3-year-old boy who was physically and verbally abusive to a black woman on a bus and whose mother refused to intervene. When this was pointed out to the mother she accused the black woman of 'having a chip on her shoulder' (9). The Macpherson Report on the Stephen Lawrence murder noted that inquiry members had heard 'about the racist attitudes of very young children' during the public hearings (10). These findings are immensely disturbing and practitioners need to be vigilant to all aspects of children's behaviour that indicate prejudice. Initially, however, children may be simply interested in difference. Three-year-olds may comment openly that 'That man has a black face'. Four-year-olds will be socially more aware and whisper this comment to the adult they are with. In both cases this is simply an interested observation and not a value judgement or indeed the start of racist attitude. As we support young children to share their observations in other situations we should not encourage them to turn a blind eye to physical differences. When carefully handled, these observations can become expressions of worth. Children will learn easily about bigotry and prejudice if it is modelled for them and parents can provide a powerful role model for children. It is only natural that they should take their values on all sorts of issues from what they observe from people who are close to them.

Case Study 14.2

In conversation with Hugo, aged four, he told me earnestly that he knew that he must never ever get into a car with a stranger. 'Except', he said, 'if the person was driving a Volvo or Mercedes car because only rich and good people drive those cars'.

Comment

Hugo loved and admired his father very much; his one ambition was to become like his father who was a wealthy and successful businessman. I did not know the make of car that Hugo's dad drove but I could guess.

Reflection Point

How would you respond to Hugo's comment?

As a consequence of what very young children will observe and hear and assimilate within the family setting, they will arrive at a nursery with their individual package of beliefs which will then influence how they view themselves and their attitudes towards others. This will include the way in which children view children with physical disabilities.

Case Study 14.3

I was sharing with 4-year-old Rosie a book about a small boy who was restricted to a wheelchair. Rosie pointed out that this was like Dom, a boy in her class: 'I know that he can't walk', she said, 'but instead of good legs he is very good at painting. I told him that'. The previous month, Andrew, a new boy in the reception class, had refused point-blank to sit next to Dom at circle time. When pressed, he protested that he was not going to sit next to someone with poorly legs because 'It's not nice'. As Andrew became used to life in the nursery, he observed Dom's good relationships with the other children. He also watched Dom painting with confidence and skill. A few weeks into the term Andrew stood painting next to Dom. He looked at Dom's work and leaning over said, 'You've drawed a good man, Dom. Do you like my picture?'

Comment

On her first visit to the nursery Rosie had noticed Dom. She had talked about his 'bad legs' with her mum who had explained that some people have bits of their bodies that do not work very well. Rosie's rapid and genuine recognition of Dom's difficulties and talents helped Dom to see himself as a full member of the nursery group. Andrew's fear of physical disability had an equally powerful effect. Initially Dom responded to Andrew's negative comments about poorly legs by refusing to remain in the circle; he repeatedly asked to be wheeled into the book area where he sat silently watching the group. Staff rapidly realised the reason for Dom's action; Andrew's attitude had made him for the first time in the nursery feel different and deficient. As Andrew became more familiar with Dom he began to realise and admire his social skills and talents in painting. The wheelchair became irrelevant; Andrew wanted Dom for a friend.

Reflection Point

How do you as a team encourage children to view difference in a positive sense?

Adult Expectations

Early years staff need to find out about children's beliefs about themselves and others. They also need to work to strengthen each child's self-image, particularly those who may be vulnerable to bias and prejudice. One of the most effective ways of doing this is through staff demonstrating their high expectations of all children. Practitioners are invariably skilled in this aspect of work. However, occasionally where a young child is led to believe that the adult has only a low opinion of what he can do, like Ben who truly came to believe himself to be physically incompetent, the child's confidence drops and he only achieves what is expected of him. This then becomes a self-fulfilling prophecy.

Cooper distinguishes between self-fulfilling prophecies and sustaining expectations. He suggests that the self-fulfilling prophecy occurs when an inaccurate expectation of a child influences the behaviour of that child so as to make the expectation accurate. A sustaining expectation follows an initially accurate judgement, which is maintained despite other influences (11). The concern is that a self-fulfilling prophecy can lead to an expectation of a child which is sustained in later years.

Most nursery settings will make shrewd and accurate judgements of their children based on skilled observations and sound information about what the child knows and understands already. However, this process takes time. Staff in reception classes know that they must determine each child's starting point for learning in order to pitch experiences appropriately and provide suitable and sensitive support. Nevertheless, hasty assessments made too early often mean that judgements are being made and recorded before children have made a sound transition to school. The consequence of this is that those children are not yet sufficiently confident and settled to demonstrate their skills and competencies. This is compounded where a practitioner has received insufficient information about a child's previous experiences and is unable to spend much time with individual children because of a large class size. In these situations practitioners themselves know that there is a danger of making an inaccurate judgement about children's abilities and their potential for learning.

These circumstances can, of course, occur in any setting. Furthermore, without any other information, adults' judgements may be unduly influenced by children's social competencies rather than what they can do. A resulting halo effect can operate and cause over-optimistic views. For example, one Scottish study of multicultural nursery schools suggests that, in the absence of detailed observations of individual children, teachers made assessments of them based on their ethnic group membership. Thus a quiet, hardworking and well-behaved Asian child was regarded as competent and her difficulties with language were overlooked (12). Conversely, a child who is awkward with people, who finds conversation difficult or who speaks colloquially, may, in the absence of other evidence, be judged to be of limited ability. Expectations are also influenced by what people find familiar and identifiable. Practitioners may spot ability in middle-class children more easily than they do in children from less advantaged backgrounds, simply because they may be more attuned to the former. On the other hand, children who have English as an additional language may have their behaviour misinterpreted or their abilities underestimated because of their struggle with a new language. Reflection and puzzlement may be interpreted to be sulky and uncommunicative behaviour. Children's difficulties with expressive language may lead adults to be unaware of the extent of their understanding of spoken language. Those children who are not only new to a school or nursery, but also face a new culture and have communication difficulties, need to be observed particularly carefully and given the necessary time to adapt. Government guidance recognises the importance of the home language and recommends that practitioners provide opportunities for children whose home language is not English to use their mother tongue (13).

Equality between Boys and Girls

Any setting concerned about equality should be aware of how they can make it possible for boys and girls to have a similar entitlement and learn to adopt positive attitudes towards each other. Young children's awareness of their gender develops over time. Three-year-olds are usually able to recognise and label themselves as boys or girls, but it can take another couple of years before they can begin to understand that their gender is stable, e.g. 'I am a boy and boys don't grow up to be a mummy'.

Children may also learn in the home how to behave differently as boys and girls and will take this behaviour into the setting. As Siraj-Blatchford wisely comments, many parents and staff conclude from children's behaviour that they are naturally different, without considering their own contribution to the children's socialisation or the impact of role-modelling (14). The ways in which parents dress children, talk with them, decorate their rooms and the toys they buy them, will give messages about their sex identity. Some parents can have strong views about children having what they consider to be unsuitable responses for their sex, for example they can subject their child to public ridicule. Banjeree suggests that this type of reaction can be a strong inducement for the child to behave in a gender stereotypical manner (15).

In these instances it is difficult for parents to accept that there is a very different approach in the setting, based on the belief that children should be encouraged to develop all aspects of their personality. Margy Whalley, head of the Pen Green Centre, recounts an episode one Christmas when the mother of a 4-year-old child was angry and distressed as a consequence of Father Christmas presenting her son with a picnic set which was what he wanted. Whalley concludes that it is necessary to move slowly when attempting to influence parents. Young children will only become confused if the values at home and nursery are in direct opposition (16).

Case Study 14.4

Andrea was sitting, sorting out cutlery in the kitchen area of a well-resourced role-play area. Aaron entered and settled himself in an armchair to 'read' the newspaper. He went through all the motions of a reader, turning the pages and appearing to scan the print. Glancing up from the paper he saw Andrea: 'Get off your bum and make me a cup of tea', he ordered. Andrea promptly picked up the kettle and looked for the teapot. On observing this Ann, the teaching assistant, asked Andrea if she could come in to join them for a cup of tea. 'Perhaps we could ask Aaron to wash up afterwards?' she suggested. Frowning slightly, Aaron agreed.

Comment

Aaron's behaviour reflected what he had observed at home. (When the episode was recounted to his mum she wryly admitted that Aaron would have heard similar comments directed to her from his three much older brothers.) Clearly it was not consistent with the equal opportunities ethos that the nursery was trying to develop. Ann promptly invited herself into the area

(Continued)

(Continued)

in order to steer the play towards giving Aaron a more equal role. Ann also hoped that she was offering a role model to encourage Andrea to be more assertive in future situations.

Reflection Point

How do you encourage parents to recognise how their behaviour and attitudes shape the beliefs of their children?

The World

Outside

In moving outside of their familiar home children will encounter another environment. This second aspect of 'Understanding the World' focuses on the inter-relationships of people and communities and of living and non-living things. It supports children in experiencing the natural world and in understanding the difference between the natural and man-made world (17). In a delightful film sequence produced by the Siren team of babies outdoors, Bobby's mum takes her 3-month-old daughter into the garden. Mum observes how Bobby takes in aspects of this new world as she faces sensations of moving tree branches and bright light and explores the cool moving air with her tongue. Bobby also has other rich experiences of the local outdoors, in the high street and the park, with unhurried time and gentle conversation from mum about the different features around them. At five months Bobby focuses for longer periods on things of interest. She notices how things are present and then disappear, i.e. shadows and pigeons as they fly off into the air. At seven months Bobby explores the outside in more detail, and from a different perspective as her mother helps her to stand. She enjoys the sensation of soft grass under her feet and mum supports her to move and touch some interesting grasses (18).

All babies and young children need these leisurely and simple excursions in order to build up valuable information about the world outside. Jan White suggests that babies have an inborn affinity, curiosity and fascination with the natural world: sky, wind, rain and shadows; plants, trees and leaves; dogs, birds, beetles and people (19). Babies and infants benefit from repeated short visits to the same localities. The young child is relaxed in the security of revisiting a familiar environment and can concentrate on looking at things more closely: the natural environments are ever-changing through the seasons and weather, and each child's stage of development and maturity means that more and more information becomes available.

A local urban or built environment also offers great scope for investigation, as a short walk along the road reveals shops, flats, houses, front gardens, postboxes, traffic and traffic lights, all of which are of interest to children. They observe workmen digging up the road, painting, constructing or demolishing buildings, and notice how this changes the area. Babies and infants simply absorb these scenarios but older children are keen to discuss what is happening, deepening their observations through asking questions.

Habitats

Young children are naturally drawn to find out about living things, i.e. how they move, what they eat, and where they live. Alison Gopnik states that her studies have found that children know a lot more about the biological world than was originally thought. She describes a study where children received goldfish to care for and watched them live and die and developed a sophisticated understanding of the way in which the natural world works. However, children don't necessarily need additional resources: Gopnik quotes other studies showing that children on Indian reservations in Wisconsin, because of their environment and lifestyle, have deep understandings of the workings of the world and an intuitive sense of biology (20).

Mini-beasts are always fascinating and easily available in most outdoor spaces. Young children need to be aware of how to handle them gently and by observing them closely will discover so much about their lifestyles.

Case Study 14.5

Two-and-a-half-year-old Noah was fascinated by snails that inhabited the dry stone wall in his child-minder's garden. He lay on the ground watching them for ages and gently touching their shells. He discovered how they ate young plants and left shiny and slimy snail trails. Noah announced to his child-minder Zoe, 'I make home for snaileys – lots', and without more ado he started to collect the snails in a large plastic bowl. Without prompting, Noah handled the snails carefully and placed each one deliberately in the bowl. He then set about collecting various leaves and twigs 'for dinner' and placed several stones in the bowl 'for bed'. Noah observed the snails crawling up the sides of the bowl and was clearly worried as two clambered over the rim and escaped. He readily agreed to Zoe's suggestion that they place a net cloth over the bowl to keep the snails safe. However, despite this, the next morning the bowl was empty – not a snail in sight! Noah was initially daunted and asked again and again 'Where they gone?' Noah then decided that the snails had 'Gone play. I see them'. He patiently caught

(Continued)

(Continued)

further specimens and this time gave them different food, i.e. grass, mud, and some fir cones. Noah also decided that the snails 'need drink' and added a saucer of water to the bowl. This time Zoe found a piece of rigid plastic to place over the bowl.

For three days Noah was absorbed with his snail friends; he talked to them, brought them more food and was fascinated by the way they clambered up the sides of the bowl. He gave them names: daddy, mummy, big boy, Toby, baby. Initially he was not interested in using a magnifying lens provided by Zoe, but by day two he started to use it, intrigued by how it enabled him to change the size of his view of the creatures.

After three days Zoe suggested that the snails might like to be freed in order to find their friends. Noah reluctantly agreed. He placed each one on the stone wall and bade it goodbye. 'They happy go home', he announced.

Comment

Noah's absorption with the snails led him to learn a great deal about their movements and eating habits. Zoe was careful to allow him uninterrupted time to study the snails and develop his concentration. Noah showed care and concern for the snails in the way he handled them and made provision for their comfort. He persisted with his interest by collecting them again and this time made a personal link by giving each one a name. Although he needed some persuasion to release the snails, having done so he seemed to have sated his curiosity. However, his interest in mini-beasts continued and within an hour Noah was searching a pile of damp logs for woodlice and beetles.

Reflection Point

How well did Zoe support and extend Noah's interest in mini-beasts and how might she have extended his investigations?

Investigating stuff in the natural world

Once children become interested in something they often want to know more. They pursue their interest and explore in more detail. Noah, initially curious about the snails, learned more about their habits through observing their movements and food preferences. His initial awareness had deepened into enquiry-based learning.

Imaginative play and role play can often lead children into enquiry. Mixing and combining natural materials is an age-old activity, and soil, water, pebbles, twigs, leaves and other natural materials are easily available. Young children are naturally inclined and will delight in exploring the

Figure 14.1 The Mud Girl

stuff of the earth and learning about how materials behave and what they do. Mud holds a special attraction and building a mud kitchen transfers elements of domestic and cooking play to the world outside. White suggests that imagination and creativity grow from building on concrete cause and effect experiences to posing and predicting 'What if … ?' (21).

Exploring scrap and reclaimed materials

As children become aware of the world they should be encouraged to develop a respect for their environment. In today's world natural resources are becoming more limited, people still throw-away materials too easily, and the waste collected is destined for landfill. The positive development and use of scrap stores linking with industries and businesses across the country has made these same materials available for children to use. The House of Objects Recycling Centre in the North of England takes this work a step forward as it promotes the view that waste and discarded articles are valuable re-usable resources. Groups of children visit the centre where environmental issues are discussed and children face the harsh reality of landfill that is used to get rid of unwanted materials rather than using them inventively. The

House of Objects has adopted the ethos and values of the Ramida centres in Reggio Emilia. The centres help to generate radical thinking around scrap and unwanted materials and how they might be used creatively (22).

Practical Suggestions

Listen and observe what children think

- Observe how babies respond to meeting different people and to different experiences.
- Listen to children as they play with each other and share books; what do they notice and what observations do they make? Note any derogatory names that children use towards each other if they are angry or upset.
- Use these comments to develop teaching points, e.g. a comment overheard ('Lisa's fat') might lead to the adult bringing in posters of children and well-known media figures of different sizes in order to talk about the range of physical shapes and relative importance of body shape and size against what a person is really like.
- Note the investigations that children select outside, e.g. which surfaces babies like to touch and crawl on.

Respect every child

- Ensure that you use children's correct names and that these are pronounced properly.
- Take care to record a child's full name when that child enters the nursery. Ask parents how they and their children would like to be addressed and listen carefully to how the name is pronounced. For the benefit of other staff, a child's personal name should be underlined on the record and if necessary spelt phonetically.
- Show a genuine interest in children's backgrounds. Ask them to bring in something that is special for them from their home. Share these precious things informally during circle times (these are most effectively organised for older children in small groups of six to eight where all children are encouraged to join in and ask questions).

Help children to see themselves in relation to others

- Create a personal book for each baby which has photographs of them with other close family members: talk to them about each photograph and the loving relationships that are depicted. Add more photographs as they bond with new adults and children.
- Use images (photographs/pictures/postcards) which show children in their own homes, other children and their families in the local environment, and those from other parts of the world. Use these images

to interest children in other people and places and to develop balanced views.

- Display and discuss examples of similarities in the stages of growing up, in the daily aspects of life (washing, dressing, eating, celebrating) and the common emotions we experience; common problems experienced in all countries (people who are homeless and poor); and the differences in homes, physical appearances and dress, and different customs.
- Use routines to help children identify how they are alike and how they are different, e.g. when grouping children or dismissing them from a group use physical characteristics as well as items of clothing ('All those with red socks, black, curly hair, two thumbs').

Provide role-play settings to reflect different lifestyles

- Provide materials which will encourage children to construct various types of home (a tent, caravan). Help children to appreciate the special circumstances of living in these homes (cooking, washing, collecting water) in order for them to use their play to develop understandings.
- Provide examples of men and women doing different jobs. Invite adults into the nursery whose roles can help to counter stereotypes, e.g. a father with a baby, a woman bus driver, a man who assists with a cookery activity.
- Use stories, jigsaw puzzles and photographic displays to show adults in different roles.

Confront exclusion

- Using photographs of the adults and children in the nursery, make stick puppets. Introduce these to the children and then ask each child to select a stick puppet and then choose other puppets to play with that morning. This activity may identify those children who are being excluded: discuss what it feels like to be left out, and then make a brief but clear reference to any issues which involve ethnicity or disability.
- Leave the puppets in the book area for children to play with; observe any activity with the puppets or change in the children's play partners. Repeat this activity after two weeks.

Plan your outside area to introduce environmental issues

- Think carefully about the environmental investigations you want to offer children.
- Even a limited space can provide for raised beds or tubs of plants and bird feeders; vegetation to attract butterflies and insects; rocks or logs as homes for mini-beasts; cobbles and sticks for children to arrange in

(Continued)

(Continued)

different patterns; access to water; and regular activities which include looking at shadows at different times of day, noting the different position of the sun and clouds and measuring puddles before and after rainfall.
- Encourage thoughtful ways to use recycled materials.

Professional Practice Questions

1. How far do we as a staff understand and promote the issues to achieve equality of opportunity for all children?
2. How far does my response to children depend on whether they are boys or girls?
3. How much do I use my knowledge of each child's cultural background in my work with the children?
4. How often do we plan simple, local excursions for babies and children which will help to deepen their understandings of the world around them?

Work with Parents

Suggest to parents that, when going on a walk together, they provide an empty paper bag for their child to find and bring home a treasure (a leaf, stone, twig, empty snail shell).

References

1. Department for Education (DfE) (2012) *Statutory Framework for the Early Years Foundation Stage*. London: DfE, p. 9.
2. Department for Children's Education, Lifelong Learning and Skills (2008) *Foundation Phase: Framework for Children's Learning*. Cardiff: Welsh Assembly Government, pp. 31–3.
3. Northern Ireland (2012) *The Revised Northern Ireland Primary Curriculum: Foundation Stage, Understanding the World*. Available at nicurriculum.org.uk
4. Learning and Teaching Scotland (2010) *A Curriculum for Excellence: Building the Curriculum 2, Supporting the Early Level*. Edinburgh: Learning and Teaching Scotland.
5. Department for Education (DfE) (2012) op.cit. (see note 1), pp. 6–7.
6. Bronfenbrenner, U. (1979) *The Ecology of Human Development*. Cambridge, MA: Harvard University Press.

7. Moylett, H. and Stewart, N. (2012) 'Understanding the Early Years Foundation Stage', *Early Education*, p. 29.
8. Lindon, J. (1998) *Equal Opportunities in Practice*. London: Hodder & Stoughton, pp. 11–12.
9. Lane, J. (2008) *Young Children and Racial Justice*. London: National Children's Bureau, p. 85.
10. Macpherson, W. (1999) *Inquiry into the Matters Arising from the Death of Stephen Lawrence* (The Macpherson Report). Available at http://news.bbc.co.uk/1/hi/_special report/1999/02/99/stephen_lawrence/279746.stm
11. Cooper, H. (1985) 'Models of teacher expectation communication', in J.B. Dusek (ed.), *Teacher Expectancies*. London: Lawrence Erlbaum Associates.
12. Ogilvy, G.M., Boath, E.H., Cheyne, W.M., Johoda, E. and Schaffer, H.R. (1990) 'Staff attitudes and perceptions in multicultural nursery schools', *Early Childhood Development and Care*, 64: 1–13.
13. Early Education (2012) *Development Matters in the Early Years Foundation Stage*. Available at www.early-education.org.uk, p. 20.
14. Siraj-Blatchford, I. (2006) 'Diversity, inclusion and learning in the early years', in G. Pugh and B. Duffy (eds), *Contemporary Issues in the Early Years*. London: Sage, p. 111.
15. Banjeree, R. (2005) 'Gender identity and the development of gender roles', in S. Ding and K.S. Littleton (eds), *Children's Personal and Social Development*. Oxford: Blackwell.
16. Whalley, M. (1994) *Learning to be Strong*. London: Hodder & Stoughton, p. 53.
17. Moylett, H. and Stewart, N. (2012) op.cit. (see note 7), p. 29.
18. Siren Films (2011) *Babies Outdoors: Play, learning and development*. Available at www.sirenfilms.co.uk
19. White, J. (2011) 'Outdoor Provision for Very Young Children', quoted in Siren Films, *Babies Outdoors: Play, learning and development*. p. 9.
20. Gopnik, A. (2009) 'Teaching young children', *National Association for the Education of Young Children: News from the Field,* 3 (2).
21. White, J. (2013) *Making a Mud Kitchen, Muddy Faces,* 40 Oivet Road, Sheffield, S88QS. Available at www.muddyfaces.co.uk
22. Pace, E. (2013) 'Exploring the House of Objects', in *Early Years Update* 106. Available at www.optimus-education.com, pp. 9–10.

FIFTEEN Working with Families

> - Whatever form a family takes, it is immensely important for each child.
> - Parents' views about bringing up their child may not always coincide with the aims of the nursery. If each party knows where the other stands, this is more likely to lead to shared tolerance and respect.
> - Practitioners need to value parents and recognise the pressures of parenthood.
> - The successful nurturing of young children depends on practitioners and parents working closely together on a day-to-day basis.

In 2007 the Early Years Foundation Stage reminded us that families are unique: 'Children may live with one or both parents, with other relatives or carers, with same sex parents, unmarried partners, divorced and married partners with families' (1). This diversity remains, although generally families are smaller and the role of the extended family in many cases has dwindled. For children their family consists of the people who are closest to them and care for them on a daily basis. These may include neighbours, family friends and partners or birth parents, and in settings, the key person. Any one of these may be the 'significant' person for the child; these are the people that we as adults remember so vividly when recalling major influences in our childhood. Early years staff are also significant for young children but they can never take the place of the family. However, if families and staff work closely together children will benefit.

This chapter explores the particular role of families in young children's personal and social development. It also considers how early years staff can learn from families and support and work closely with them.

Families Matter

However it is made up and however imperfect, for a young child her family is critically important. The relationship between a young child and her immediate family is recognised by its very nature to be personal, intense and long lasting:

> Parenting has a strong influence on emotional and physical health and wellbeing in adult as well as child life. There is a growing body of evidence that the quality of care that babies and toddlers receive depends on the sensitivity, insight, attitudes and resilience of parents or carers. (2)

Parents invest so much in their children because they matter to them. They are, and should be, biased in favour of their child. The Newsons, writing over thirty-five years ago, stressed how important this is:

> The best that community care can offer is impartiality – to be fair to every child in its care. But a developing personality needs more than that; it needs to know that to someone it matters more than other children; that someone will go to unreasonable lengths, not just reasonable ones, for its sake. (3)

Throughout this book we can see how adult models of behaviour impact on the way children think and behave. Long before a child starts at a nursery, her early personal experiences in her family will be a powerful influence on her attitudes to living and learning as one of a group.

Case Study 15.1

Rick was used to making decisions about how to use his time in play and sharing with others while he stayed with a neighbour who was his childminder; his dad, a single parent, encouraged Rick to help with the daily chores of clearing up after meals and sorting clothes out for washing. Rick and his dad also talked about what they had done each day and sang songs and looked at books before bedtime. Dad took Rick and the neighbour's child swimming every Saturday morning. Rick was used to taking some responsibility and being treated with respect. At four years old, he was confident and secure within himself.

Jez was seemingly also confident, but at four years of age he was learning different lessons. His older brother Ned shoplifted regularly and he taught Jez how to easily transfer a bar of chocolate from the shop counter into his pocket. When these episodes were recounted at home Jez's dad was tolerant and amused, saying that he 'had done the same as a kid'. Jez initially settled into a nursery well but was confused and angry when he was gently

(Continued)

(Continued)

taken to task for removing toys and sweets from other children's pockets and lunchboxes.

Comment

Jez was very much in awe of his older brother Ned, who he described as 'awesome and powerful'. Ned's activities were starting to influence Jez's behaviour in the nursery.

Reflection Point

How could the nursery staff help Jez understand that 'awesome and powerful' behaviour can be achieved by being honest, brave and kind?

We can be sure that the family provides the young child with an influential example of what things are important and interesting in life, how to conduct oneself and how to live with others. Most significantly, the ways in which the family members regard and treat the child provide her with a view of herself.

The value of the home and family life in helping young children to develop empathy and learn about right and wrong behaviour has already been discussed (see Chapters 4 and 12). Classic studies also show the significance of daily life at home where children listen, converse, interrupt, question and learn from members of their family (4, 5). The Effective Provision of Pre-School Education (EPPE) study found that parents' interest and involvement in their children's early learning at home has a significant impact, with the quality of the home environment the key factor: in short, what parents do with their children is more important than who they are. For example, one of the numerous factors that seemed to lead to children developing higher intellectual, behaviour and social skills is the opportunity to have friends to play with at home (6). Moreover, it seems that an initial investment in the early years can have long-term benefits. Ongoing EPPE research has shown that parental involvement with their young children can have positive advantages which are still apparent for children at age seven and ten (7). Charles Desforges' study suggested that parental engagement can account for up to a 12 per cent difference between the outcomes for individual children (8). Increasingly, we recognise that fathers matter to young children and can have a profound impact on their children as they grow up. Studies show that where dads are involved early in their child's life:

- there is a positive relationship to later educational achievement;
- there is an association with good parent–child relationship in adolescence;
- children in separated families are more protected from mental health problems. (9)

The research evidence for all ages of children in school is constant in showing that when schools, families and communities work together to support learning, children tend to do better, stay in school longer, and enjoy school more (10).

The sheer amount of time that young children spend with their families is persuasive. Even though family members work, or are at school, in the long-term most of them have a lot of contact with their youngest children. Apart from those in full-time day-care, young children spend the bulk of their time at home.

Approaches to Parenting

We have all had parents, and if and when we become parents, our experience of being 'parented' is probably the strongest influence on our attitudes and behaviour. This can work in two ways. Some people may, consciously or not, dismiss their parents' approach, believing that their own style of parenting is preferable to what they had. Others, deliberately or unconsciously, will base their style of child management on what they have known.

Although practitioners increasingly understand that parents may have clear views about raising a child, Jane Lane points out that this wasn't always the case. For example, in the past it was considered good parenting practice to establish a routine of a set early evening bedtime. Where this didn't happen parents, commonly from black or working-class families, were often regarded as irresponsible or inadequate. Now more relaxed attitudes are evident, the more important concern being that children have enough sleep and awake refreshed. Lane concludes that 'the idea that there is one best way ... is rightly being questioned ... So long as a child is content and thriving most parents accept that there is no definitive way to bring up a child and feel little pressure to conform to specific ways' (11). Parents may also have different views between them about how to raise their children. Blamires refers to those parents who have children with special educational needs. She suggests that when parents are faced with highly emotional issues and significant concerns regarding provision for their child who has difficulties, they may think and react very differently (12).

Case Study 15.2

Four-year-old Wang-Hoi was waited on heavily by his three older sisters at home. They tidied away his toys and clothes and responded to all his needs. At the nursery however Wang was encouraged to be self-sufficient; he found this very difficult and resisted all attempts to encourage him to fend for himself. When changing clothes to go outside, Wang would dangle his wellington

(Continued)

(Continued)

boots in front of a member of staff; he became confused and cross when asked to tidy equipment away and started to hide at tidy-up time. It was not until his mother and key person discussed Wang's behaviour that they became aware of each other's different expectations. After that they agreed that Wang should be helped to conform with nursery practices and his family would encourage him to 'do as his friends did'. However, his mother insisted that at home Wang would remain the 'little prince' and his sisters would continue to do things for him.

Comment

The nursery and the family respected each other's viewpoint, although initially Wang-Hoi found it difficult to adjust to these dual expectations. However, he carefully observed what other children did. Three weeks later, Wang joyfully pulled at one of the helper's hands and showed her how he had stacked bricks away. After that, he appeared to have accepted the nursery routines and took great pleasure in learning how to cope for himself. Wang's mother laughed when she heard this development and reported that his dependent behaviour was unchanged at home.

Reflection Point

Consider how far children face consistent expectations at home and from all staff in your setting.

Pressures on Young Families

Choices and possessions

Being a parent of a young child is an unmatched wonder; all parents experience the joy, excitement and fun of sharing life with a newly emerging personality. These are the precious rewards for the difficulties and challenges of parenting. It is tempting for professionals, working for limited and planned periods of time with children who do not belong to them, to criticise what parents do and do not do. The reality is that bringing up children today is not easy even when one has the support of a loving partner or family, no financial worries, and your children are loved and wanted. Being a parent can be a frightening, exhausting and lonely job if the person concerned is young, inexperienced or alone. Most parents, whatever their circumstances, find the job a heady combination of delight, frustration and despair; some of the time it is simply tedious. Being a parent has always meant responsibilities and the job has become even more demanding. Lillian Katz wrote:

> Many of the stresses of parenting stem from the wide range of choices, alternatives and options available to modern Americans in virtually every aspect of life. It is not difficult to imagine how many fewer arguments, heated discussions and reductions in demanding behaviour on the part of children would follow from having to live with minimal or even no choices in such things as food, television shows, toys, clothes, and so forth. (13)

These stresses are evident in the UK and have certainly not lessened in the last twenty years (14, 15). Busy parents, sometimes only too aware of the lack of time they can spend with their children, try to compensate by providing their children with material possessions, whether they be sweets or other goodies advertised by the media as essential to make every little boy or girl happy. Asha Phillips, an experienced child psychiatrist, while sympathising with parents' need to indulge their children, suggests that this may actually deprive a child of learning the important lesson in life of doing without: 'Without this ability, he (the child) will always be at the mercy of wants that can never all be satisfied. Having and discarding possessions easily also robs him of the feeling that anything is special' (16).

Relationships

A wide group of parents cope with turbulence and demands in their personal and professional lives, namely separated partnerships, single parenthood, and full-time jobs and careers. While none of these factors in themselves is necessarily harmful for children, they can mean that at times it becomes difficult for parents to provide their young child with the necessary undivided attention and unqualified love. Constant disharmony between parents can be particularly disturbing. When parents stay together, but in an acrimonious relationship, children can be hurt emotionally. Goleman's work shows that the way a couple handle feelings between them will have a clear effect on their children, who from a young age are very sensitive to the feelings of people close to them (see Chapter 8). The alternative, parental separation, can also cause damage: the risk of a relationship breakdown is noticeably high for some groups such as teenage parents (17). If parents do decide to go their separate ways, even young children will need to have matters explained to them and to feel involved in decisions if at all possible (18). The Good Childhood Enquiry Report goes to the heart of the matter when it recommends that, in order to reduce conflict in families, parents must give more priority to relationships (19).

The challenges of being a parent go across all sectors of society: with a grossly unequal distribution of work, children may be living with parents who, as Charles Handy describes, may have plenty of resources and no time, or plenty of time and no resources (20). Young children need access to both.

In wanting the best, most parents are ambitious for their children to achieve well. Seaman and colleagues found that many parents saw 'doing well' in education as a key measure for their children's success and wanted their children to do better than themselves (21). Liz Brooker's study of a group of 'hard up' Anglo and Bangladeshi families whose children were starting school showed that all recognised the importance of education for their child's future and believed that parental involvement in their child's learning had an influence on their academic success (22). These positive aspirations and support are surely helpful for children who will be better motivated by parental encouragement. However, where this develops into a culture of competition, aspirations can cause stress. Contributing to evidence for the Cambridge University Primary Review, parents of young primary school children described feeling under intense pressure to read to their children and help them with school work. They struggled to find the time but felt guilty if they did not do so (23). Others, zealous to push their infants onto the ladder of success, became helicopter parents, intervening in every aspect of their child's life (24).

Penelope Leach paints a picture of the child who comes to recognise that she is only loved for what she does rather than for who she is. Leach suggests that this has extremely damaging consequences for any child's self-esteem (25).

Offering Support for Families

The first principle of the Children's Plan in 2007 was that 'government does not bring up children – parents do – so government needs to do more to back parents and families' (26). Since then there has been a flurry of initiatives, preceded by consultations, although the responses to proposals, for instance the Standards for Early Years Educators and Teachers, suggest that the government is not listening to the workforce.

Financial support with childcare

Recognising the spiralling costs of childcare, the government has made clear its intention to support families through new tax benefits and credits:

- *Universal credit*
  - From 2015, six million parents will be eligible for 85% child care costs if they each earn £10,000 or more and work more than 16 hours a week. Many families in the lower income bracket will not earn enough to claim the benefit.
- *Tax-free childcare vouchers*
  - From 2015 parents earning an average income of £50 a week and a joint income of not more than £30,000 a year can claim 20%, to a maximum of £2,000 per year for every child, towards childcare costs.

o Families of service personnel deployed on operations and families with a disabled child where one parent works more than a 16 hour week can also claim this benefit.

o These proposed changes are contentious: they are administratively complex and will benefit higher paid earners considerably more than those who are low paid (27).

- *Support for specific groups*

  o Although there are increased numbers of children being adopted, there remains a shortage of adoptive parents and a growing number of children awaiting adoption. The government has released £150m to tackle this problem of which £100m will be ringfenced to allow local authorities to meet most urgent needs. Adopted children are also entitled to a free nursery place at two years old. The new Statutory Guidance on Adoption helps to simplify and fast-track the adoption procedure, and a 'National Gateway for Adoption' provides a first point of reference for those interested in adoption (28).

Information for parents

At times being a parent of a young child can be confusing and parents need help. 'Families in the Foundation Years' provides an on-line gateway which offers straightforward advice to parents from pregnancy to children age five. It includes a Parent's Guide to the EYFS (29).

Face-to-face fully funded training courses are also still available, although less so due to budget cuts.

Trials of 'CANparents' started in 2012, in four areas aimed at parents of children under five years old. The principle was ambitious, i.e. that parenting support should be available to all families, rather than only those in crisis. However, an evaluation of the scheme one year later showed that only 2 per cent of parents in the pilot areas had signed up to classes due to their lack of awareness of the scheme and confusion in its setting up. The researchers concluded that the programme needed more time to become established (30).

One successful training event to support parents with their children's behaviour was led by their peers. Parents attending (having children aged two to eleven years) were positive about the sessions and maintained attendance. They found the sessions helpful and relaxed and reported changes in their children's behaviour as a result of what they had learned (31).

Support from Children's Centres

Historically, social care, health, childcare and education had operated separately; too often parents had to negotiate their way through different services, replicate information for different professionals, and often receive conflicting advice and support. The notion of bringing together agencies to support families in a unified way gained impetus in the late 1990s with the introduction of early excellence centres and Sure Start programmes. These paved the way for Children's Centres with their central agenda to put children and families first.

Evidence is strengthening to show that Sure Start Children's Centres make a difference to parents. A report from the All Party Parliamentary Sure Start Group included evidence from Ofsted which stated that the best centres:

- focused on developing parenting skills;
- used the views of children and families;
- knew how much progress children had made;
- could show families where parents were better able to work with their children as a result of their intervention (32).

Parental and community involvement has been a feature of Children's Centres from the beginning, although with stronger practice in some centres than others. Evidence from the Children's Centre Census showed that the number of volunteers had increased substantially between April 2011 and 2012 (33). One council described in their evidence the use of parents as outreach workers, thereby allowing these individuals to support people 'like themselves'. The report recognised that the huge resource of volunteers had enabled centres to increase their 'reach' and offer more facilities to parents. Parents also recognised the benefits to them of volunteering in terms of personal growth, increased experience, and improved employability.

The report's recommendations included the following measures to ensure that all centres could enhance the lives of babies, children and their families:

- increase volunteer involvement across the country;
- centre staff to work with parents in 'Stay and Play' sessions, and encourage them to talk and sing to their babies and share stories in ways that will encourage their development;
- dads to be encouraged to take an active and equal role in parenting their children;
- the Department of Education to provide materials to give to parents advising them on how best to engage with their babies.

The All Party Group stressed that the investment put into Children's Centres needed time to have an impact and warned that cutting back provision to the most disadvantaged areas would be a backward step.

Despite these messages local authority cuts are having a detrimental effect. Restricted budgets have forced Children's Centres to reduce their universal services for all families and focus on targeting the most needy. The last evaluation report found that the climate of austerity had caused centres to change dramatically: many were now organised in networks and clusters, services were thinly spread, and fewer staff were under stress with too much to do and too little time to do it (34).

Practitioners and Families Working Together

Against this picture of increased expectations and limited funding streams, all nursery settings and schools have the responsibility and challenge of working with families practically on a daily basis. Frameworks and policies are in place to steer practice, but it is the direct contact that they have with the practitioners that can influence the way in which parents feel supported to bring up their children. Similarly, the impact on what happens to children in settings is largely dependent on what parents are prepared to condone or actively support.

Staff in nursery settings have traditionally understood the inextricable links that exist between young children and their families. When Margaret McMillan opened her nursery school in Deptford in 1911, she was a firm believer that parents should take a strong role in all aspects of the work (35). McMillan was ahead of her time. While over the years nursery settings have developed some exciting and innovative ways of working with families, it has taken a century to ensure that this work is beginning to become common practice. Even now, terms such as 'parental involvement', 'partnership' and 'open door policy' are used in a variety of contexts and to cover different purposes in discussing and documenting aspects of nursery life. Some nurseries and schools would cautiously acknowledge that parents have a right of access but little more. Others are proud of the daily presence of a number of parents tackling different tasks with children during the nursery day. When one looks more closely, though, it is often difficult to see any planning or purpose to this involvement, other than the view that 'an extra pair of hands is always useful'. Yet other nurseries may have a detailed written policy for parents, e.g. a stack of paperwork may be produced to keep parents informed but this does little to generate the spirit of working together.

Work with parents can take many forms and will be undertaken for various and legitimate reasons. These can include meeting the requirements of government in order to be eligible to receive nursery grants, or capitalising on parents' fundraising initiatives. However, if staff really wish to work closely with parents and share in the upbringing of their children during the critical early years, this requires an approach with three important ingredients:

Exchanging information with families.

Tuning in together to understand children's personal and social development.

Respecting and supporting families.

Exchanging information with families

Whatever parents believe about and do with their children, it cannot be assumed that this will coincide with what happens in early years settings. Unless staff and parents are aware of each other's beliefs and practices, they could be working at cross-purposes. Early years staff do not have the right to tell families how to bring up their children, or indeed to insist that the setting's way is the right way. However, both parties need to know about each other's views. Early years settings and schools go to great efforts to inform parents about their priorities and practices, but it is still less common for practitioners to find out what families consider to be important for their children. The introduction to the statutory framework and Section 1 emphasise the need for partnership working (36) and there are several more references to work with parents throughout the document, particularly in regard to the responsibilities of the key person (37) and sharing information from assessments (38). The section on Safeguarding and Welfare requires parents to have access to information and records and to benefit from a two-way flow of information (39). However, apart from this last requirement the emphasis is heavily weighted towards keeping parents informed and supported rather than having a reciprocal dialogue. Guidance from the previous Framework gives a clearer message: 'Successful relationships become partnerships when there is a two-way communication and parents and practitioners really listen to each other and value each other's views and support in achieving the best outcomes for each child' (40).

Nevertheless, no legislation or guidance is likely to meet the real and unique concerns of any new parent when their baby or child moves from home for the first time. Any parent of a young baby will be anxious that the key person has understood the baby's non-verbal signals. Those with older children may worry about how they will adapt to a new regime and environment; what will be expected of them; how they will get on with other children and adults; how much they will miss the familiarity of home life.

When parents hand over their child they are demonstrating a great act of faith in the people who will be acting *in loco parentis*; in turn, they should be informed about their concerns. It is not surprising that their child's welfare, happiness, personal development and behaviour will feature highly. Essentially, although parents need to be given information about policies and daily procedures, what they want is reassurance about the staff who will be working with their child. When settings asked parents what they needed from practitioners, their responses included 'Someone who really likes my child and knows them well, gives me time to talk, has a sense of humour and keeps me informed' (41).

It seems, then, that in order to respond to parents' real questions and concerns, nurseries must try to communicate the ways in which staff bond with the children, get to know them, support their behaviour, and help them develop good relationships. The key person should be available to talk informally; in this way parents will get to know the qualities of the key person, observe how she relates both to their child and to others, and see how their child might make an attachment.

In some family circumstances, for example where parents have separated, it can be difficult to keep both partners informed. It is worthwhile for a setting to try to maintain contact with both parents and, so long as there are no access issues regarding the child, to encourage involvement from both.

Case Study 15.3

Three-year-old Jake's parents had terminated an acrimonious relationship and his dad, Gus, moved 70 miles away to start a new job; this severely restricted his access to Jake. The boy clearly missed his dad and on several occasions said sadly that he had dreamt about his daddy.

The Children's Centre was holding a 'dads and kids' day as part of a programme to encourage fathers to take a key role with their children. Following several discussions with Jake's mum they found out Gus's address. With her agreement they wrote a personalised invitation for Gus to attend the day, and in consultation with Jake attached a recent photo of him to the invitation. Gus managed to take a day off work and travelled to spend the entire day with Jake at the centre. The little boy was delighted to see his dad and wanted to show him everything. By the end of the day Gus had chatted at length with Jake's key person and arranged to attend future dads' days which were held monthly. The key person also promised to send Gus regular updates of Jake's well-being and progress.

Comment

All parties gained from the arrangement which continued for nearly two years when Jake moved into the reception class. A few months after Gus's initial visit to the centre, Jake's mum in discussion with Jake's key person admitted that he had really benefited from seeing his dad more often: 'He tells me that he shows his dad his pictures and gives daddy a big kiss when he sees him'. Gus was delighted to feel that he was 'playing his part as a proper dad and seeing my son grow up'. The centre's initiative had enabled partners in a fractured relationship to maintain an aspect of their role as parents.

Reflection Point

Consider the steps your setting might take to help a child maintain a relationship with two separated parents, and the potential difficulties that might arise in taking such actions.

Settings must also be aware that the exchange of information is two-way. Staff need to tap into the fund of knowledge that families have about their children, e.g. how children have spent their time during the earliest years of life. Have they been used to being parted from their parents, perhaps staying at granny's for occasional nights, spending weekdays with a childminder, or staying with a whole range of neighbours or friends on account of parents' busy social or work lives? The establishment of children's hotels means that some young children will have had the experience of being 'boarded out' while their parents are away; this is in sharp contrast with children who have never been separated from their parents until they join a nursery.

Parents can potentially play the ace card when it comes to having information about their children's personal development. Because of the close relationship that they have, they know about their child as a person in a way that no outsider could. Parents and other close family members are aware when children feel pleased with themselves, when they are confident or fearful, and when they are truly interested. Unless parents are estranged from their children they know how they tick and can predict how they might feel and act. They may not be aware of how their child is prepared for early literacy and numeracy but they have invaluable and intuitive knowledge about their child's personal attributes. It is unlikely that an adult working with children in a group setting will easily have access to such intimate information. The key person needs this information from parents in order to help them form a rapid and meaningful bond with each child. Such details can highlight children's behaviour in different situations and throw light on a completely different world of learning at home. They can complement the information that staff glean in the nursery or school and contribute towards a three-dimensional view of each individual. Staff and parents need time together in order to encourage parents to respond to the request, 'Tell me about your child'. Parents will respond if they are convinced that their knowledge is not only valuable for staff, but also important in helping their child to settle happily, feel known, and make progress. The key ingredient to a successful meeting will be the teacher's evident and genuine interest in getting to know their child.

Tuning in together to young children's personal and social development

Although parents and carers are likely to have unparalleled information about their children, there will be times when they find it difficult to interpret why they are behaving in a certain way. As children struggle to find out about and understand their world they become absorbed in certain activities and ask what appear to be bizarre questions. Parents love their children; they find many of their responses endearing and amusing as they repeat them to friends. However, they do not always recognise the significance or the underlying messages behind what they are describing. Early years staff who have been trained in child development may understand better the reasons for a child's actions; nevertheless, they will only see a very limited slice of behaviour while the child is in the nursery. If staff and parents share their observations of children in the nursery and at home they will be in a stronger position to understand what is happening.

Chris Athey's timeless work with parents in 1990 introduced them to their children's schemes of thought. The study aimed at gaining further information about how young children developed their understandings at home and in the nursery. Information was shared freely with parents, who were asked to attend discussions and outings with their children. Parents were also asked to note what their children did and said at home. Chris Athey admitted that initially parents treated the professionals as the experts. However, as they became better informed and gained confidence, parents were able to take an equal part with staff in tracing their children's patterns of understanding. Although parents' levels of understanding and participation in the project varied, they stressed that all became more and more interested in observing their child: 'Nothing gets under a parent's skin more quickly or permanently than the illumination of his or her own child's behaviour' (42).

Respecting and supporting families

The government has stated clearly that it recognises the challenges of parenthood: 'There is no doubt that children enrich our lives but raising them is hard work. The hours are lousy, there's no annual leave and crucially you don't get training' (43). Perhaps it was always naive to assume that the biological fact of producing a child made for good parenting. However, now parents are urged to consider their responsibilities and to capitalise on their child's responses from birth to such a degree that the joy and spontaneity of the role are in danger of disappearing. Some parents are confused as they become steeped in literature which may offer conflicting advice; others are isolated and in danger of feeling desperate and powerless as a small child appears to take over their lives. By sharing the child with parents the early years setting is in a key position to help.

Adults can indulge children as a consequence of their own guilt. They may naturally be worried about the effects on a young child of a family break-up or the lack of time that they spend with their child as a result of their long working hours. As a result they may condone behaviour which they would normally regard as unacceptable. This can lead a child to feeling in an uncomfortable position of holding power. Parents sometimes need reassurance that a good way of showing their love for their children is to establish clear boundaries. This helps young children to feel secure and cared for, while a lack of guidance can lead a young child to experience a freedom which is heady but frightening. Lillian Katz reminds us that it is not so much the different family pattern that the child grows up with that will affect her psychological and social development, as the way in which she regards that arrangement (44).

Despite the unique role that they have, parents are at least very modest about their influence, and in some cases still remain unaware of how essential they are to their children's personal growth. Perhaps the single most important thing that staff, particularly key persons, can offer all parents is to help them recognise this.

Work with families is complex and sometimes frustrating. Being realistic, the single largest variable that affects children's lives is the one over which practitioners have the least control, i.e. their home circumstances. So there is a stark choice to be made here, i.e. to give up or to regard it as a fundamental challenge. Edwards pointed out that committed practitioners see this aspect of their work as a long-term investment (45). If parents are respected, supported and informed during the earliest years of their children's education, they are likely to be stronger parents as they grow older, and their parenting skills will also be used with younger children in the family.

Practical Suggestions

Listen and observe

Note how relaxed parents are when they enter the setting and how easy they are when approaching you. Occasionally a parent will need time to talk to you immediately and in private and staffing arrangements should allow for this.

Ensure that your environment is family friendly

- Have clear signposts to the office/reception area and to a parents' room.
- Design paths which are wide enough for double buggies, and a covered area for prams and pushchairs. Also provide photographs of all staff members with brief descriptions of their roles (including domestic and administrative staff).
- Have comfy chairs and a playpen with toys for parents and children waiting in the reception area.
- Display a prominent welcoming sign in different languages.
- Display information about meetings/courses for parents (in various languages) with photographs of any recent family events.
- Provide a library of books/booklets for families to borrow.

Share respective standpoints about young children's personal and social development

- Through informal chats/discussions/seminars (whatever term is likely to appeal to your family group), invite parents and carers to share their views about how they would like their children to develop, e.g. how important is it for their children to become self-confident, assertive, sensitive, competitive, obedient, self-critical?

- Ensure that families are clearly informed about the setting's aims for fostering personal and social development.
- You may never reach a full consensus but an open discussion can help all parties to reflect on their views.

Help families to support their children in personal and social development

When you have established a trusting relationship with parents, it may be helpful if you encourage them to consider some of the following questions (it is extremely important that these are offered in a spirit of friendly mutual discussion and that any suggestion of 'testing' parents is avoided):

- *Helping confidence.* How carefully do you listen to what your child is telling you? How do you show that you respect (i) your child's views, and (ii) your child's drawings/paintings/models? How do you show your child that she is very special?
- *Supporting behaviour.* How consistent are you in how you expect your child to behave? When are you likely to be too hard on your child? When are you likely to be over-indulgent? What rules are non-negotiable? How often do you praise/give attention to your child when she is behaving well?
- *Aiding independence.* How well do you encourage your child to be personally independent, e.g. dressing/washing/going to the lavatory? How much choice does your child have in daily routines, e.g. choosing a cereal for breakfast, which clothes to wear, which way to go home? What decisions does your child have in how she uses her time at home?
- *Developing social skills.* How many other adults and children does your child meet during the week? How often do you invite other children to play with your child at home? How often does your child visit other people's homes?
- *Encouraging care for the environment.* How do you help your child care for growing things, e.g. through having her own patch of garden/windowbox, providing food for the birds, helping to care for a pet? How do you help her to become responsible for keeping the environment tidy, e.g. through picking up litter in the park, on camping holidays?
- *Priority.* How often do you show that you really enjoy being with your child?

Set up communication links to suit parents

- Parents' different circumstances will influence the way in which they will wish to exchange information about their child with the nursery. Some

(Continued)

(Continued)

will prefer a daily and informal personal contact with their child's early years practitioner; others will relish completing a home diary or having a visit at home. It is helpful if the nursery makes clear that there are a number of options. The most effective link will show a good regard for family preferences.

Professional Practice Questions

1. How much do I know about what young children enjoy and learn at home?
2. What are the barriers to dads participating in their young children's lives in our setting?
3. How do I show families that I use the information they share about their children?
4. How do I know that parents are fully satisfied with what I provide for their babies and children?

Work with Parents

Discuss with parents their aspirations for their children and how these might be fostered both in the nursery and at home.

References

1. Department for Education and Skills (DfES) (2007) *The Early Years Foundation Stage: Principles into Practice Cards*, 2.2. London: DfES.
2. National Service Framework for Children, Young People and Maternity Services (NSFC) (2007) *Rationale for Standard 2*. London: Department of Health.
3. Newson, J. and Newson, E. (1976) *Seven Years Old in the Home Environment*. London: Allen and Unwin.
4. Tizard, B. and Hughes, M. (1984) *Young Children Learning*. London: Fontana.
5. Wells, G. (1984) *Language Development in the Pre-School Years*. Cambridge: Cambridge University Press.
6. Sylva, K., Melhuish, M., Sammons, P., Siraj-Blatchford, I., Taggart, B. and Elliot, K. (2003) *The Effective Provision of Pre-school Education (EPPE) Project: Summary of Findings*. London: Institute of Education, University of London.

7. Sammons, P., Sylva, K., Melhuish, E., Siraj-Blatchford, I., Taggart, B., Grabbe, Y. and Barreau, S. (2007) *EPPE 3–11 Project. Influences on Children's Attainment and Progress in Key Stage 2: Cognitive Outcomes in Year 5.* DfES research brief RB828, February.

8. Desforges, C. and Abouchaar, A. (2003) *The Impact of Parental Involvement on Pupil Achievement.* DfES Report 433.

9. Department for Children, Schools and Families (DCSF) (2006) *Sure Start Children's Centres Practice Guide.* London: DCFS, p. 81.

10. Department for Children, Schools and Families (DCSF) (2007) Haris, A. and Goodall, J., *Engaging Parents in Raising Achievement: Do Parents Know They Matter?* in DCSF research report RW0O4. London: DCSF.

11. Lane, J. (2008) *Young Children and Racial Justice.* London: National Children's Bureau, p. 132.

12. Blamires, M., Robertson, C. and Blamires, J. (1997) *Parent-Teacher Partnership: Practical Approaches to Meeting Special Educational Needs.* London: David Fulton.

13. Katz, L. (1995) *Talks with Teachers of Young Children.* Norwood, NJ: Ablex, p. 162.

14. Palmer, S. (2006) *Toxic Childhood.* London: Orion.

15. National Children's Society (2008) 'Good Childhood Inquiry reveals mounting concern over commercialisation of childhood', *Good Childhood Inquiry*, February, National Children's Society. Available at www.childrenssociety.org. uk

16. Phillips, A. (2008) *Saying No.* London: Faber and Faber, p. 138.

17. Department for Education/Department of Health (2011) *Supporting Families in the Foundation Years.* London: DfE, para 81.

18. Department for Education and Skills (DfES) (2004) *Parental Separation: Children's Needs and Parents' Responsibilities.* Available at www.dfes/gov.uk/childrensneeds

19. Layard, R. and Dunn, J. (2009) *A Good Childhood: Searching for Values in a Competitive Society.* London: The Children's Society.

20. Handy, C. (1994) *The Empty Raincoat: Making Sense of the Future.* London: Hutchinson.

21. Seaman, P., Turner, K., Hill, M., Stafford, A. and Walker, M. (2005) *Parenting and Children's Resilience in Disadvantaged Communities.* York: Joseph Rowntree Foundation.

22. Brooker, L. (2002) *Starting School: Young Children Learning Cultures.* Buckingham: Open University Press.

23. Curtis, P. (2007) 'Hard pressed parents struggle to help with school work', *Guardian Unlimited*, 23 November. Available at guardian.co.uk/primaryeducation/story

24. Honore, C. (2008) *Under Pressure: Rescuing our Children from the Culture of Hyper-Parenting.* London: Harper Collins.

25. Leach, P. (1994) *Children First.* London: Michael Joseph.

26. Department for Education and Skills (DfES) (2007) The *Children's Plan: Building Better Futures.* London: DfES, p. 5.

27. HM Treasury (2014) 'Millions of parents to get help with childcare costs', Gov.uk News Story. Available at www.Gov.uk/government/news/millions-of-parents-to-get-help-with-childcare-costs

28. Department for Education (2013) *Statutory Guidance on Adoption*. London: Department for Education.

29. 4Children (2012) *Parents' Guide to the EYFS*. Available at www.foundation years. org.uk

30. Morton, K. (2013) 'CANparents Study reveals low take-up of Government-Funded Scheme', *Nursery World,* March.

31. Day, C., Michelson, D., Thomson, S., Pennoy, C. and Draper, L. (2012) 'Evaluation of a peer-led parenting intervention for disruptive problems in children', *British Medical Journal*, 344, e1107.

32. Report from the All Party Parliamentary Sure Start Group (2013) *Best Practice for Sure Start: The Way forward for Children's Centres*. London: 4Children.

33. Report from the All Party Parliamentary Sure Start Group (2013) op.cit. (see note 32), pp. 19–20.

34. Gaunt, C. (2013) 'Children's Centres move away from universal services to target the poorest', *Nursery World,* July.

35. Dowling, M. (1992) *Education 3–5*. London: Paul Chapman, p. 6.

36. Department for Education (2012) *Statutory Framework for Early Years Foundation Stage*. London: DfE, Introduction, 1.1.

37. Department for Education (2012) op.cit. (see note 36), 1.11, 3.26.

38. Department for Education (2012) op.cit. (see note 36), 2.1–2.9.

39. Department for Education (2012) op.cit. (see note 36), 3.67–3.74.

40. Department for Education and Skills (DfES) (2007) *The Early Years Foundation Stage: Principles into Practice 2.2,* CD Rom *in depth*. London: DfES.

41. Department for Education and Skills (DfES) (2007) op.cit. (see note 40).

42. Athey, C. (1990) *Young Children Thinking*. London: Paul Chapman, p. 66.

43. Department for Education and Skills (DfES) (2007) *Every Parent Matters: Helping you to Help your Child*. London: DfES, ref. LKAW, p. 1.

44. Katz, L. (1995) op.cit. (see note 13).

45. Edwards, E. and Knight, P. (1994) *Effective Early Years Education*. Buckingham: Open University Press, p. 111.

SIXTEEN Vulnerable Children and Fragile Families

- National documents emphasise the need to reduce the gap between wealthy and poor families and improve life chances for vulnerable children.
- Early years practitioners should be aware of signs of abuse and neglect of young children and must act to protect children and support their families.
- Close links with other agencies can assist a broader approach to early intervention.

In this book we have cited research that highlights the early years as a crucial time of life where investment can benefit both every child and the wider society. However, in today's complex and fast moving world we have to recognise that children's life chances differ. Parents invariably want the best for their children but sometimes their own circumstances prevent them from acting in those children's interests.

The Reality of Huge Inequalities for Young Families

The gap is widening between those families who live in comfortable circumstances and those living in poverty. Being poor has a profound effect on a child's life chances. Children from poorer homes do worse in terms of achievement and behaviour than those from more affluent backgrounds.

Young children from the poorest families are 30 points behind others in terms of school readiness and score 20 points lower in their vocabulary. The poorest 20 per cent of children are more likely to have conduct problems at five years of age and show risky behaviour later in school such as smoking and truanting. Schools don't appear to close the gap and those who arrive in school as poor performers tend to stay there (1). Working families are poorer when their children are young partly due to the cost of childcare. Despite some financial support from the government (see Chapter 15) the costs of childcare are high. In order to avoid this expense, parents juggle with part-time jobs with anti-social hours which prevent them from being able to be with their children and chat and read to them in the evenings (2).

Messages from national documents

The government's interest in focusing work on families who are in the greatest need has been reflected in various documents commissioned and published within the last five years. All reviews and reports are united in their call for early intervention:

- Eileen Monro reviewed the guidance for Child Protection (3). She reported that the system had become too focused on compliance and procedures and did not focus on the experiences and needs of individual children. In response the revised statutory guidance published has reduced prescription and makes it much clearer who should do what to keep children safe and promote their welfare (4). Northern Ireland (5), Wales (6) and Scotland (7) have separate guidance for safeguarding, and all four countries of the United Kingdom have their own guidance on how to carry out a serious case review where abuse or neglect of a child is believed to be a factor.
- Claire Tickell's review of the Early Years Foundation Stage highlighted the critical nature of the first years of life and recommended that, in collaboration with parents, a progress check should be carried out at two years old which identified a child's level of development including any strengths and concerns (8). This recommendation was adopted in the current EYFS (9).
- Frank Field's review on the effects of poverty stated that what a parent does is more important than what he earns but that poverty, in whatever form it takes, has a corrosive effect on a child's health and achievement (10). Although the government had commissioned this document it took no actions in response to the recommendations for more financial investment.
- Graham Allen's independent report to the government argued just as powerfully for investment in early years to prevent the costs of later intervention. However, recognising that no public money would be made available he proposed that early years projects should be funded by private investors (11).

- The Department for Education expressed a vision for Children's Centres to improve the lives of the most disadvantaged families (12). This was followed by a report from the Institute of Health Equity which prioritised three areas of focus for centres: children's health and development, parenting, and parents' lives. Recognising that Children's Centres already measure some aspects in these areas, the report provided an Outcomes Framework which reframed and suggested additional measures which would help to indicate success (13).

Very young children at risk

A range of research has now shown that the first two years of life (including conception) is an exceptionally crucial time and needs the optimal conditions for healthy development.

However, babies and very young children are particularly vulnerable. The NSPCC's recent report *All Babies Count* makes clear that the risk factors highlighted above for fragile families don't necessarily lead to child abuse, but they do increase the likelihood that it might occur. The report cites evidence estimating that:

- over a third of Serious Case reviews relate to babies under the age of one year;
- in England and Wales babies are eight times more likely to be killed than older children;
- In the UK:

  - 19,500 babies under one year are living with a parent who has used class A drugs in the last year;
  - 39,000 babies under one year live in households affected by domestic violence in the last year;
  - 93,500 babies under one year live with a parent who is alcohol dependent;
  - 144,000 babies under one year live with a parent who has a mental health problem (14).

- Studies find, not surprisingly, that if babies and infants experience these dangers early in life they can have extreme detrimental long term costs on their development (15). The 0–2 Special Interest Group supported by the Departments of Education and Health recognising these findings emphasise the urgency to intervene early (16).

Financial assistance for families with very young children?

The 2-year-old entitlement

The government now provides a free nursery place for 20 per cent of 2-year-old children from less advantaged families and intends to extend this number up until 2015. Eligible children are currently those in families who meet the criteria for free school meals, looked after children, those in care, and others from more needy families at the discretion of local authorities (17).

Although this support is very well received by many parents there are some concerns about providing a consistent quality for these very young children, particularly as numbers increase. Eligible providers are mainly those who are rated good or outstanding by Ofsted. However, local authorities do not always rely on Ofsted as there is a widespread belief that judgements are too infrequent and not always reliable (18).

Children's Experience of Stress and Trauma

NICE defines vulnerable children as those who are at risk or those who are already experiencing social and emotional problems and need additional support (19).

We should recognise that a huge number of young children fare well in life, but equally every day there are children everywhere who are stressed and anxious, although the degree of stress can vary.

Common stresses

Many young children suffer the tensions of living with harassed family members who are constantly busy and do not always give the time and attention needed to nurture a growing personality. These children are rushed through their young lives and are expected to adapt to daily transitions often to multiple caregivers. Children may also become tense and anxious if they move house or a new baby arrives. These tensions, whilst worrying at the time, are *positive* stress responses and a normal part of healthy development.

Crises

All children, like adults, can be confronted with tragedies in their lives which can be particularly problematic if they are unexpected. Young children will face bereavements whether of a much loved family pet or a much loved grandparent. Their parents may separate and they will have to come to terms with a mum or dad who no longer lives with them. Severe financial difficulties may lead to a loss of home and children having to face living in an unfamiliar and possibly less pleasant environment. These situations can lead a child to show a *tolerable* stress response to the pain caused. However, most children will adapt and even recover given time and the loving attention of a close adult.

Living in a Fragile Family

Where children live with families who lead troubled lives they can face persistent stress and anxiety. Parents who find life overwhelmingly difficult may sink into a depression or resort to crutches such as alcohol, drugs or gambling in order to blank out daily problems. Children are then overlooked and feel abandoned, or worse may suffer abuse by being the targets of their parents' despair and anger. Types of abuse can include:

- *physical abuse*, where by various means children are subjected to suffer bodily harm;
- *emotional abuse,* where a child is persistently bullied, led to feel worthless, inadequate or frightened;
- *sexual abuse,* where a child is forced or enticed to take part in sexual activities involving physical contact or viewing sexual images and actions;
- *exposure to neglect,* where failure to meet a child's basic physical and/or psychological needs leads to the possible serious damage of that child's mental and physical health or development (20).

All children are susceptible to some degree, but the higher number of on-going and persistent stresses that any child faces will sap their natural capacities to cope and will cause *toxic* stress. This can have an important and cumulative impact on a child's physical and mental well-being, causing depression, developmental delay and later health problems (21).

What makes a family fragile?

Definitions of a fragile or troubled family vary, but a recent joint report using Cabinet data from 2007 suggests that a family is at risk if it shows at least five of the following indicators:

- Worklessness.
- A low income.
- Material deprivation.
- Poor quality housing.
- Disability, and physical, emotional or long-term illness.
- A mother with mental health problems.
- No qualifications.

Wider and often related risk factors include: family separation or breakdown; drug and alcohol problems; homelessness or transient lifestyles; abusive relationships; criminality; and isolation (22). However, there are dangers in making simplistic assumptions about families based on membership of groups and complex needs must be carefully considered on an individual basis.

Case Study 16.1

Billy, at 3-years-old, had been on the register of the Children's Centre for six months. His attendance was irregular and he usually arrived late with his mum, Annie, who looked harassed, saying that they had overslept.

After some initial problems Billy had settled at the centre, appeared relaxed and interested, but was noticeably reluctant to go home at the end of the day.

Annie then told Olive, Billy's key person, that she had a new partner, Jake, and was expecting his child. She confided that Jake has alcohol problems and had lost his job as a result, but that she wanted to stay with him for the baby's sake and to give Billy a proper daddy. Billy talked about his new daddy and appeared happy with the arrangement.

Annie, never an attentive parent, now had less time for Billy and rushed in to leave and collect him, giving no opportunity for conversation. Olive noticed a gradual change in Billy's behaviour. He was more withdrawn and tearful and often hid when Annie came to collect him. He ate his snack but refused to sit down to eat lunch. Olive suspected that Billy was losing weight and confirmed this when she started to weigh him regularly.

When questioned about these changes Annie said that Jake was trying hard to be a good dad but sometimes found Billy to be difficult and disobedient. She thought that this was due to Billy being jealous about the forthcoming baby and that his changed behaviour in the nursery was attention seeking.

The health visitor, who had visited the house twice, reported that it was bare but tidy and that Jake spoke warmly about Billy, his 'new son'. She returned when Billy was at home. Jake had brought him a football that morning, but Billy had ignored the gift. He sat cuddling a new puppy and told the health visitor that it was called Bonzo. Curling up with the dog, Billy refused to talk further.

Comment

Olive was not easy about Billy's welfare but she lost contact with Annie. As Annie's pregnancy developed she arranged for a neighbour to bring and collect Billy from the nursery. Olive believed that her priority was to ensure Billy's attendance.

Reflection Point

What concerns you about this scenario?
What do you believe Billy is experiencing?
What is he likely to be feeling?
What are Annie and Jake experiencing?
What further actions, if any, should Olive (the key person) take?

Working with all fragile families and vulnerable young children

It is not possible to think about the needs of vulnerable children without considering their families. The quality of relationship between a parent and child is the best determinant to ensure that child's life chances. By supporting families we may help children.

Inter-agency work has become increasingly important as we recognise that contact with another service opens up a wider system of assistance. The Marmot Report recommended 'proportionate universalism' to address health inequalities (including mental health). This means making services available for all families and children with targeted and bespoke help to meet specific needs (23). Many local authorities have plans in place but information sharing is variable. However, the Manchester Common Assessment Framework is a revised scheme which bravely attempts to bring together midwives, outreach workers and health visitors to identify parents and babies in need. Parents are visited eight times until the child reaches the age of five and regular inter-agency joint meetings assess needs, including the provision for further support. Participants are deter-mined to show that this is the best way to identify problems early on and reduce costs to support families in later years (24).

Children's Centres have suffered badly from financial cuts (see Chapter 15) but still offer valuable support to families by accessing a wide range of specialist support. Research suggests that parents value co-ordinated ser-vices so that information can be shared and does not have to be repeated (25). An integrated programme is particularly helpful for fragile families who need a range of support. Designated programmes which require families to fit into a one-size-fits-all mould are often not successful for families with complex and multiple needs. Families also require different levels of information and help as their situations change: for example, tran-sition times when a child starts at a nursery or school and is expected to arrive on time, when a child has to adapt to a parent being taken into custody, or with the development of an abusive relationship. Children's Centres are well placed to co-ordinate support which can be tailored around families in non-stigmatising ways.

Reaching out to fragile families

A lack of awareness of Children's Centres is a problem in some areas of disadvantage. A recent survey revealed that of those who had never used a centre, 42% said that this was because they had never heard of them. Two factors stood out here: men were found to be less aware than women of the services on offer; also those families with English as an additional language. The survey highlighted a need to engage with fragile families who were isolated, such as those from minority ethnic backgrounds (26). It also underlined the importance of Children's Centres knowing their families and identifying the neediest within their reach.

The recent opportunity for parents to register live births at a Children's Centre should help the centre to link with families at the start of a child's life. Information also needs to be passed on from other agencies. The survey quotes an example from a Children's Centre where police kept health visitors and schools informed of local domestic violence incidents but did not inform the centre. This meant that staff could not identify why some families had stopped using the centre or not allowed them to offer specific help which might have prevented this happening (27).

Even if parents become aware of the services on offer they have to take the big step of visiting a setting for the first time. Smaller nursery settings are not so likely to have the resources to provide support from a home visit or family worker and a parent may be on her own when she first visits. Many parents will have had poor experiences of their own schooling and will naturally be apprehensive about entering an educational institution. It is a scary prospect to join a strange group of people and that first visit can determine whether a parent returns. Several parents told me how they felt intimidated entering a building. Others recounted how they felt left out and were not welcomed by others. These parents never repeated their first visit and sadly refused to try another setting.

Fathers are also sometimes daunted by female-dominated environments. One lone father who had been supported to place his little girl at a Children's Centre described his experience thus: 'I waited to collect Charmaine and tried to be friendly and chat with a mum, just about kids and that. A bit later I heard her whispering to her friend, saying "That creepy bloke over there was trying it on with me, so be careful"'. Needless to say, the dad refused to visit the centre again.

Establishing trust

Parents appreciate feeling comfortable and welcome in a setting and an important factor in this is having easy relationships with staff. Building positive and trusting relations with all families makes it easier if difficult issues need to be raised at a later stage. All agencies involved with fragile families will work hard to maintain good working links, but the key person has a critical role in that she usually has regular and frequent communication with parents and is their first point of contact. Even when these contacts are brief they provide an opportunity for friendly exchanges. The National Children's Bureau sums it up: 'Parents need to know, and internalise, the feeling that they are important, that they are known to those working with them and that their difficulties are understood and acknowledged' (28). If this is achieved parents are more likely to relax and be honest about tensions and problems in their lives which invariably affect their young children.

A child's need for a secure attachment is well recognised, but many fragile parents will have lacked this themselves and will desperately need the experience of being cared for through professional love.

Studies suggest that home visits are probably the most effective way of establishing a strong initial link with the family. Ideally a friendly welcome note addressed to the young child should make parents aware of an intended visit. Most are likely to feel more comfortable and in control chatting in their home rather than in a strange environment.

It is particularly sensitive establishing and maintaining trusting relationships when parents are suspected of abusing their child and are involved in a safeguarding investigation. The child's needs are most important and she is likely to benefit if a positive and reciprocal relationship has been established between the family and key person. However, there is a delicate balance between maintaining support for the family and ensuring child protection. Overconcentrating on a friendly link with a parent may be to the detriment of the child. At worst staff may be manipulated to ignore suspicious evidence and believe the best of a situation. An horrific example of this was the case of 4-year-old Daniel Pelka who was starved to death while teachers were led by his mother to believe that his extreme thinness was due to an eating disorder (29).

Nevertheless, if communication breaks down it makes it less likely that practitioners can work to improve matters. It is worth remembering that hostile and aggressive reactions from parents are likely to mask anxiety, guilt and resentment. These strong emotions should be accepted calmly, and where possible not allowed to deflect any discussion.

Key persons involved need strong interpersonal skills, empathy, determination and their own resilience when matters aren't resolved and families opt out of contact with the setting. Close links with other agencies will ensure another connection with the child and parents.

Case Study 16.2

At the start of each week Katy organises a conversation time with her reception class. Children are encouraged to share any interesting items of news and also ask each other questions.

Suki, usually very quiet, suddenly burst out with her news: 'On Sundays I go through windows; sometimes the windows are very tiny and my daddy helps me through. There's no-one there [in the house] and it's dark. I open the door for my dad and sometimes it's really, really hard cos I can't reach'.

Everyone received the news in silence and then Ben, who was sitting by her, stated firmly, 'That's not good'.

Suki rushed out to the cloakroom, sobbing that she didn't want to go through windows any more.

Katie immediately reported the matter to her headteacher who liaised with the police and social worker. Suki was attached to her father and was allowed to remain with him (a single parent and odd-job worker) while

(Continued)

(Continued)

an investigation was carried out. Katie managed with great difficulty to establish a positive relationship with the father while giving priority to Suki's welfare.

Comment

The trusting and supportive climate in the reception class contributed to Suki feeling able to openly divulge her stress and receive support.

Reflection Point

What actions might Katie now take to successfully maintain her key person role with both the child and the father?

Practical Suggestions

Having difficult conversations with parents

Before any safeguarding issues come to light, there may come a time when suspicions occur about a child's welfare. A change in behaviour, a bruise that is unaccounted for, irregular attendance at the setting all indicate the need for an initial, cautious investigation. There is no right way to approach a parent in these circumstances but the following guidance might help.

Possible areas of concern

- A weak attachment with their child – lack of interest/indifferent attitude/ apparent detachment.
- Indications of possible abuse – physical, emotional, sexual, neglect.

Preparation for a meeting

- Be clear about your concerns and keep written evidence with dates and observations from colleagues.
- Ensure privacy, space, and a mutually convenient time to meet.
- Make sure that your absence is covered and that there are no interruptions.
- Be familiar with family circumstances.
- Try to meet on a one-to-one basis, but if you anticipate antagonism or need the conversation to be verified ask a senior colleague to join you.

The conversation

- Start on a positive note by choosing common ground, for example what the child enjoys doing.
- Share concerns but limit these at any one time: keep messages brief and supported by evidence, and ask for a response after making a couple of points.
- Be aware of non-verbal communication, both yours and that of the parents.
- Show that you are listening carefully: be attentive and avoid butting in.
- Receive negative messages with empathy: try to understand the parents' concerns.
- After listening, 'reframe' your understanding of what has been said and respect comments from the parents.
- Do not attribute blame: show that you understand the circumstances but avoid 'red herrings'.
- Emphasise the parents' unique and central role in their child's development.
- Summarise, ensuring that the parents have understood the main messages and have had a good chance to offer their point of view; finish with some suggestions for action and agree a date for a review.

Having difficult conversations with staff

We expect staff to carry out their responsibilities with fragile families, but we should never underestimate the daily stress of working with children who do not appear to be thriving, and trying to approach and link with evasive or volatile parents. It's a wonder that practitioners do such a magnificent job. But occasionally a staff member is not sufficiently vigilant and does not pursue suspicions that something is amiss. It is critical that senior managers are aware that in this respect the quality of provision for families and children is lacking.

Possible areas of concern

- Insufficient knowledge of each unique child and a consequent inability to 'read' her behaviour.
- Failure to recognise potential abuse, e.g. attributing fractious or withdrawn behaviour, bruises, minor fractures to the child being 'off-colour' or 'prone to accidents'.
- Reluctance to enquire from parents about a child who appears to have an injury/bruise that is not accounted for.
- Avoidance of parents who are difficult to approach and failure to follow up issues of concern.

(Continued)

(Continued)

- Inadequate records of observations and a lack of insight following the observations.
- Lack of communication with other parties which delays a multi-agency approach to support fragile families.
- Personal beliefs and judgemental attitudes about childcare and children's welfare which restrict openmindedness.

Provide a programme of assistance

- Regular sessions of supportive supervision – each key person has a weekly supervision session where she discusses vulnerable key children with a senior colleague and shares field notes, observations and her contact with family members.
- Annual Performance Management: the agenda should include targets to protect vulnerable children and work with fragile families.

The Conversation (between Senior Staff and Key Persons)

The approach

- Know staff as individuals and be familiar with their work.
- Ensure confidentiality and encourage staff to feel safe and speak honestly.
- Have a collegiate conversation with the message that you are a professional companion rather than a leader who 'knows it all'.
- Listen carefully without judging.
- Encourage and model reflective practice, helping staff to feel that they are valuable team members.

The meeting

- Prepare thoroughly and be clear about what you need to communicate.
- Understand how you are going to convey messages, e.g. through eye contact, and using simple, straightforward language.
- Concentrate on what is important and don't be deflected.
- Start with strengths but be frank about concerns (giving specific examples of practice).

Conclusion

- Keep to time.
- Agree and record two or three actions to be discussed at a follow-up meeting.
- End on a note of encouragement, e.g. that we can all improve our practice.

The prospect of having a difficult conversation can be stressful and cause sleepless nights. However, in certain circumstances it is an essential task for key persons and leaders and is in the interests of children and families. In the best instances a conversation will strengthen a relationship with a parent or staff member and also improve the quality of parenting and practice.

Professional Practice Questions

1. How aware are we in our setting of those children who are at risk and the degree of risk that they are exposed to?
2. How clear are we as staff of our responsibilities to safeguard young children?
3. How well do we support new colleagues in this aspect of their work?

Work with Parents

Enlist the help of parents to raise awareness of the children's services on offer:

- Suggest that they encourage parents to register a new baby's birth at a local Children's Centre.
- Ask them to accompany a parent when she makes a first visit to an early years setting.

References

1. Waldfogel, J. and Washbrook, E. (2008) *Early Years Policy.* London: The Sutton Trust.
2. Centre for Longitudinal Studies (2013) *Millennium Cohort Study: Age 11 Survey.* Swindon: Institute of Education, Economic and Social Research Council.
3. Monro, E. (2011) *Review of Child Protection Final Report: A Child Centred System.* London: HMSO.
4. Department for Education (DfE) (2013) *Working Together to Safeguard Children: Revised Statutory Guidance.* London: DfE.
5. Department for Culture, Arts and Leisure (2009) *Guidance on Safeguarding Children.* Belfast: Northern Ireland Assembly.
6. Wales (2012) *Protecting Children in Wales: Guidance for Arrangements for Multi-Agency Child Practice Reviews.* Cardiff: Welsh Assembly Government.
7. The Scottish Government (2010) *National Guidance for Child Protection in Scotland.* Available at www.scotland.gov.uk
8. Tickell, C. (2011) *The Early Years: Foundations for Life, Health and Learning.* London: HMSO.
9. Department for Education (DfE) (2012) *Statutory Framework for the Early Years Foundation Stage.* London: HMSO, p. 10, paras 2.3–5.
10. Field, F. (2010) *The Foundation Years: Preventing Poor Children becoming Poor Adults.* London: HMSO.
11. Allen, G. (2011) *Early Intervention: The Next Steps – An Independent Report to HM Government.* London: Cabinet Office.
12. Department for Education (DfE) (2012) *The Core Purposes of Sure Start Centres.* London: HMSO.
13. Institute of Health Equity (UCL) (2012) *An Equal Start: Improving Outcomes in Children's Centres.* London: UCL.

14. Cuthbert, C., Rayne, G. and Starkey, K. (2011) *All Babies Count: Prevention and Protection for Vulnerable Babies,* NSPCC, Executive Summary, p. 5.
15. Department for Education/Wave Trust (2013) 'Californian Adverse Childhood Experiences (ACE)', quoted in *Conception to Age 2 – The Age of Opportunity. Wave Trust: Tackling the Roots of Disadvantage.* Available at www.wavetrust.org
16. Department for Education/Wave Trust (2013) *Conception to Age 2 – The Age of Opportunity.* Wave Trust: Tackling the Roots of Disadvantage. Available at www.wavetrust.org, p. 4.
17. Department for Education (DfE) (2013) *Early Learning for 2-year-olds: Information for Local Authorities.* London: HMSO.
18. Department for Education (DfE) (2010) Gibb, J., Jellicle, H., La Valle, I., Gowland, S., Kinsella, R., Jessimon, P. and Ormston, R., *Rolling out Free Early Education for Disadvantaged 2-year-olds: An Implementation Study for Local Authorities.* Research report DfE: RR131.
19. National Institute for Health and Care Excellence (NICE) (2012) *Social and Emotional Well-being: Early Years.* Public Heath Guidance (PH 40).
20. HM Government (2013) *Working Together to Safeguard Children: Revised Statutory Guidance,* op.cit. (see note 4).
21. American Academy of Paediatrics Centre on the Developing Child (2013) *Toxic Stress: The Facts,* Cambridge, MA: The President and Fellows of Harvard College.
22. Reed, H. (2012) *In the Eye of the Storm: Britain's Forgotten Children and Families.* Action for Children, Children's Society, National Prevention of Cruelty to Children, p. 11.
23. Department for Education (DfE) (2013) op.cit. (see note 4).
24. Watt, J. (2013) Joined up Care Strategy making 'tough love' work, *The Guardian,* 30 December.
25. Siraj-Blatchford, I. and Siraj-Blatchford, J. (2010) *Improving Development Outcomes for Children Through Effective Practice in Integrating Early Years Services.* London: Centre for Excellence and Outcomes in Children and Young People (C4EO).
26. Royston, S. and Rodrigues, L. (2013) *Breaking Barriers: How to Help Children's Centres Reach Disadvantaged Families.* London: The Children's Society, p. 7. Available at www.childrens society.org.uk
27. Royston, S. and Rodrigues, L. (2013) op.cit. (see note 26), p. 8.
28. National Quality Improvement Network (2010) *Principles for Engaging with Families.* London: Early Learning Partnership Parental Engagement Group, National Children's Bureau, p. 35.
29. *BBC News* (2013) 'Starved boy "invisible" to professionals', 17 September. Available at www.bbc.co.uk/news/uk-england-coventry-warwickshire-24106823

Conclusion

Mick Waters, well respected educator and thinker, in his book *Thinking Allowed on Schooling*, likens our current educational system to the story of Chicken Licken who is followed by a whole group of creatures, including Henny Penny, Goosey Loosey and Foxy Loxy. They believe that the sky is falling in and run around in panic to tell the king. But before they arrive 'the sky fell in' (1).

Waters asserts that schools are beset by accountability – and so it is in early years. Heads and managers have become obsessed with data, measuring their success on the basis of spurious assessments and tests, a supreme example being a phonics screening check at the end of Year 1 when children are required to sound out words, some of which don't make sense. Interestingly, in an evaluation of the screening, 'Most teachers interviewed as part of the case study visits reported that the check would have minimal, if any, impact on the standard of reading and writing in their school in the future' (2).

There also remains a culture of fear around Ofsted visitations. Everyone is working faster and harder to 'prove' that they are doing a good job. Many staff are worn out and children become frazzled and frustrated in 'busy' settings when they are given too little time to absorb things and learn properly.

We should recognise the real dangers of pushing the workforce to achieve more and more and gain less and less satisfaction in doing the work they are trained in and needed for.

The premise of this book is based on helping young children to become resilient and self-regulated people who can survive, succeed and enjoy life in a world full of uncertainties. Young children have inbuilt mechanisms to grow, but their progress and development also depend on support from close adults who know what they are doing.

'The single, biggest factor that determines the quality of childcare is the workforce' (3). This belief is undoubtedly shared by all leaders in early years. And yet as we have seen, we still have a long way to go in gaining the highly qualified staff that are needed for the work and achieving the pay and conditions that they deserve. Abbott's quote is passionate: 'I would fight to the death the view that anybody can look after young children; they have got to be the finest minds and the best trained people' (4).

So what particular qualities do these people have?

Self-reflection

We all have our beliefs, values and attitudes based on our own experiences and which have served us well enough in our lives. Work with young families however can shake these beliefs and assumptions. Parents and carers may have different ways of conducting their lives; children may not behave as expected or respond to overtures. Colleagues may have different views about ways of caring for and educating children. All this can be discomforting, shake our self-confidence, and cause defensiveness. To avoid these negative feelings we need to be prepared to be open-minded, re-examine what we believe, learn from others, and sometimes adapt attitudes in the light of what we have learned. Once we are brave enough to reflect on and learn from experience we grow professionally though broadening, clarifying and strengthening the principles for our work. It can be helpful to use a particular format to guide reflections. A document on Social and Emotional Aspects of Development (SEAD) includes a useful audit which is intended to help practitioners make a judgement about how they look after and promote personal, social and emotional well-being for everyone in the setting. The important message is that as practitioners we need to take good care of ourselves in order to care for others (5).

Flexibility

One of the joys of working with young children and their families is that it is dynamic. Edgington describes the work as 'unpredictable and the best laid plans have a habit of going entirely awry'. She also points out that if control and predictability are what make you feel comfortable it is likely that you will find working in early years threatening (6). Practitioners should have planned intentions for what they offer, but must be prepared to adapt or even abandon plans in order to follow children's thinking and go with the tide of their motivation.

Emotional Maturity

Involvement with powerful and harrowing issues such as family break-ups and issues of child abuse (see Chapters 15 and 16) can cause practitioners to feel disturbed, upset, angry and frustrated. Although it is not easy to handle these feelings it is important to remain outwardly calm and in control, being able to cope with complexity.

Empathy

Goleman describes empathy as our 'social radar' (7). Empathetic practitioners are able to see into the child's world and when permitted enter it.

They tune into the dilemmas experienced by parents and acknowledge and respect their feelings. Empathy cannot in itself solve problems but it can help a person feel that they are not alone. Goleman suggests that highly developed empathy goes even further than this by recognising the issues or concerns that lie behind another's feelings. When this happens it becomes possible for practitioners to offer children and their families more tangible support.

Communication

The ability to read young children's behaviour and to connect with them is at the heart of successful practice. Trevarthen describes this so well, as being able to 'dance with the children' (8). This implies harmony, recognising the steps a child is taking, being able to anticipate the next move, and adapting our response accordingly.

Optimism

Practitioners work with children who have had different starts to life and who enter a nursery at different stages of development. The exciting thing here is that although we can recognise what a child achieves today, we can never be sure of the potential that child might realise tomorrow. This gives cause for optimism. Practitioners understand that, regardless of children's different abilities, given the climate described in this book their personal growth will flourish, thereby helping progress in other aspects of their lives.

Commitment

Returning to the tale of Chicken Licken and her friends, we can surely rely on a workforce with the qualities mentioned to prevent the worse scenario of the sky falling in. The main strength of these practitioners is a quiet certainty that they are carrying out important work which can make a difference to children at a very impressionable time of their lives. Ill thought-out initiatives from the centre and restrictive budgets make their work more difficult and frustrating but they will not be deflected. The work is hard and often unremitting. It requires huge physical and emotional energy as well as intellectual endeavour and it can easily lead to burnout. This job is not for the faint-hearted. And yet the commitment evident in our best practitioners is there because they recognise the privilege of sharing the world of childhood and accompanying children in their very early stages of growing up.

A Note about Changes to Early Years Policies and Procedures

The reader needs to be aware that the government and Ofsted have introduced many changes which relate to Early Years practices since I completed this book.

References

1. Waters, M. (2013) *Thinking Allowed on Schooling.* Carmarthen: Independent Thinking Press, p. 329.
2. Walker, M., Bartlett, S., Betts, H., Sainsbury, M. and Mehta, P. (2013) *Evaluation of the Phonics Screening Check: First Interim Report.* London: DfE/ NFER, p. 7.
3. Department for Education and Skills (DfES) (2004) *Every Child Matters: Change for Children.* Nottingham: DfES, para. 43.
4. Page, J. (2005) 'Working with children under three: the perspectives of three UK academics', in K. Hirst and C. Nutbrown (eds), *Perspectives on Early Childhood Education: Contemporary Research.* Stoke-on-Trent: Trentham, p. 110.
5. Department for Children, Schools and Families (DCFS)/The National Strategies Early Years (2008) *Social and Emotional Aspects of Development (SEAD).* London: DCSF, Appendix 2, p. 53.
6. Edgington, M. (2004) *The Foundation Teacher in Action.* London: Paul Chapman, p. 4.
7. Goleman, D. (1998) *Working with Emotional Intelligence.* London: Bloomsbury, p. 133.
8. Trevarthen, C. (1992) 'An infant's motives for thinking and speaking', in A.H. Wold (ed.), *The Dialogical Alternative.* Oxford: Oxford University Press.

Index